HAND LETTERING ON THE IPAD WITH PROCREATE:

Ideas and Lessons for Modern and Vintage Lettering

Liz Kohler Brown

rockynook

Hand Lettering on the iPad with Procreate: Ideas and Lessons for Modern and Vintage Lettering
Liz Kohler Brown
lizkohlerbrown.com

Editor: Kelly Reed
Project manager: Lisa Brazieal
Marketing coordinator: Mercedes Murray
Copyeditor: Joan Dixon
Interior layout: Gary Hespenheide
Interior design: Malea Clark-Nicholson
Cover production: Malea Clark-Nicholson
Cover design: Liz Kohler Brown

ISBN: 978-1-68198- 582-4
1st Edition (2nd printing, April 2021)

Rocky Nook Inc.
1010 B Street, Suite 350
San Rafael, CA 94901
USA

www.rockynook.com

Distributed in the UK and Europe by Publishers Group UK
Distributed in the U.S. and all other territories by Ingram Publisher Services

Library of Congress Control Number: 2019950818

This book is printed on acid-free paper.
Printed in China.

Contents

CHAPTER 8

Combining Letterform Styles 152

CHAPTER 9

Sharing and Critiquing Your Work 162

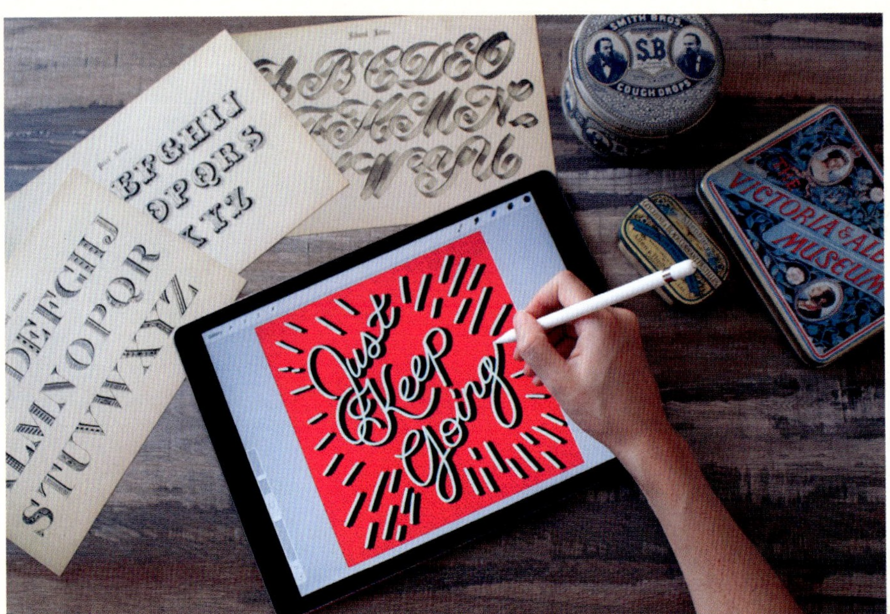

CHAPTER 1

Introduction

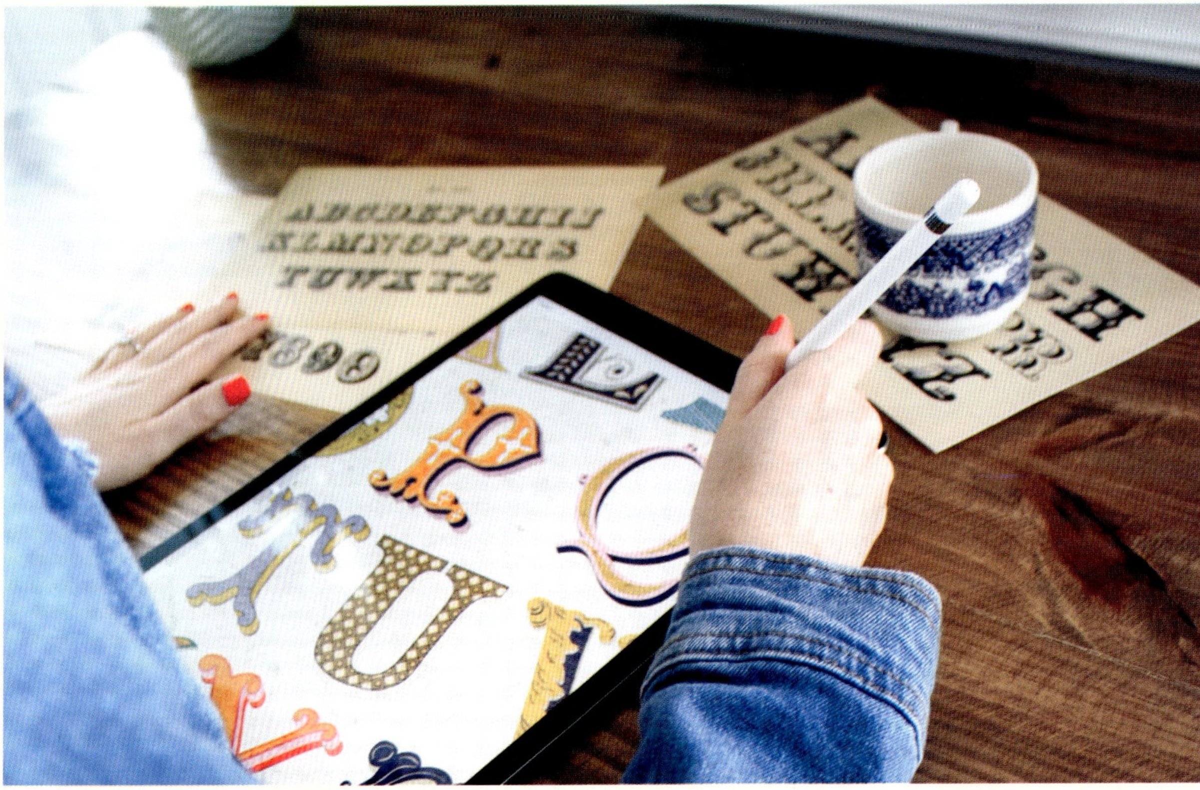

Whether you're a complete beginner to the practice of lettering or a seasoned pro in search of some fresh ideas, this book will provide all of the tips, practice pages, and composition layouts necessary to get your lettering juices flowing and to take the quality of your work to the next level.

HOW TO USE THIS BOOK

As a teacher and lifelong student of art and design, I'm a devout believer in learning by doing. We can understand design principles by reading about them, but the only way to truly master the application of those principals is through the process of trial and error. Therefore, you'll notice throughout this book that every single step and tip is part of an interactive learning method that will allow you to immediately use, and then easily remember, each lesson in the book.

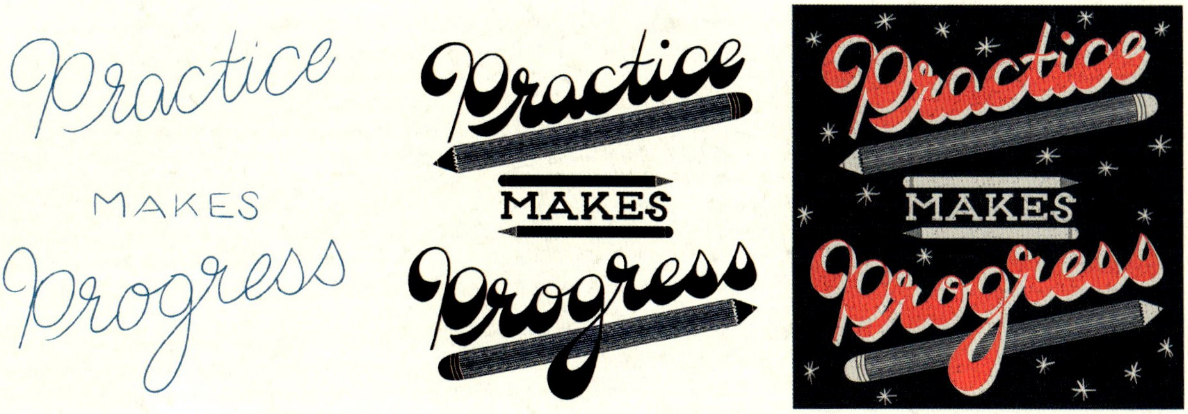

As you work your way through the book, I'll show you every step of the hand lettering process, from idea to rough sketch to finished project, so you can create your own unique compositions. However, before jumping into a new technique or approach, you might find it helpful to skim through a chapter to get an idea of what is to come.

I recommend working through the chapters in sequential order because the projects have been designed to get progressively more difficult. This will allow beginners to slowly build confidence and tackle increasingly more challenging design principles without ever feeling uncomfortable or underprepared. If you're itching to try a specific type of lettering—like scripts in chapter 6—or you need some ideas for decorating your lettering (chapter 7), then feel free to jump ahead. I will teach you all the important "rules" of lettering while recognizing that creatives are rule-breakers by nature, so don't feel badly if you've already gotten the urge to check out the later chapters.

Precision vs. Perfection

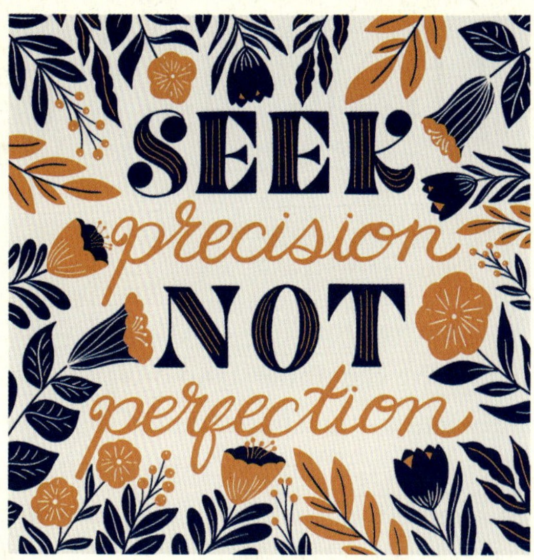

As you complete the projects in the book, remember that hand lettering is not supposed to be perfect. If you want perfection, you could use a tried-and-true font like Times New Roman. What makes hand lettering beautiful is its authenticity and unpredictability, which occurs because of its imperfections, not in spite of them. The widely varying textures, swirls, and idiosyncrasies created by the human hand are what give lettering compositions a personal touch, allowing them to stand out from the mechanical perfection of a font.

However, this doesn't mean hand lettering should be messy. The goal is to set your rules and boundaries for your lettering, and then stay within those boundaries using precise guides and careful attention to detail. If you find yourself obsessing over details and having trouble finishing projects because you think they aren't perfect, remember that the goal is precision not perfection!

Why Go Digital?

When I began art school in 2004, I was given a syllabus for each class, which listed the materials I needed to buy. I had totally underestimated the cost of getting an art degree! I was prepared for the tuition and living expenses, but apparently, that was just part of the cost. I also had to purchase hundreds of dollars' worth of art supplies for every single class, every single semester. I remember so many times being hesitant to start a new painting because I was worried about wasting a sheet of expensive watercolor paper if I were to make a mistake!

How many paintings did I fail to paint because I was worried about wasting money and materials, and how much faster would I have progressed if I hadn't been overly cautious about making mistakes? For that matter, how much time is spent shopping for the perfect set of brushes or the right kind of paper?

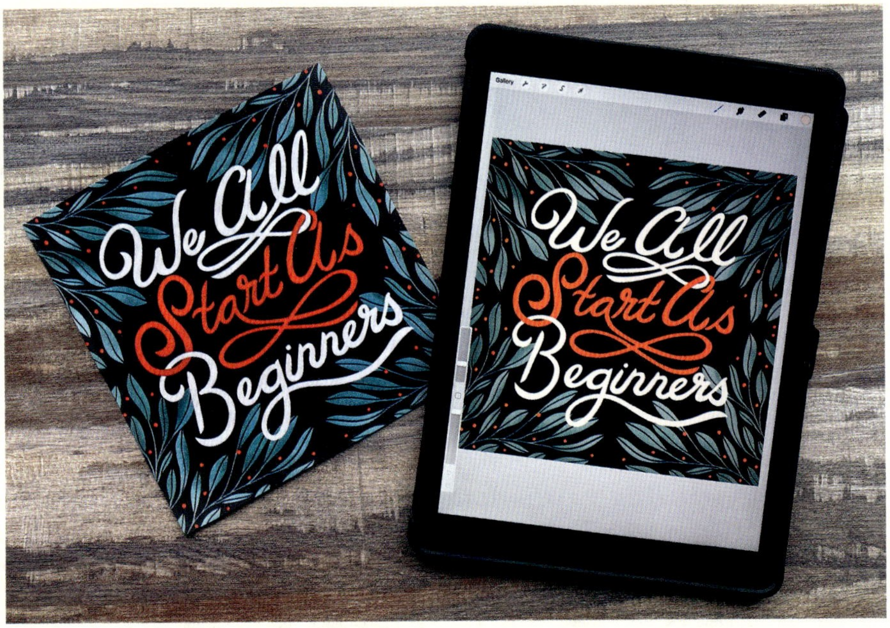

It is no secret that art supplies can be expensive, but an overlooked side effect of this is how often it prevents people from creating works of art in the first place. What I love about drawing digitally is that once you buy the device and app, you have every color, tool, and texture at your fingertips without the need for any further financial investment. You also have the ability to create or download unlimited brushes and try them out on unlimited digital canvases. You can freely create new drawings and throw them in the trash as many times as you need to in order to find your personal style. The only time you'll need actual paper is if you choose to print some of your favorite lettering pieces!

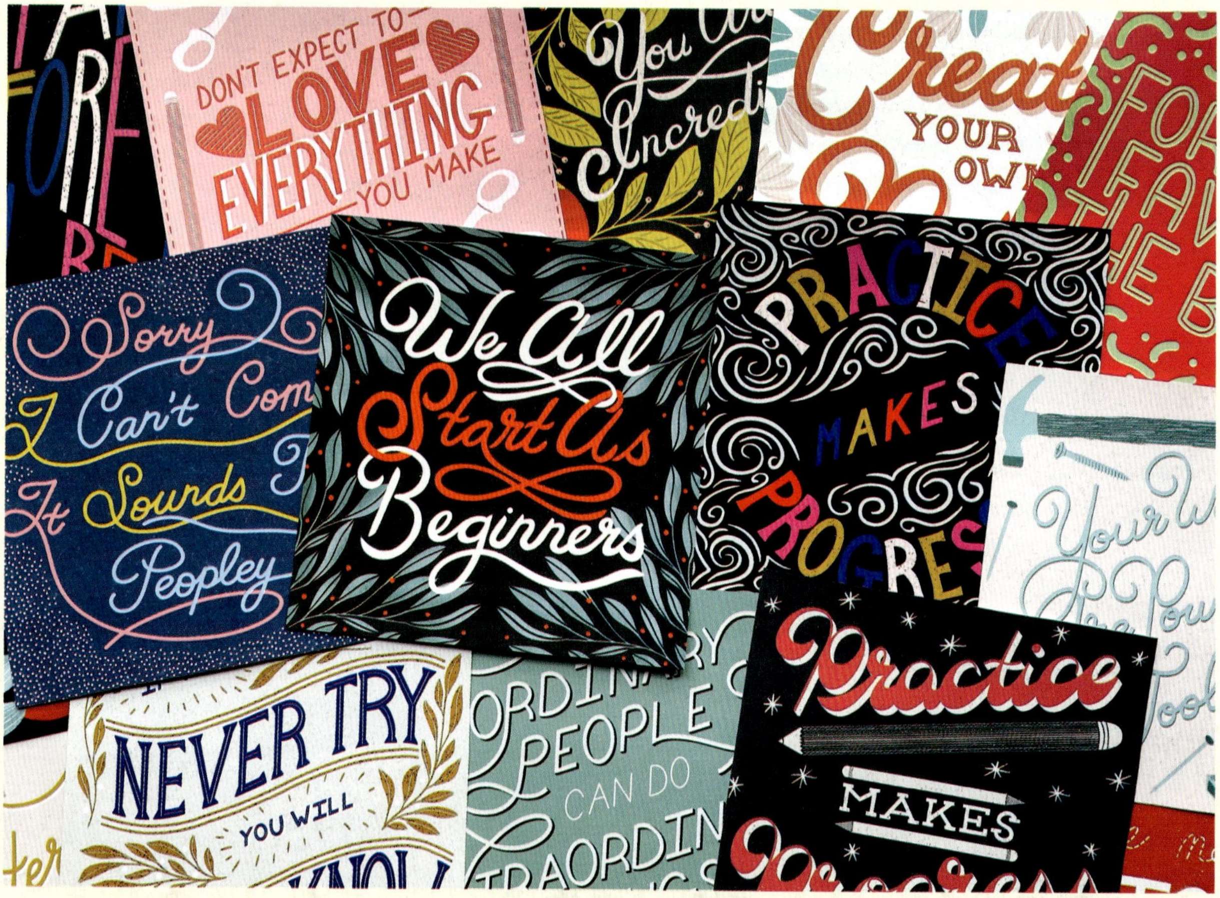

In other words, if you've been hesitant to start lettering because you don't want to waste expensive paper, paints, or ink, then working digitally is a great way for you to gain confidence in choosing colors, designing letter forms, and creating beautiful lettering compositions.

Every step in this book is done in the digital illustration app called Procreate, but this doesn't mean you have to letter digitally forever. The processes you'll learn in this book can be applied to paper and canvas, and even to the side of a building!

Why iPads and Procreate?

There are many devices and useful applications for digital artists to choose from. What I love about Procreate and the iPad is they give us the ability to produce lifelike strokes, textures, and pressure-sensitive lines all in a super mobile and easy-to-use interface. Compared to buying both a tablet and computer, which is the requirement for most computer-based drawing programs, the combined cost of an iPad and the Procreate app is a mere drop in the bucket. That being said, if you already work with a different digital drawing program, you can easily transfer the processes found in this book to your drawing tablet or computer, or even to paper or canvas.

Materials

For the projects in this book, I use an iPad Pro, an Apple Pencil, and the Procreate app, but you don't need this exact combination to complete the projects. If you don't have a pressure sensitive stylus like the Apple Pencil, you'll just need to thicken and vary the lines by hand rather than relying on the pressure of your stylus.

If you're considering which iPad to buy, I suggest getting one with the biggest screen and the most storage your budget allows. The more screen space you have to draw on, the less you need to zoom and pan around the screen while you work. The more storage you have, the less often you have to remove files in order to free up space on your device.

The only other materials you may want to have on hand are some inspirational images and/or objects. In the next chapter, we'll dive into a huge list of resources you can pull from as

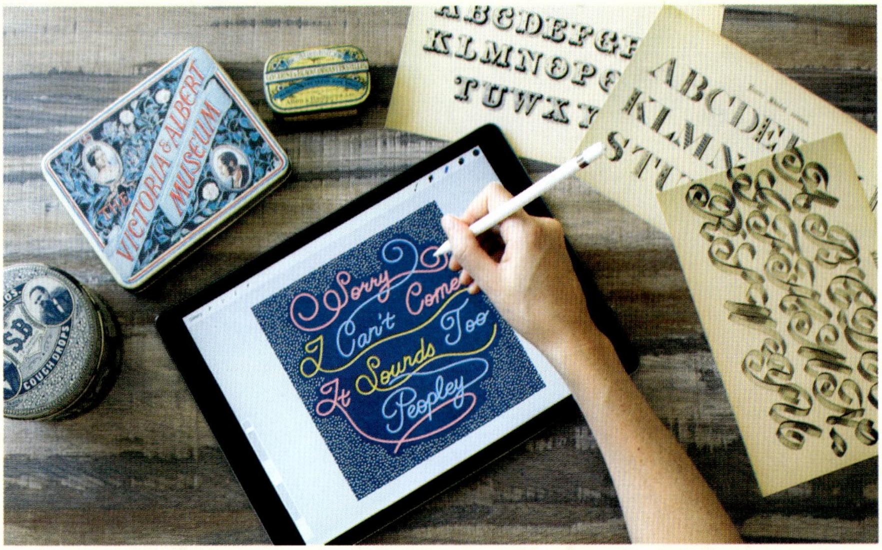

you're gathering inspiration for your next lettering project. You can save your inspirational ideas and images on your iPad, or print them out and have them nearby as you work.

Downloads and Resources

Throughout the book I'll mention the **Downloads and Resources** page on my website where you'll find practice sheets, letter style inspiration, and a link to the Facebook group mentioned below. You can find the **Downloads and Resources** page at lizkohlerbrown.com/hand-lettering-resources. Enter the following password in the field provided to open the page: *handletteredcard*.

To open the brush set and practice sheets in Procreate, tap the Download button and then select Procreate as the app.

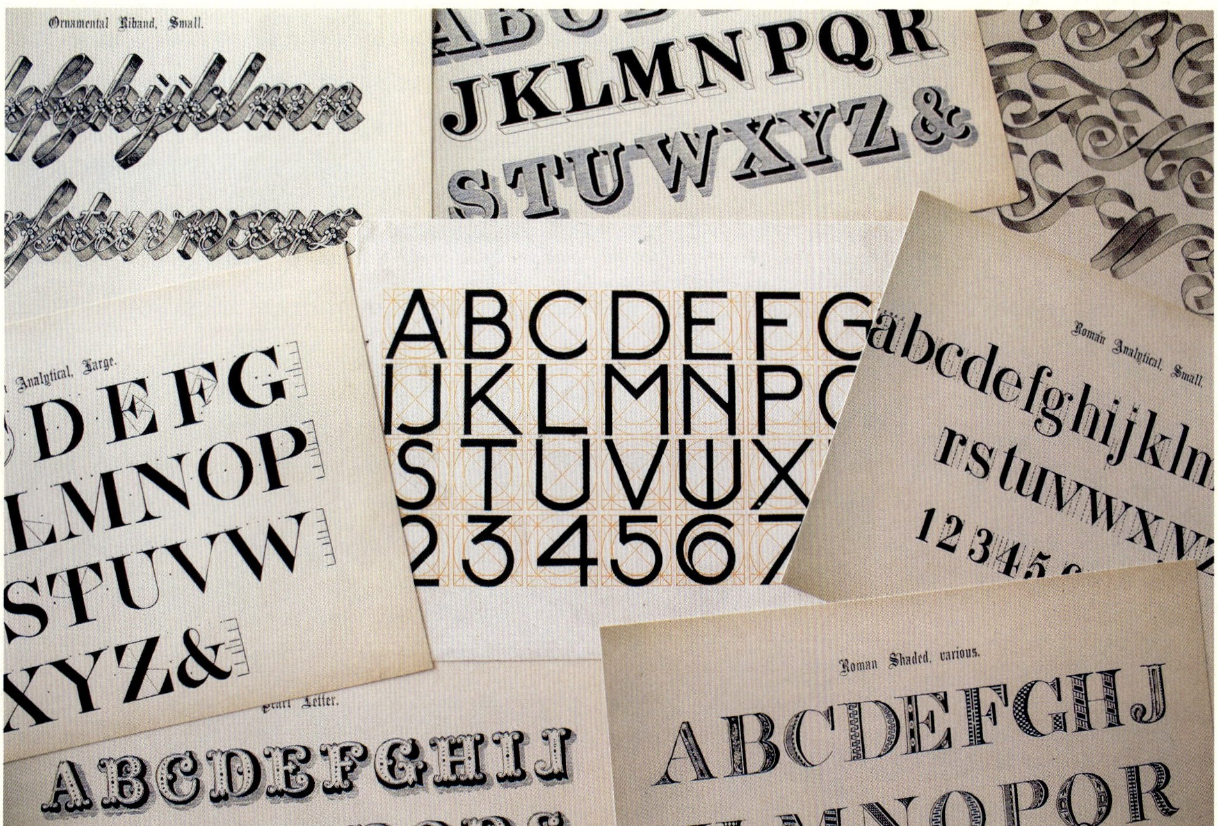

Printed vintage lettering alphabets can be a great source of inspiration.

Get Tech Support and Share Your Work

As with all technology, iPads don't always work the way we expect. Combine that with the fact that Procreate (like all digital applications) is continually changing and evolving, and it becomes inevitable that some technical questions or problems might arise while completing the steps in this book.

I've created a private Facebook group for the readers of this book so you can join other letterers around the world in conversations, idea sharing, seeing each other's work, and getting tech support from me and other iPad letterers. In the group, I share many of my time-lapse videos from the projects in the book, so you can easily view the exact steps I followed to create each composition. Join the Facebook group (using the link on the **Downloads and Resources** page mentioned above) where you can ask questions, share your work, and see creations by other letterers from around the world!

Just Keep Lettering

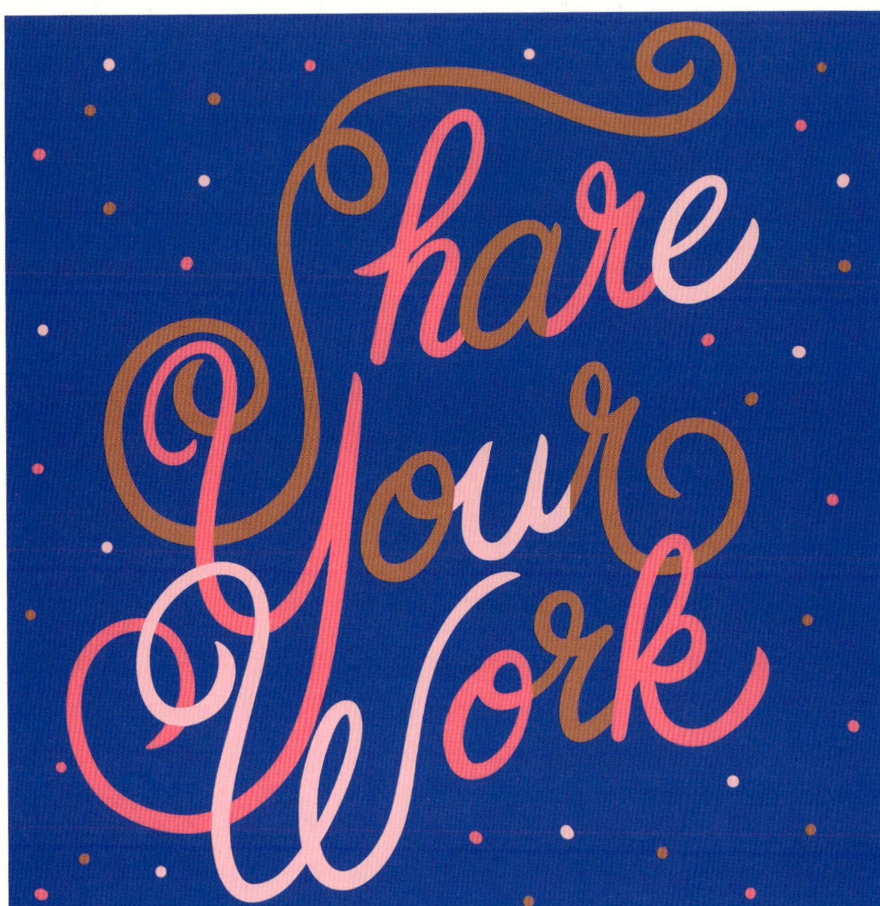

No one sits down to hand letter for the very first time and creates a beautiful lettering composition. Just like learning a language or a musical instrument, lettering is an acquired skill that can be learned and improved through practice. If you're just starting out on your lettering journey, keep in mind that not everything you make will be beautiful. In the beginning you may even feel like nothing you make is beautiful. Just remember that if you keep practicing and experimenting, your lettering will improve. At the same time, your ability to choose appealing color combinations will improve, and your sense for what makes an eye-catching composition will start to become second nature.

I once asked my college professor how many paintings it takes to become a good artist. He quickly said it would take 100. I was skeptical and asked a lot of follow up questions. How do you know it's 100 for me, when you don't even know how good my paintings are now? What if I only paint 2″ × 2″ canvases, would that be the same as painting 100 5″ × 5″ canvases? How much time do I have to spend on each painting? He thought for a moment and said, "I think for you, it will be more like 200 paintings."

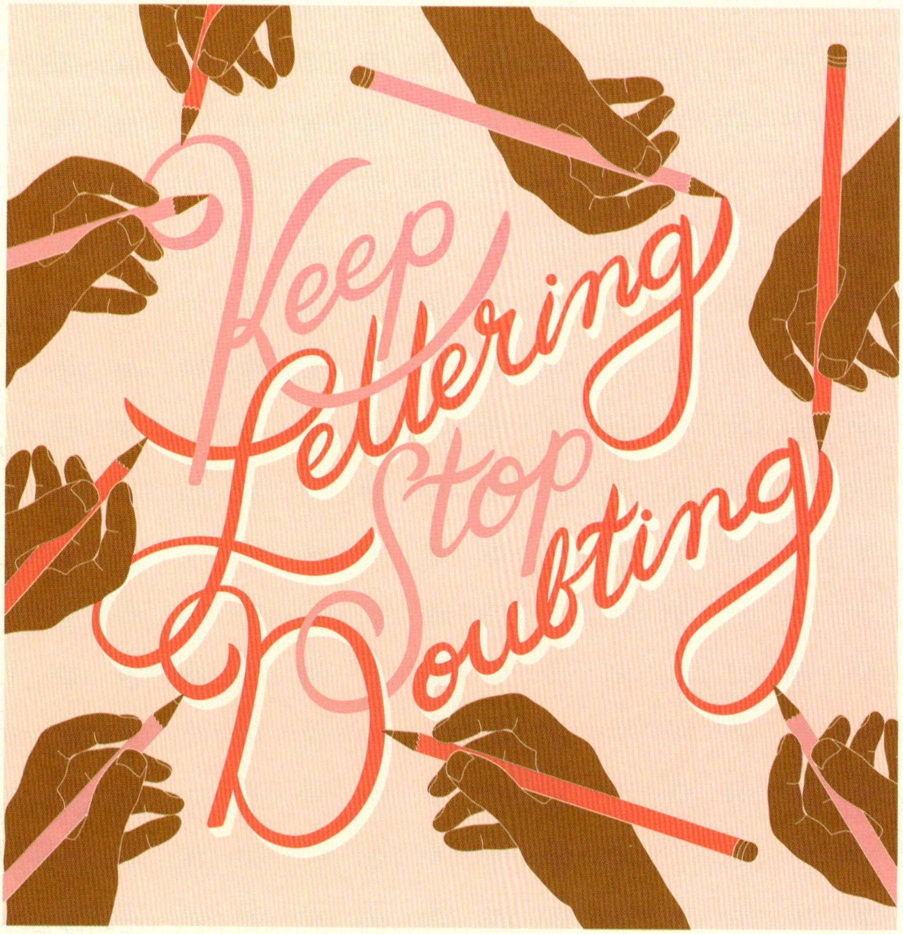

At the time I didn't understand what he meant and assumed he was just another crazy painting professor who had inhaled too many solvent fumes over the years. I realize now, after years of making art, that the important lesson he was trying to convey was to stop analyzing, stop doubting, and start doing. Your doubt will only make the process more difficult.

Allow your analytical side to recede into the background while cultivating your creative and experimental side, and embrace the inevitable uncertainty that accompanies any new endeavor. If we spend our time worrying or trying to make predictions about the speed or trajectory of our improvement, or how we might arrive at some future level of success, then we're subtracting from the time and energy we could spend creating, which is the only thing that really matters.

That being said, if choosing a personal goal or benchmark, such as completing 100 lettering compositions in a year, keeps you interested and motivated, then by all means do it! Anything that keeps you continually engaged with your newfound lettering practice and whatever helps you compartmentalize any doubts or misgivings you might have will be the most valuable components of your lettering success.

Now, let's start lettering!

CHAPTER 2

Building Your Inspiration Library

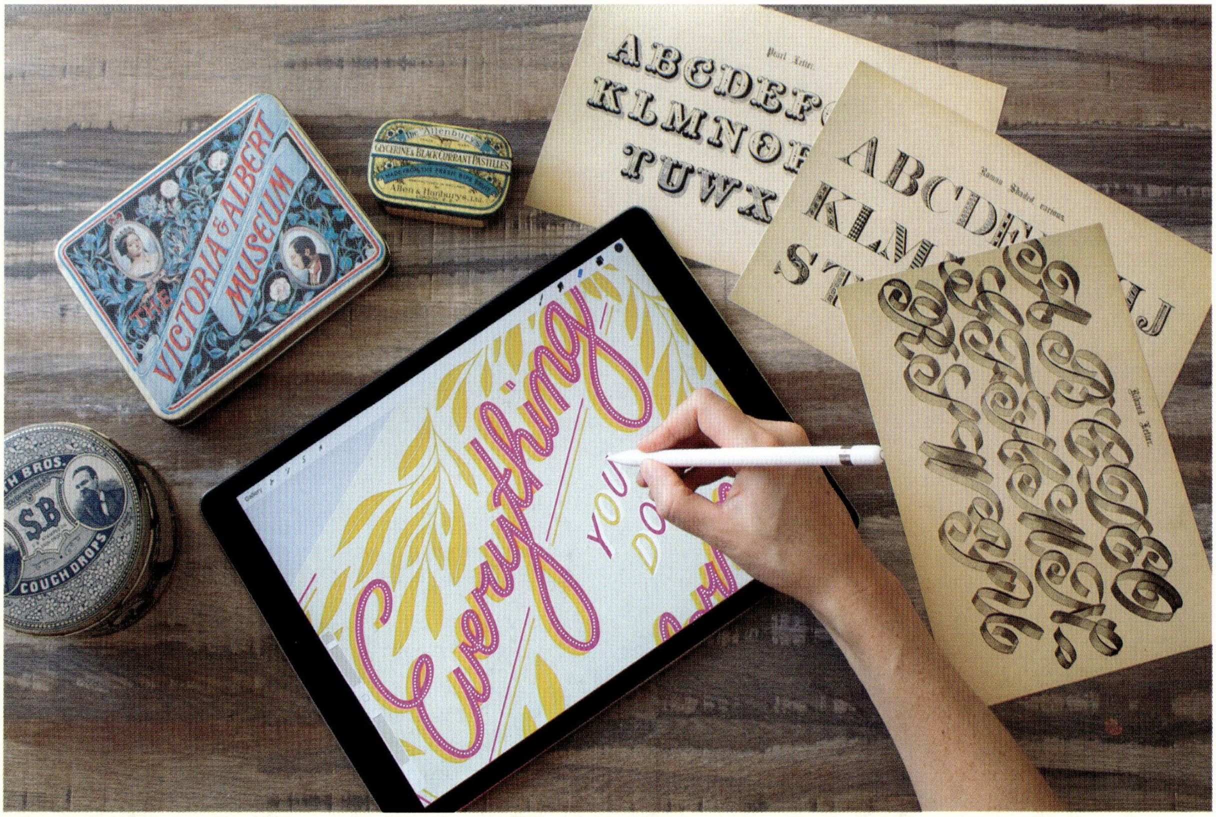

Lettering inspiration can be found all around us. It's on the chalkboard menu of your local coffee shop. It's on the vintage signs and magazine covers in antique stores. It's on t-shirts, books, food packages, and everything in between. All we have to do is keep our eyes peeled for letterforms, colors, and phrases that inspire us. We can build an inspiration library by taking pictures of whatever catches our eye and storing them on our iPads in a photo album or uploading them to an online photo album such as Flickr or Google Photos.

When we work from our own inspiration libraries we never have to worry about finding the colors, decorations, or letterforms we need. Take this composition (next page) for example. You can see how I combined the letter style of the words "Paris garters" (tall, chunky letters with ends that flare out) with the leaves of the wreath in the vintage sign. I used my photograph to create a color palette and I devised a few different color combinations.

Many of our ideas will come spontaneously by simply playing with the possible combinations of styles, colors, and decorations, which is why it is important to have these elements available before we start designing. Interrupting the creative process to search for

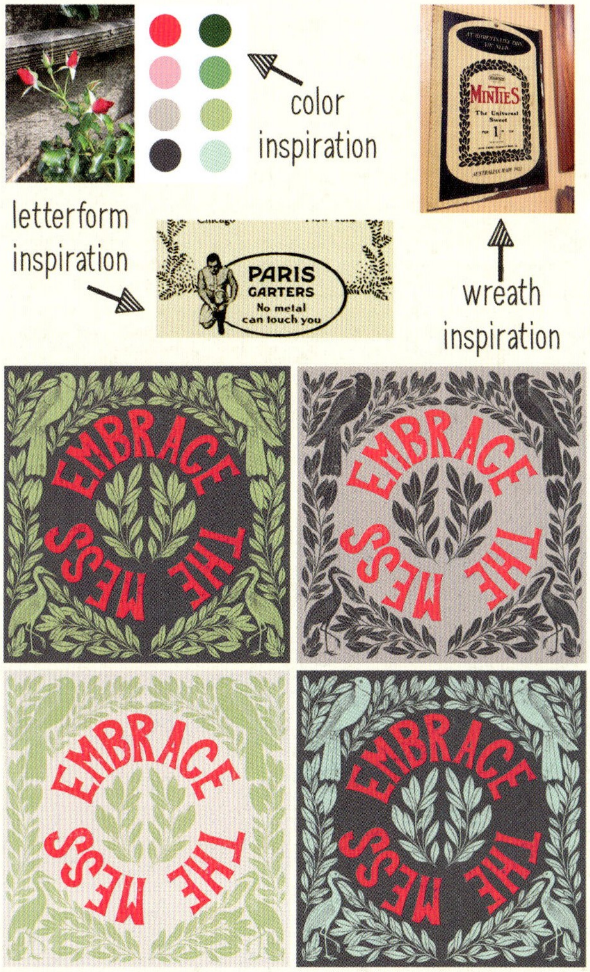

I had the idea to letter the phrase "Embrace the mess," so I needed a letter style, a decorative motif to surround the lettering, and the right color palette to tie it all together. All these elements were available to me in my inspiration library.

ideas can sometimes lead to creative block, but a little bit of preparation can make the design process fun, easy, and even addictive.

With this goal in mind, in this chapter you will learn to build your own personalized inspiration library of color palettes, words and phrases, letterforms, and decorative elements so you'll never lack the raw materials and inspiration needed to fuel your lettering hobby.

Color Inspiration and Palettes

Whether your intention for a composition is for it to be bold or subtle, or if you want a vintage feel or a modern twist, having an array of beautiful colors literally at your fingertips makes the coloring process a breeze. In this section, we'll look at how to find color inspiration, create a custom color palette, and save it in the Procreate Palette Library.

Color palettes can be found in gardens, shopping malls, magazines, and even our own homes. For an example, I will use a photograph of a flower to create a palette, but we could use this same process with most any photograph.

Follow these easy steps to create your first palette:

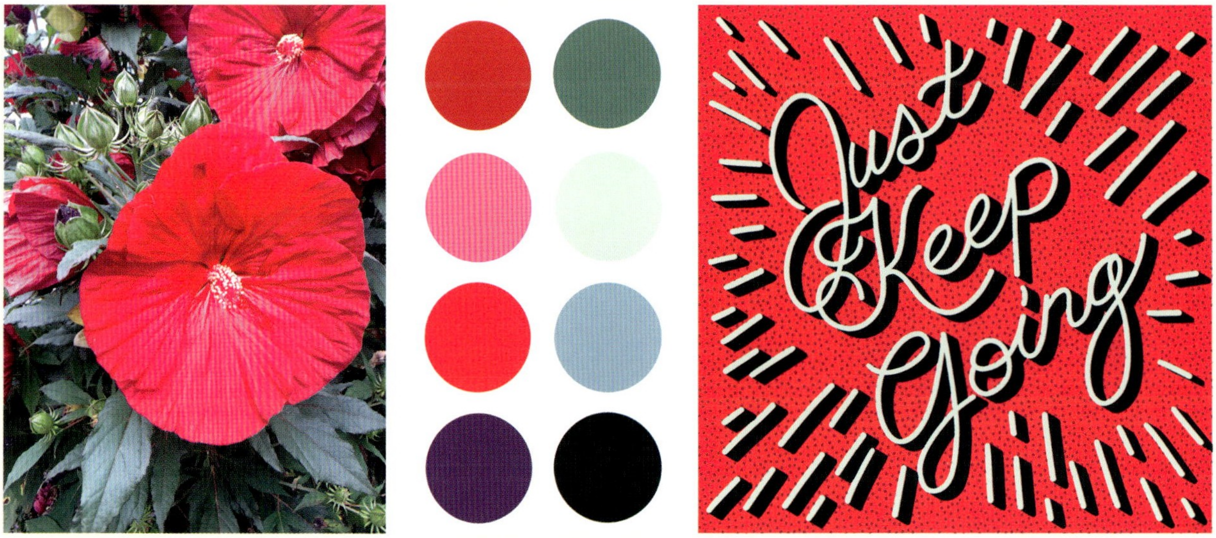

I found a flower with a gorgeous set of colors, pulled the most prominent colors from the image, and then used some of my favorites to color this composition.

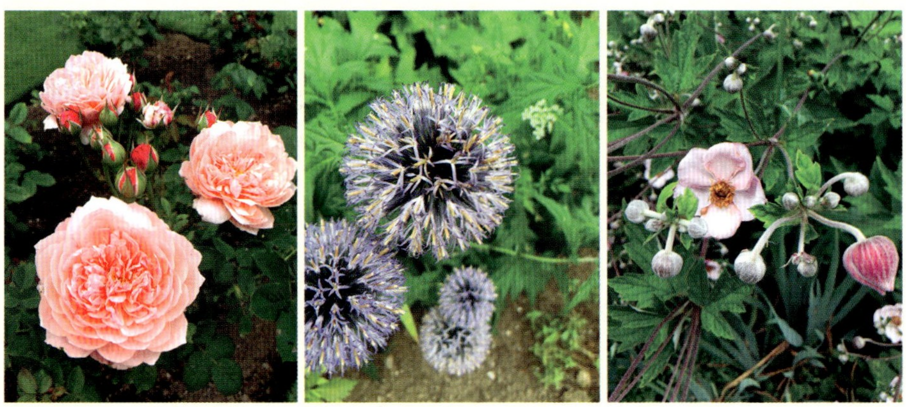

STEP 1: Take some pictures in bright lighting. When photographing outdoors, an overcast day is ideal because the sunlight is diffused and there are few shadows and no glare from the sun. For these photographs I used the camera on my phone, but you could also use your iPad or a digital camera. I went to a botanical garden on an overcast day and took hundreds of pictures like these for my future color palettes.

When I take pictures for color palettes I try to capture a wide range of colors. In these examples, everything from the bold pinks of the flowers to the dark browns of the dirt can be used in a palette.

> Tip: When photographing, get close to your subject so it almost fills the frame. Zooming in like this will make it possible to extract richer, more vibrant colors in Procreate.

STEP 2: Open the Procreate app, and tap the + symbol to create a new document.

STEP 3: Tap the **Custom Size** icon to create a custom-sized canvas.

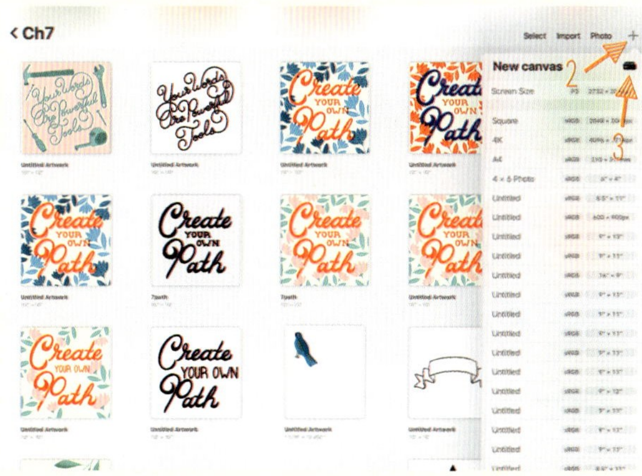

STEP 4: Select **Inches** as the measurement.

STEP 5: Tap the words **Untitled Canvas,** and enter a title. I called mine "Purple Flower Color Palette."

STEP 6: Enter 7 as the **Width** and 5 as the **Height.** (We'll talk more about image sizes and DPI in the next section.)

STEP 7: Tap **Create** to open the document.

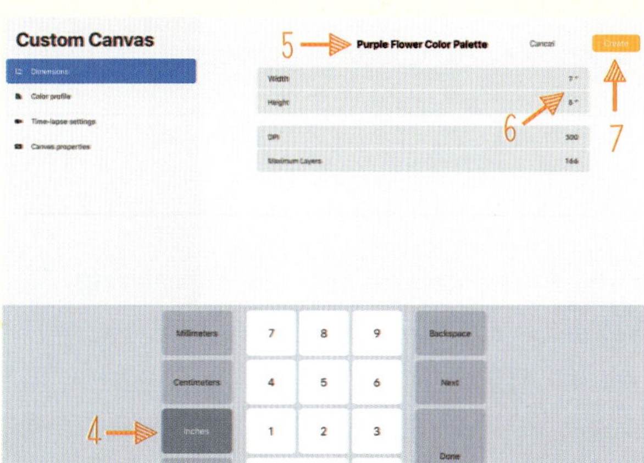

STEP 8: Tap the **Actions** menu.

STEP 9: Select the **Add** section, and then tap **Insert a photo.**

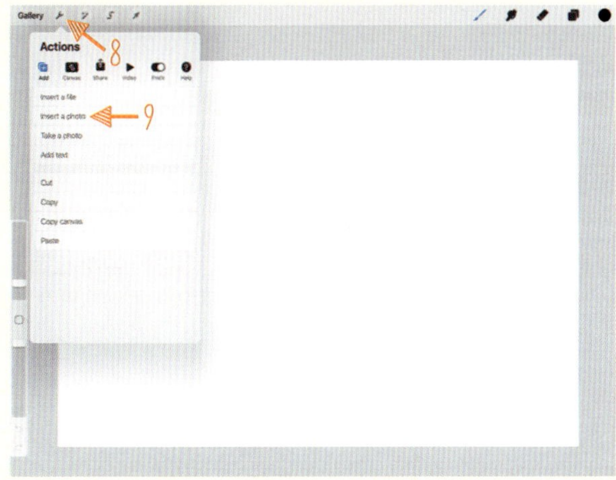

STEP 10: Find your photo in the Gallery, and tap once to transfer it onto your canvas.

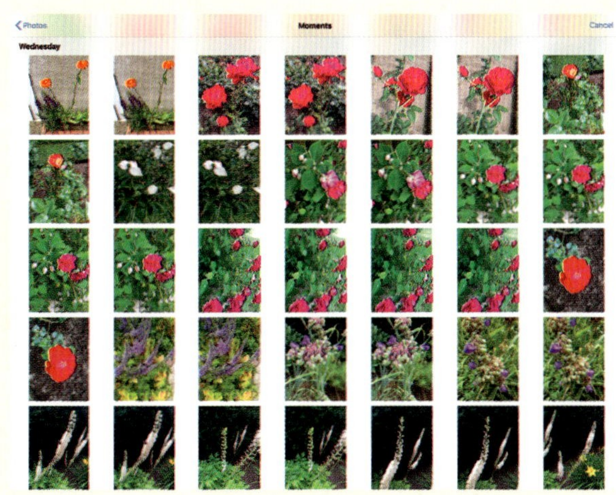

STEP 11: Tap **Snapping,** then make sure the **Magnetics** symbol is in blue, which indicates it is turned on, then use your finger to drag the image over to one side of the canvas. **Magnetics** will help your image stay aligned with the canvas borders.

STEP 12: Tap on the **Layers** panel to open it.

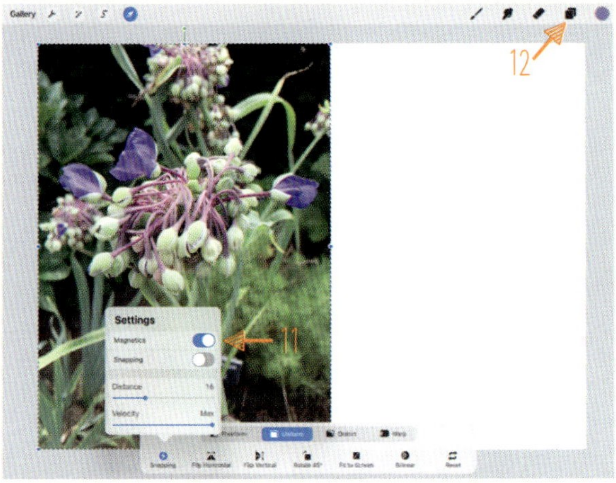

STEP 13: Tap the + symbol to create a new layer. (We'll talk more about layers in chapter 3.) Tap anywhere on the canvas to close the Layers panel.

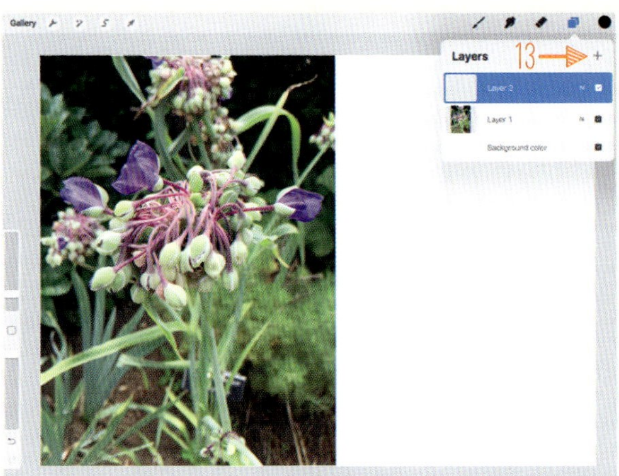

Tip: Use your finger to tap and hold anywhere on the photo, then drag your finger around to select different colors. Once you release your finger, the last color you selected will appear in the color dot.

STEP 14: Tap and hold your finger on the image to select a color (this works with your finger only, not a stylus). This step is like dipping your paintbrush in a paint color, so next time you use your brush, it will lay down that color.

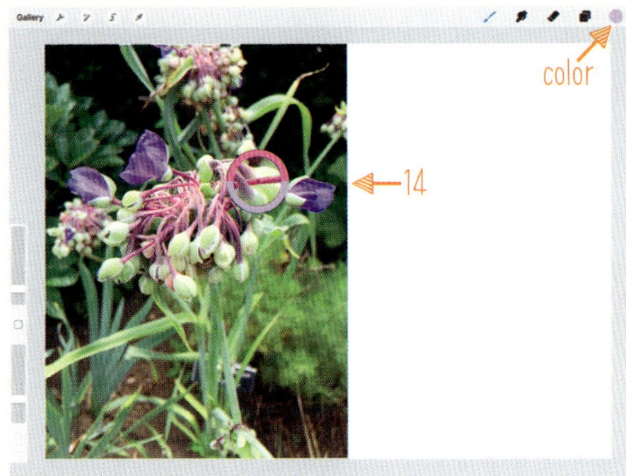

STEP 15: Once you are happy with the color shown in the color dot, tap on the **Brush** tool.

STEP 16: Tap on the **Hand Lettering** brush set. (If you do not yet have this brush set installed in your Procreate app, see chapter 1 under "Downloads and Resources" for instructions.)

STEP 17: Select the **Circle** brush.

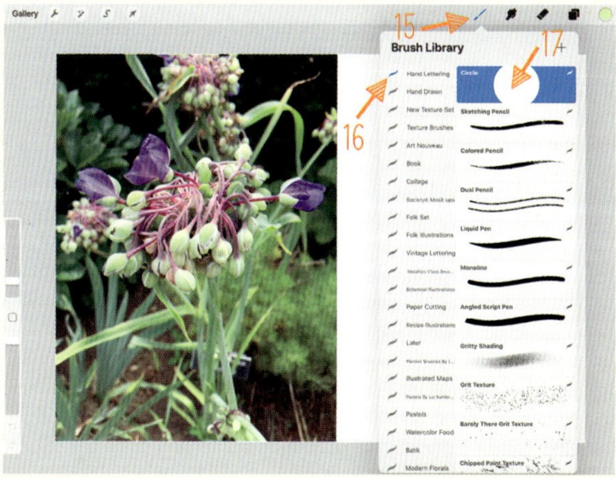

STEP 18: Use the top slider on the left to adjust the brush size. I'm using a brush size of 6%.

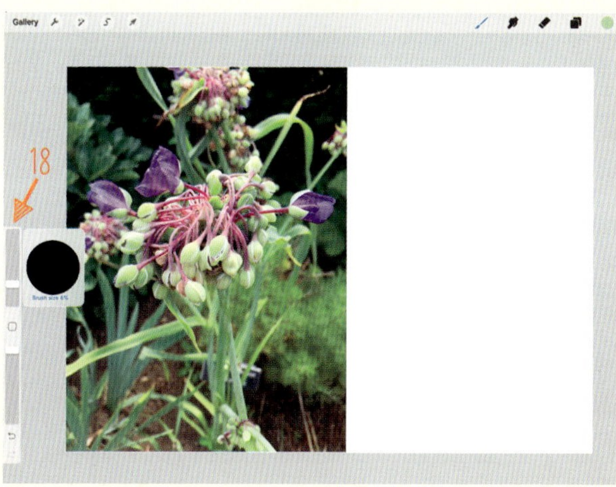

STEP 19: Tap on the white part of the canvas with one finger to create a circle. If you tap with your stylus, this brush will create a different size circle each time you tap. If you use your finger, the circle size will be the same size every time. (We'll talk more about brush settings throughout the book.)

STEP 20: Tap the **Move** tool, turn off **Magnetics** in the **Snapping** section, and then use your finger to move the circle beside the photo.

Tip: If you make a mistake, just tap two fingers on the canvas to undo the action. Keep tapping with two fingers to undo multiple actions.

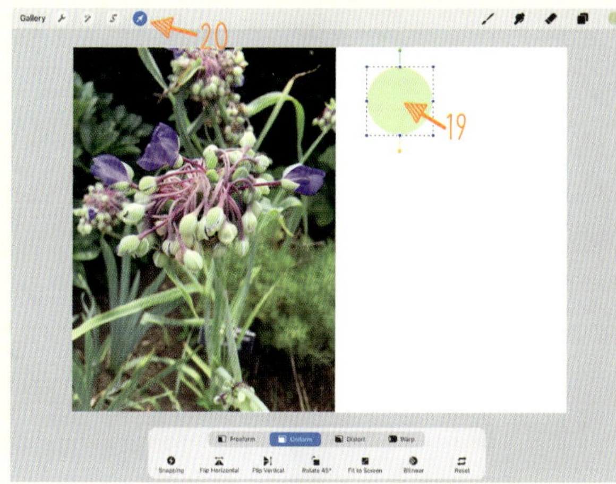

STEP 21: Repeat steps 13 through 20 until you've sampled all the colors you want to include in your palette, remembering to create a new layer before creating each color circle. Your canvas should look something like this when you're finished.

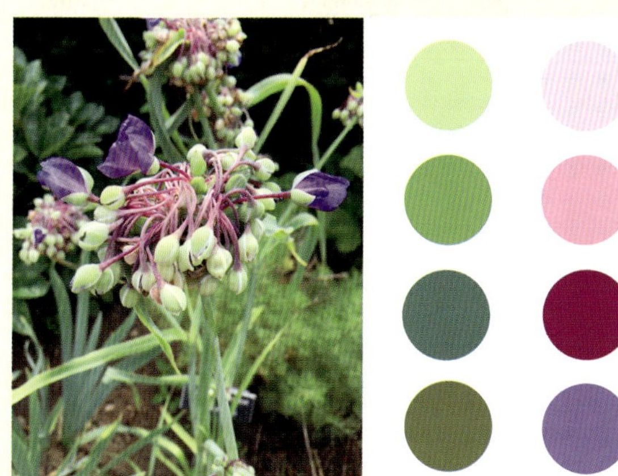

> Tip: Get a wide range of colors from each photo. You may not use all of them, but seeing them all together will help you decide which ones you want to combine.

STEP 22: Make lots of palettes. There is no such thing as having too many color options!

You can see from these examples (below) that you can find stunning multicolored scenes practically anywhere. Keep an eye out for complementary color combinations wherever you go, and don't be afraid to ask if you can snap a photo of someone's outfit!

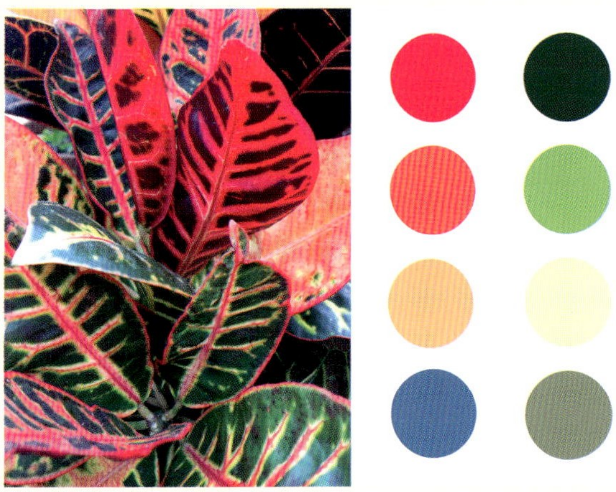

Plants and flowers display a wide range of vibrant colors, so I take pictures of any colorful botanical forms I find in gardens, arboretums, and greenhouses.

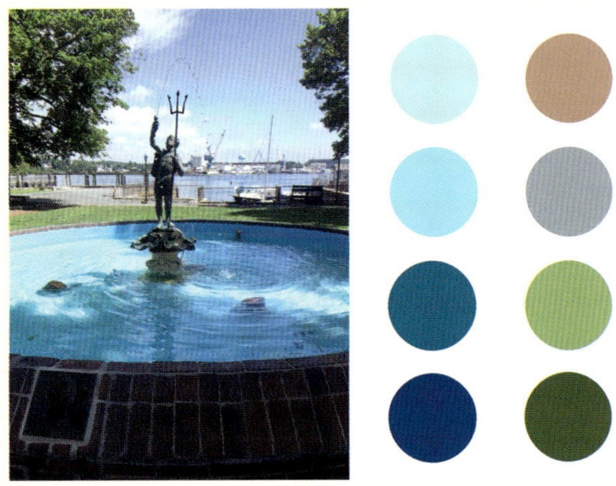

Sometimes a landscape, a cityscape, or a sunset can provide an interesting color combination.

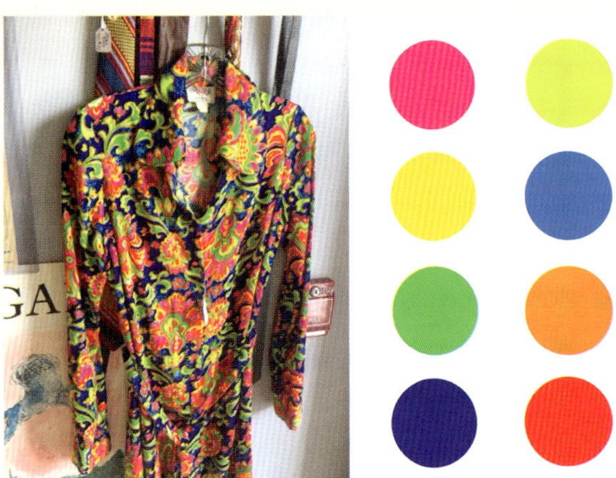

Keep your eyes peeled for beautiful color combinations in clothing and accessories.

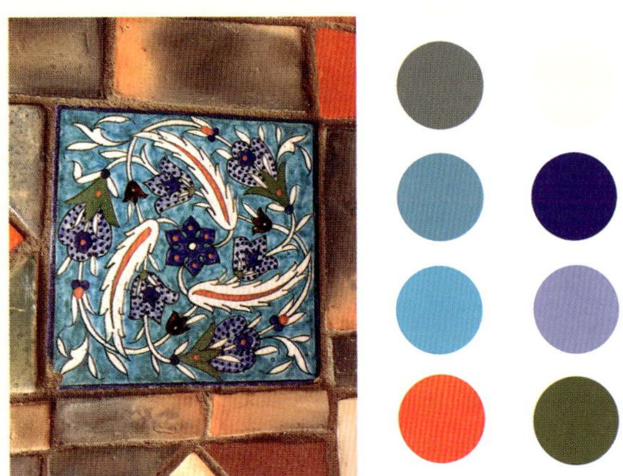

Wall tiles, wallpaper, and objects hanging on walls often display beautiful color palettes.

Save Your Palette in a Procreate Palette Library

Once you have created a color palette you like, you can save it in the Procreate app so it will be easy to access any time you use the app.

Follow these easy steps to save your color palette in your Palette Library:

STEP 1: Tap on the color dot to open the **Colors panel.**

STEP 2: Tap on **Palettes.**

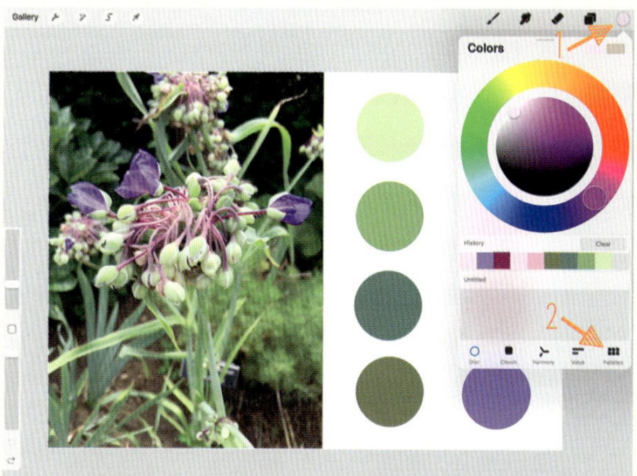

STEP 3: Tap on the + symbol, and then tap **Create new palette.**

STEP 4: Tap **Untitled,** and name your palette. I named mine "Botanical Inspiration."

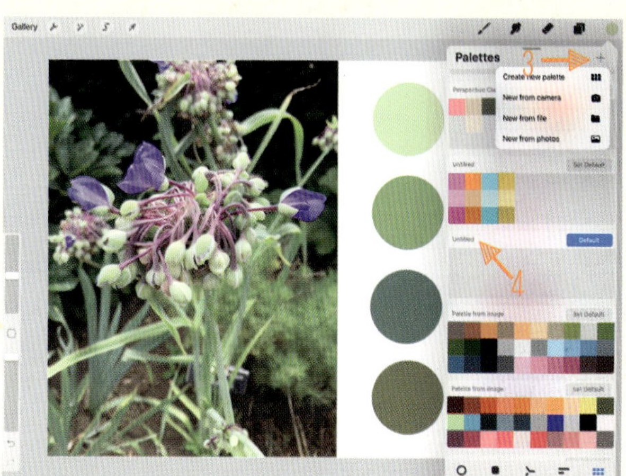

STEP 5: Tap and hold on one of the colors you created, and then release your finger (the color you sampled should be shown in the color dot).

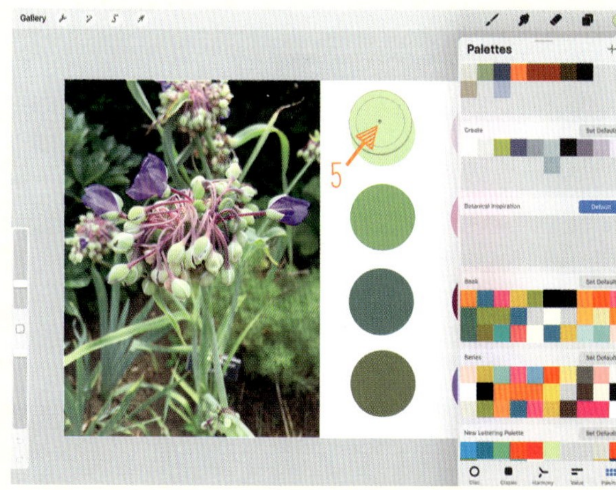

STEP 6: Tap on one of the squares in the palette to save that color.

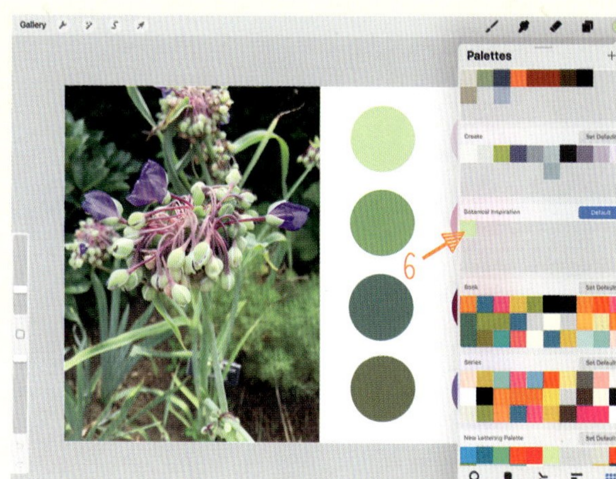

STEP 7: Repeat steps 5 and 6 for each color.

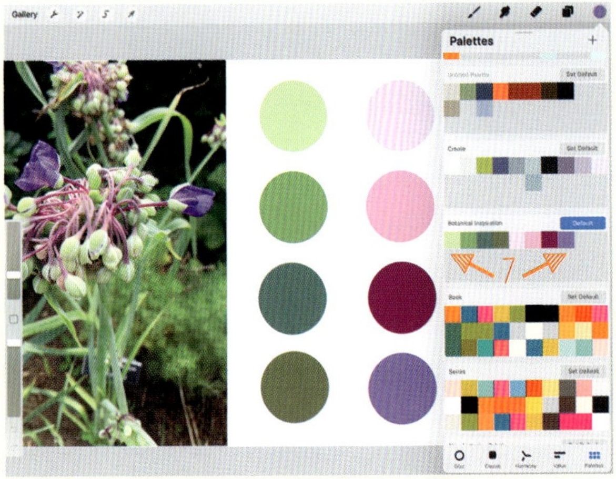

> Tips: 1.) Tap and drag your colors around the palette to organize them in the way that works best for you. 2.) Tap and hold a color square to see the option to delete it.

Now that we have created some color palettes, let's move on to the next part of your inspiration library where we'll store ideas for words and phrases to letter.

Choosing Your Lettering Content

One of the most challenging aspects of hand lettering is figuring out what words or phrases to letter. Because we'll spend so much time making the text beautiful, it's important that the content of the lettering is something we want to share with the world. In this section we'll brainstorm for lettering content so you can create a library of your favorite quotes and phrases to hand letter.

Safety First! Intellectual Property Basics

There are two types of hand lettering projects: personal and commercial. *Personal* means you won't make any money from the project. It could be anything from a gift for a friend to an inspirational quote you just want to hang on your wall. For these kinds of projects you can use any quotes, phrases, or words you like!

"Commercial" means that you could receive financial gain (directly or indirectly) from the project. This could be an art print that you sell online or an Instagram post that you use to attract more followers. When creating commercial lettering projects, it's best to play it safe and use only your own words, unless it's a quote or phrase in the public domain. The good news is, quotes from literary works that are over 100 years old are typically in the public domain, so you are safe using material from old religious texts, ancient manuscripts, and books that are in the public domain, which includes practically everything from the 19th century or earlier.

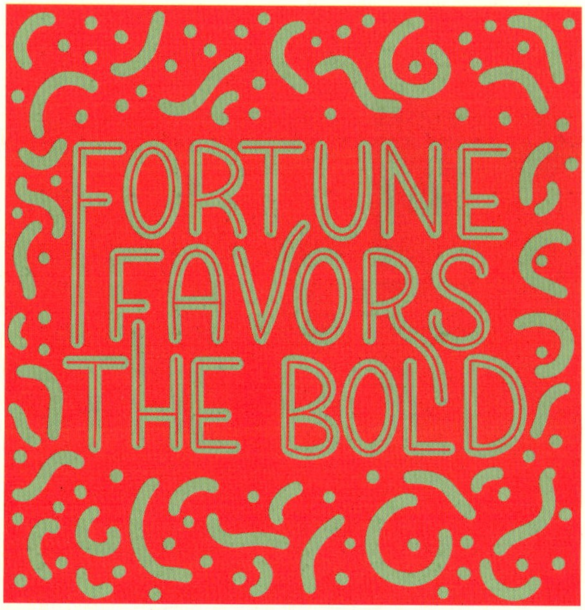

This phrase is a translation of an ancient Latin proverb, so it is available for personal and commercial use.

Who Owns a Quote?

First of all, I'm not a lawyer! If you're ever in doubt about something related to intellectual property, there is no substitute for contacting a real attorney. However, all creatives need to be aware of the basic principles of intellectual property.

Intellectual property rights protect the things we create from being used for financial gain by anyone other than the original creator or the legal holder of rights to the property. For example, if you see a poem you love and decide to hand letter your favorite line, and then if you attempt to make money from that work without written permission, you may be putting yourself at risk. The poet may have a legal right to claim most or all the profits you've made from that work, or even request additional fees for damages. That being said, most people are happy to be quoted and wouldn't dream of suing a creative for making their words look beautiful. Regardless, it's important to remember that hand lettering other people's words is risky.

Tip: If you want to use someone's quote, but are worried about violating intellectual property rights, then just contact them! They may be more than happy to be quoted by you, especially if you can show a beautiful example of the lettering you create.

Create Your Own Lettering Library

The easiest way to avoid violating intellectual property rights laws is to create a library of your own original quotes and phrases. I write down any phrase that comes to my mind throughout the day. I try to come up with ideas that speak to my unique experiences in the world and that are relatable to a wide audience. You could save your phrases in a notebook, a Procreate document, or a text document. Keep them somewhere that is easy to access, so no matter where you are, you can quickly add a new idea the moment it comes to you.

For example, my husband and I like to joke about how introverts (like us) see the world. I was invited to a party that sounded like it would be very loud and crowded, and I immediately thought of an introvert's response: "Sorry I can't come, it sounds too peopley." This is a sentiment any introvert could understand, and I thought is would be a fun and relatable phrase to hand letter.

No, *peopley* is not a word, but hand letterers can feel free to play with language to both reduce the number of words in a quote and to make a phrase humorous to a particular audience.

As you start to jot down your ideas, think about your personal experiences. What do you know a lot about? Maybe you're a parent who has some quirky or unconventional parenting advice. Maybe you're a teenager who wants to creatively explain exactly how uncool your parents are. Maybe you want to letter positive, uplifting phrases to help people who have

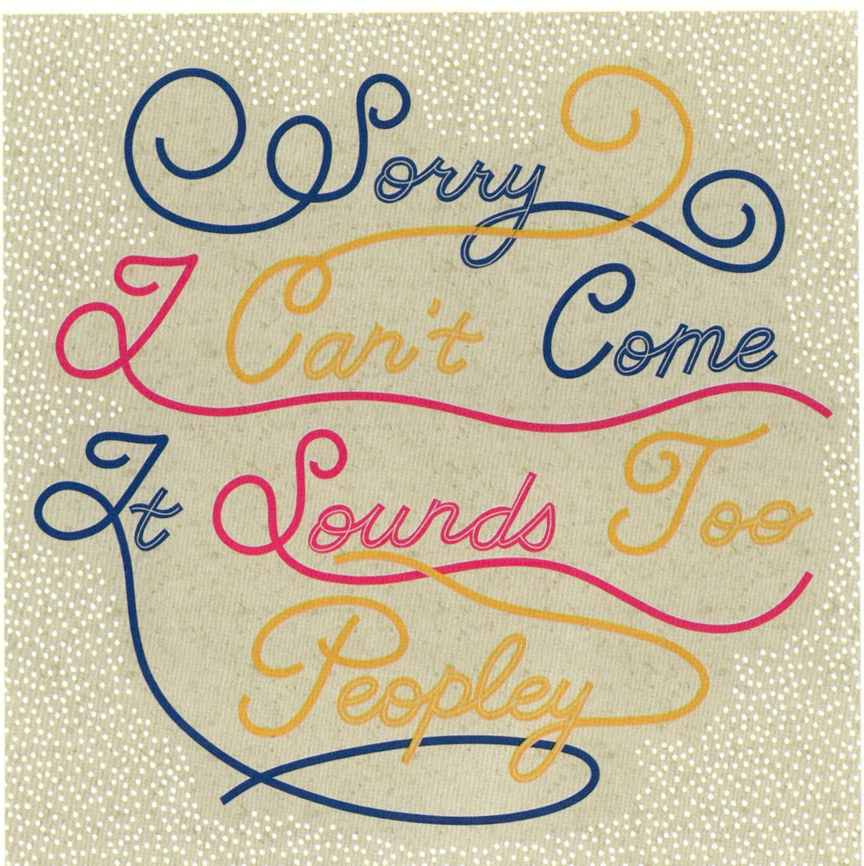

anxiety; or maybe you want to share your religious, political, or cultural views. Whatever direction you decide to go in, choose something that you want to say to the world, then think of short, interesting ways to say it.

Create Your Own Phrases

One way to come up with interesting phrases is to practice stream-of-consciousness writing. To give it a try, first write down an idea. It can be anything you think or believe. For example, "I think that some people think too much about the past and regret things that have actually helped them make good decisions in their daily lives." That would be a terribly long quote, right? Next, start writing down all your thoughts about your idea. Write down everything you can think of and don't focus on spelling, grammar, or punctuation. Even if it seems crazy, silly, or wrong, let it flow onto the page like you are talking to a close friend who really gets you. Usually, during this process ideas will start coming to the surface and soon you'll start to distill your idea into shorter and shorter phrases without losing the original meaning.

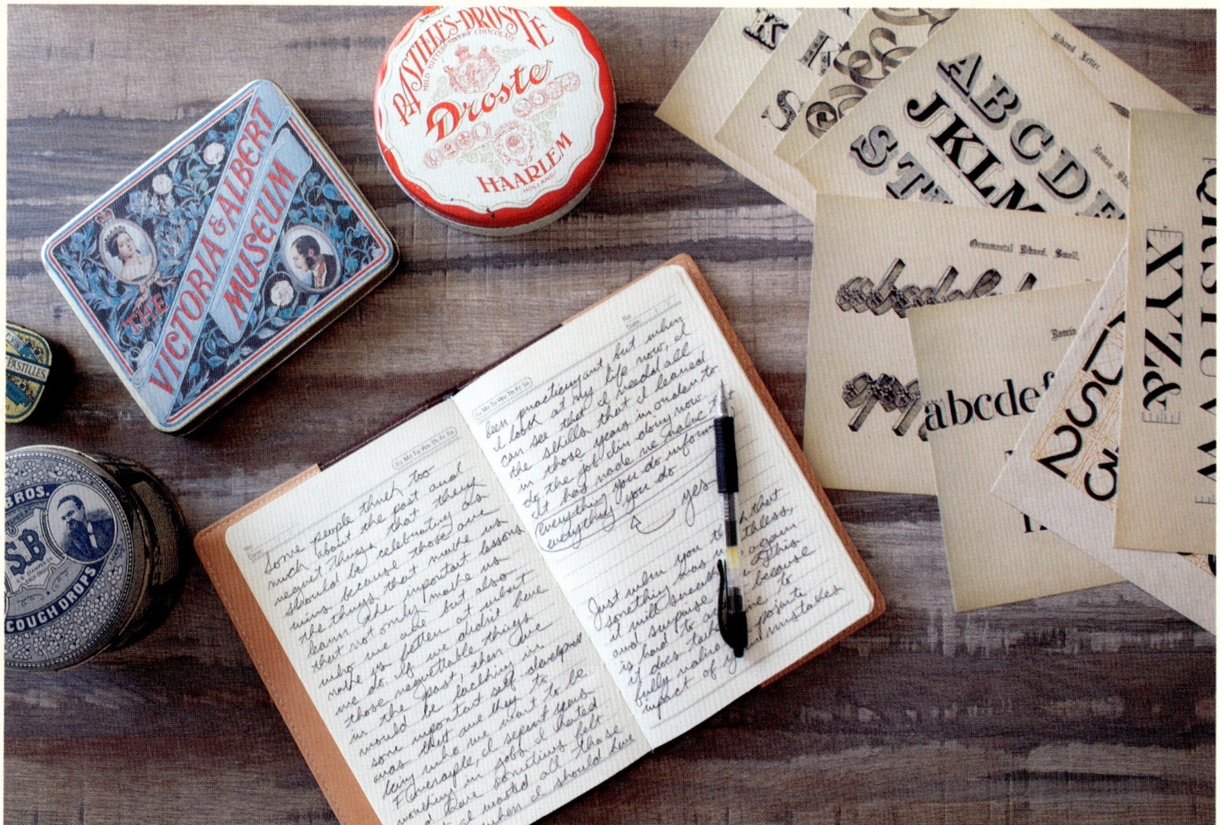

During the writing process, my idea went from, "Some people think too much about the past and regret things that actually help them make good decisions in their daily lives" to "Everything you do informs everything you do."

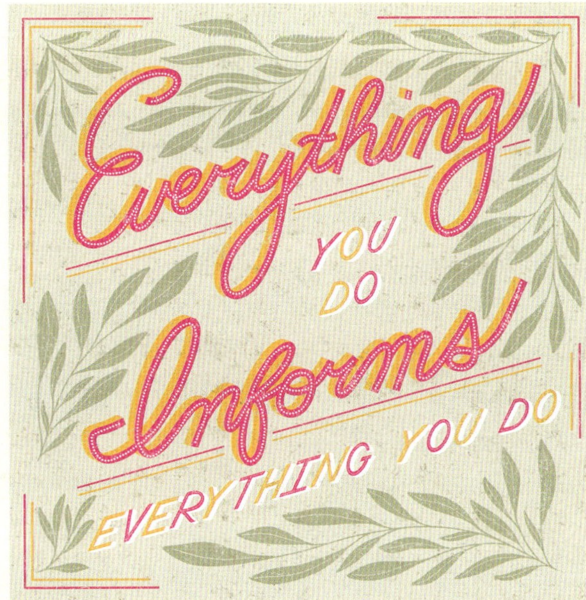

Tip: Keep it short! When you first start lettering, it's better to stick to single words and short phrases. The more words in the composition, the more complicated the design process gets.

Need some help getting started? Here are some prompts to help you create your own phrases:

When I said ______ I meant _______.
Example: When I said "date night" I meant pajamas and Netflix.

Don't ever let ______ stop you from ______.
Example: Don't ever let doubt stop you from drawing.

Life is better with ______.
Example: Life is better with naps.

Let's ______ and ______.
Example: Let's eat chocolate and snuggle.

Darling, you're ______.
Example: Darling, you're as weird as me, which is why I love you.

It's only ______ before you ______.
Example: It's only scary before you start.

Never stop ______.

Example: Never stop dancing like a toddler.

You are ______.

Example: You are more creative than you realize.

It's never too late to ______.

Example: It's never too late to start something new.

Less ______ more ______.

Example: Less Monday more Friday.

We go together like ______ and ______.

Example: We go together like ketchup and scrambled eggs.

A problem only ______ can solve.

Example: A problem only chocolate can solve.

You make me happier than ______ (and that's saying a lot).

Example: You make me happier than chocolate (and that's saying a lot).

No ______ before coffee.

Example: No talkie before coffee.

Some Ideas to Get You Started

Not ready to write your own quotes? No problem. Below you'll find a list of ideas to help get your library started:

SINGLE WORDS

- Awesome
- Beautiful
- Love
- Create
- Grow
- Breathe
- Inspire
- Incredible
- Gorgeous
- Smile
- Wonder
- Explore
- Flow
- Dance

PHRASES

- Work it
- You got this
- Oh yeah!
- Just roll with it
- Do your thing
- Choose joy
- Be lazy today
- You're a star
- You're killing it
- You deserve a nap
- Can't adult today
- You're my favorite
- Do what you love
- Embrace the mess
- It's okay to take naps
- It takes whatever it takes
- Start before you're ready
- Practice makes progress
- Let's be weird together
- I came, I saw, I left early
- Everything will be okay
- Fortune favors the bold
- Every day is a blank slate
- Start before you feel ready
- There is beauty in everything
- I have no idea what I'm doing
- Live the life you've imagined
- Be the energy you want to attract
- If you never try, you'll never know
- Everything is hard before it is easy
- Everything will turn out fine
- Your weirdness is your superpower
- There are opportunities in every failure
- You are exactly where you need to be
- Ordinary people do extraordinary things
- Everything you've done informs everything you do
- When you can't find the sunshine, be the sunshine

You could even create a series of lettering illustrations around a central theme. A series is a great way to practice your lettering while making something that is great for sharing online or selling as a set. Here are a few ideas for lettering series you could create:

- Days of the week
- Months of the year
- Seasons
- Zodiac signs
- Plant names with botanical borders
- Words in another language (bonito, amor, beso)
- Letters of the alphabet
- Various ways to style an ampersand
- Various ways to style the same letter
- The same word in various languages (hello, hola, bonjour, etc.)
- Crazy things your toddler says
- Places around the world (city names, country names, etc.)
- Animal or insect names with an illustration

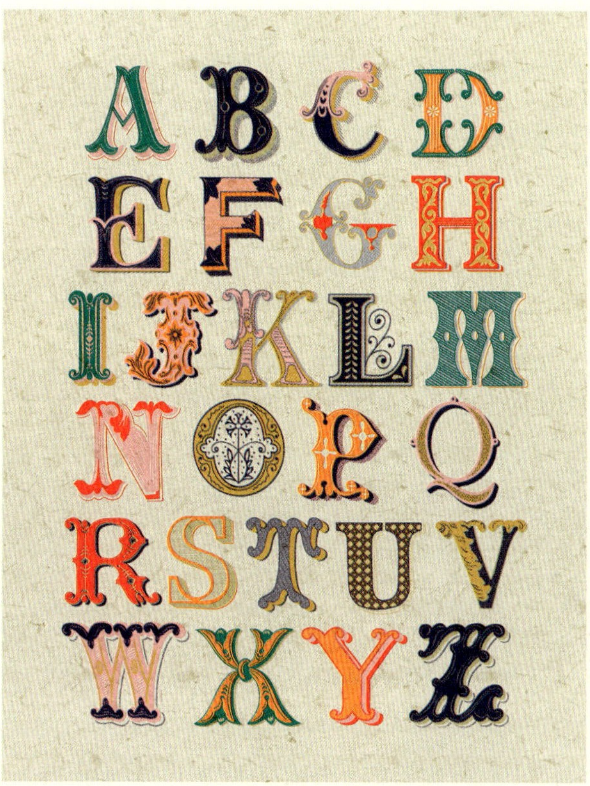

Creating a series is the perfect way to improve your lettering skills without having to constantly come up with new ideas for content. Once you choose your series theme you can just focus on coming up with beautiful ways to decorate the words or letters in your series.

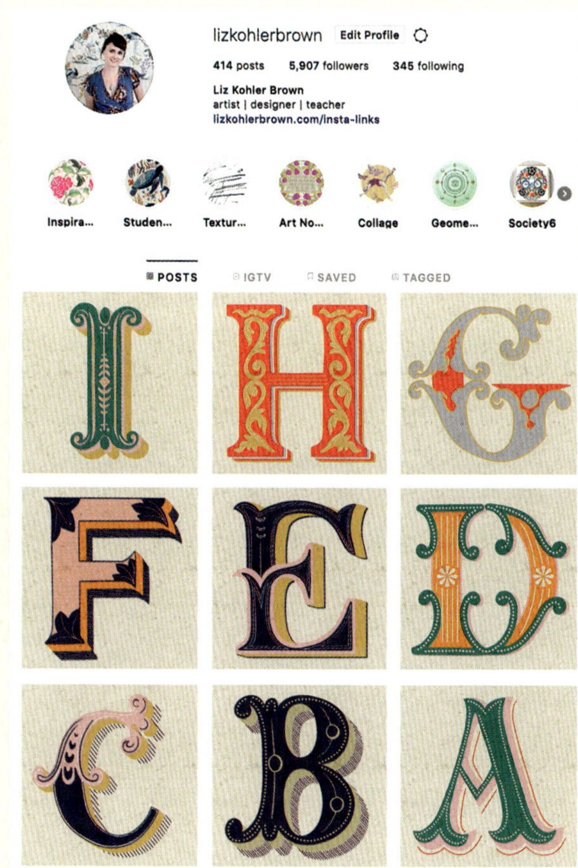

Sharing your series elements individually is a great way to present the detail work you put into each illustration.

For example, I created a series of 26 different vintage-inspired letters of the alphabet and then combined them into a single document to create an art print (opposite).

A series is great for sharing online because you can share one piece of the series each time you finish it. It can get your audience interested in your work and can help you keep up the motivation to finish the series.

Lettering in the Real World: Letterforms Are Everywhere!

The last pieces of the inspiration puzzle are letterforms and decorative shapes. There are an unlimited number of letter styles out in the world, so finding inspiration is a matter of training yourself to notice the aesthetic and artistic details of the places you visit. Every time you see a lettering style or decorative element you like, snap a quick picture with your phone or camera. You may not have a finished composition in mind when you take the picture, but when you're ready to draw you'll be thanking yourself for having created a treasure trove of resources to pull from. Here are a few photos I took in cafes, museums, and antique shops.

I love scouring antique shops and flea markets for vintage magazines, books, and packages. Each one of these vintage packages is covered in ideas for letterforms, decorative elements, and color palettes (below).

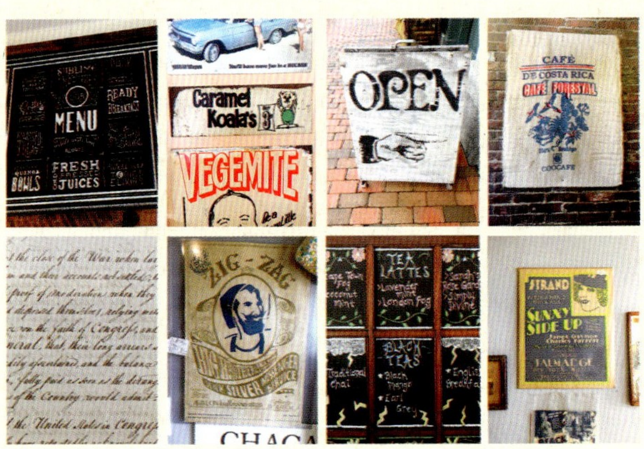

When you visit cafes, walk downtown, or peruse antique shops, keep your eyes peeled. Lettering layouts, color combinations, and letterform ideas are all around you.

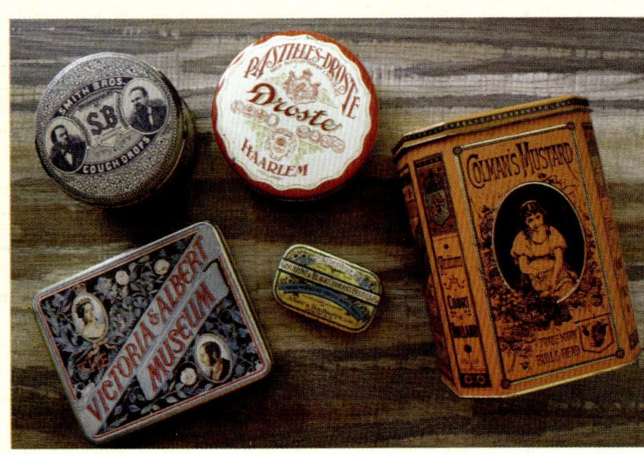

Vintage tins and packages provide some of the best resources for lettering inspiration. You can find lettering on old magazines, cigarette packages, medicine bottles, and everything in between!

Finding Inspiration Online

Don't live in a trendy city with lettering inspiration around every corner? No problem. The number of online resources for lettering inspiration is not only larger than any one person could ever use, it's also growing every day! Libraries, universities, and other educational institutions around the world are digitizing old publications to make them available online at no cost.

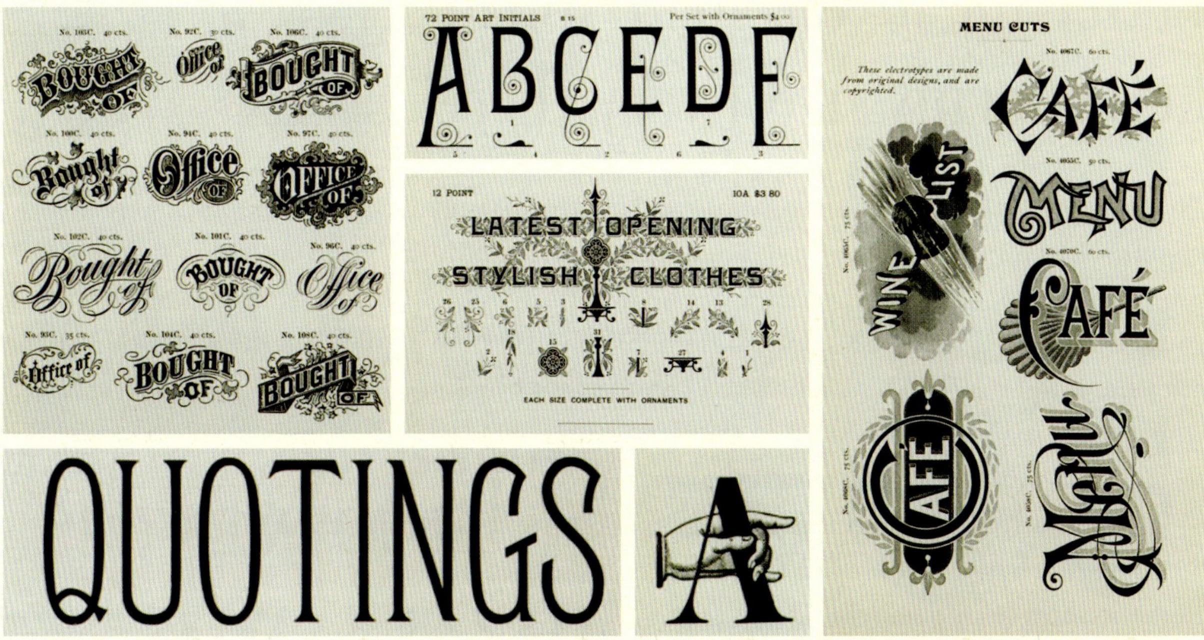

These examples of lettering from the 1897 book Specimens of Type, Borders, Ornaments, Brass Rules and Cuts *are just a tiny sample of the kinds of lettering inspiration you can find online.*

The **Downloads and Resources** page found on my website includes a Pinterest inspiration board with over 500 images of letterforms and decorations with links to download each one. You can find the **Downloads and Resources** web page using the instructions in chapter 1.

On the Pinterest inspiration board, you'll see a huge collection of alphabets you can use as practice sheets to help you learn nearly any lettering style. For example, the following alphabets are from an 1864 book called *Mediaeval Alphabets and Initials for Illuminators* (opposite top two). Can you figure out which letters of my alphabet series were inspired by these vintage resources?

On the inspiration board you'll see that you can look into history to find hundreds of beautiful alphabets in every style of lettering ranging from medieval decorative print to stylized script.

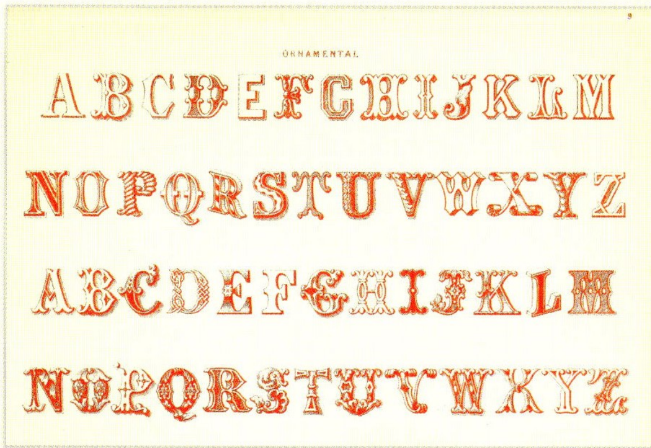

A beautiful example of ornamental letter styles.

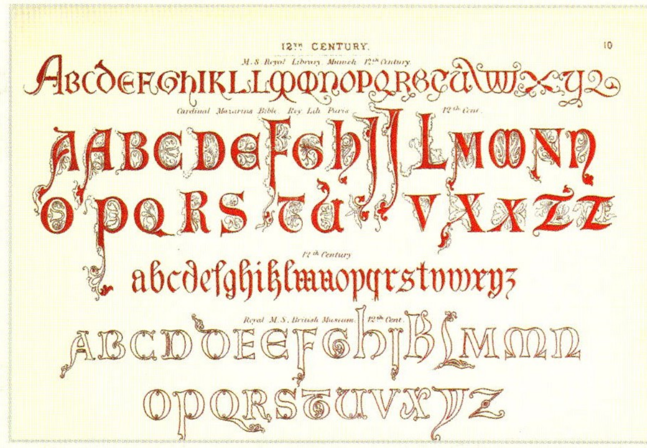

12th century style letters and decorative elements.

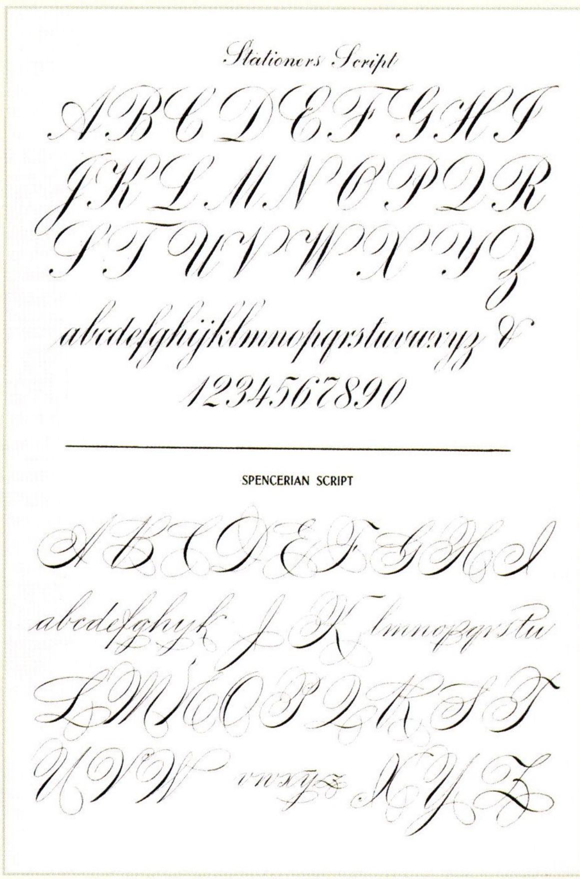

Two styles of script lettering from the 1914 book Art Alphabets and Lettering.

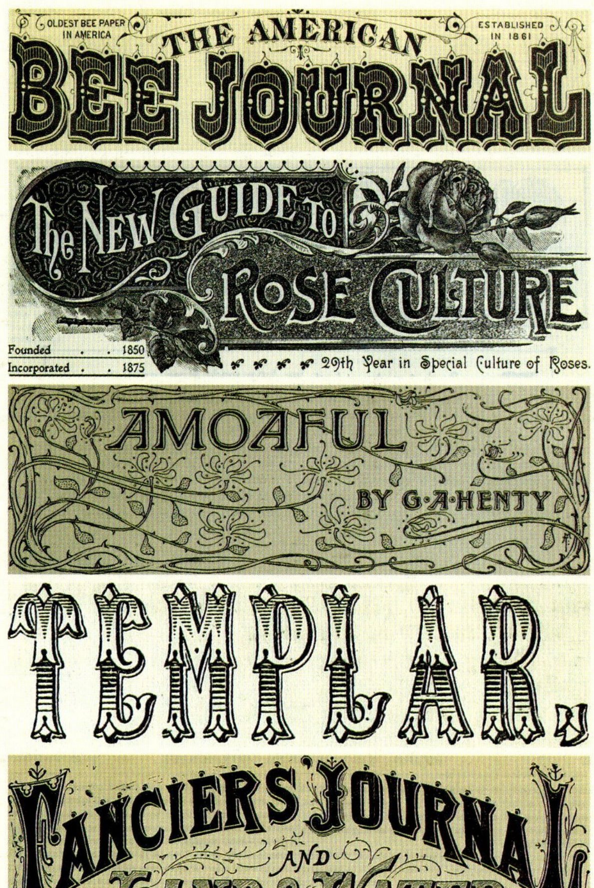

Examples of letter styles and decorations found in magazines, books, and advertisements from the 1800s.

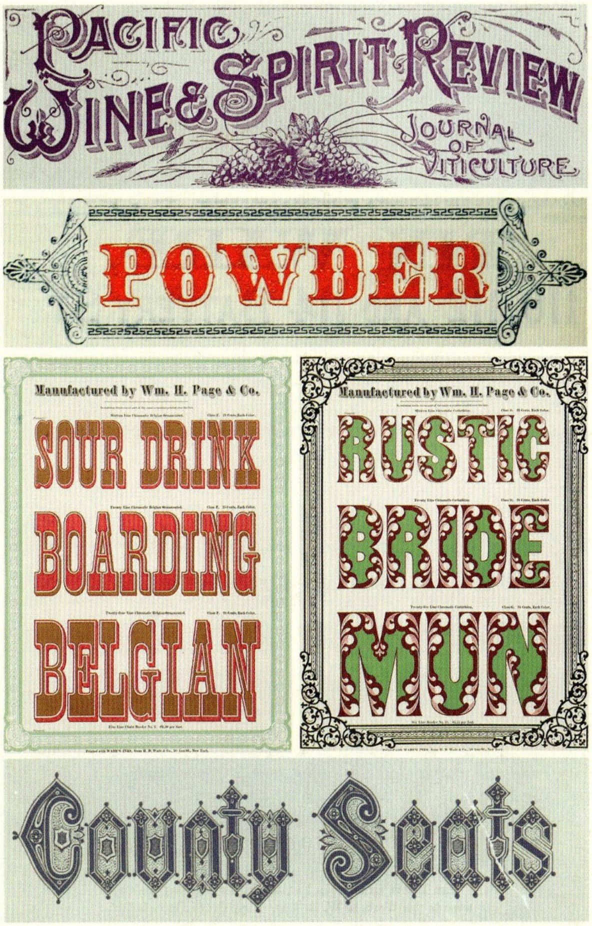

Examples of colorful lettering compositions from the 1800s.

You'll also see a huge list of vintage advertisements and signs to help inspire your lettering layouts and decorative elements.

You can save the vintage images you find online on Flickr, a Pinterest board, or just take screenshots and save them in your iPad photo album. I also like to print a few of my favorites so I have a quick reference guide beside me when I create letters.

> Tip: To take a screenshot on your iPad, press the home button and the power button at the same time. You can then crop the screenshot in the Photos app.

In the following chapters, we'll look at how to take a letterform inspiration and make it your own so that rather than copying letter styles directly, you use them as inspiration to create our own unique letters. Can you guess which vintage advertisement (left) inspired this piece (opposite)?

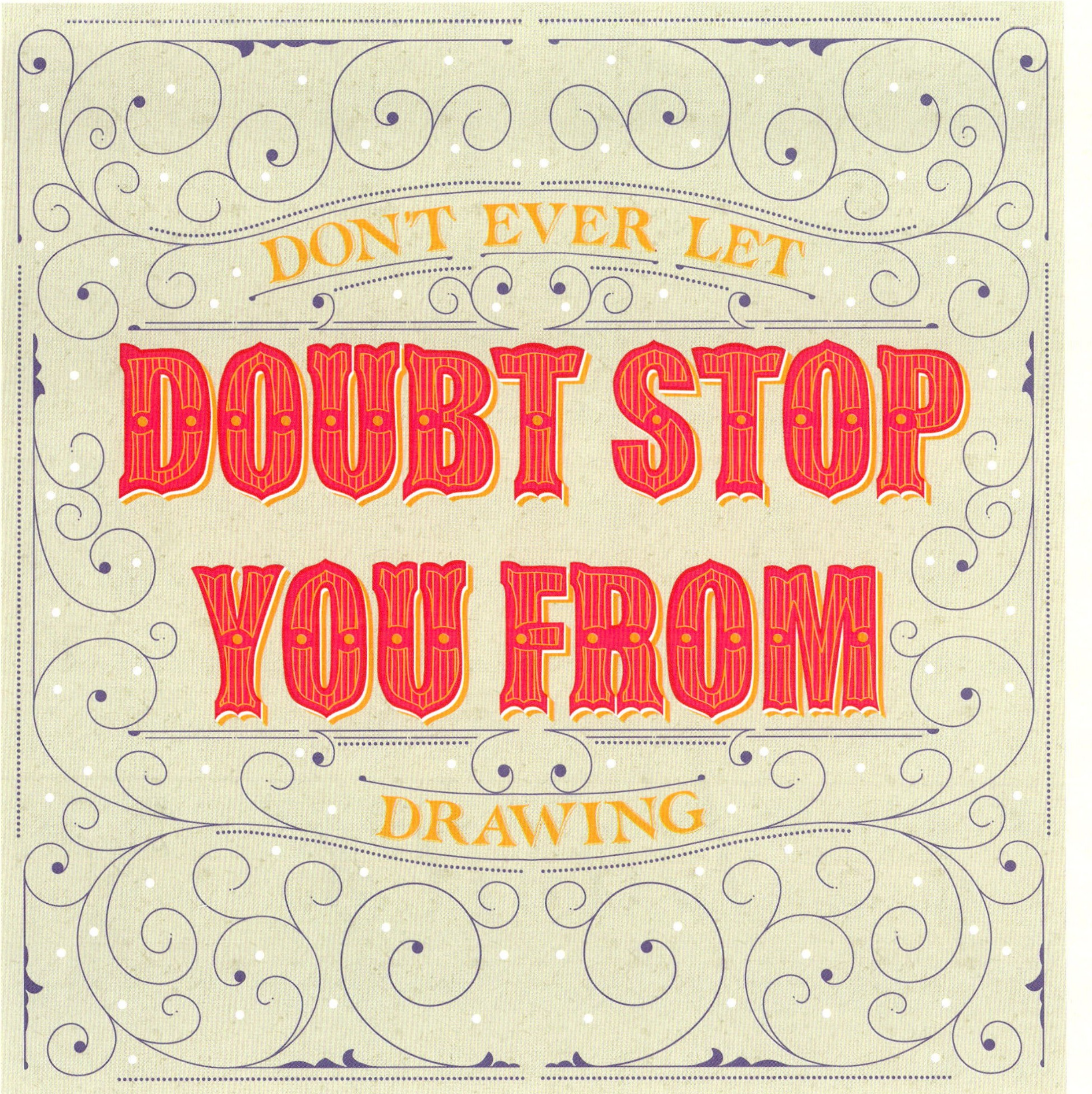

A lettering composition.

CHAPTER 3

Procreate Basics

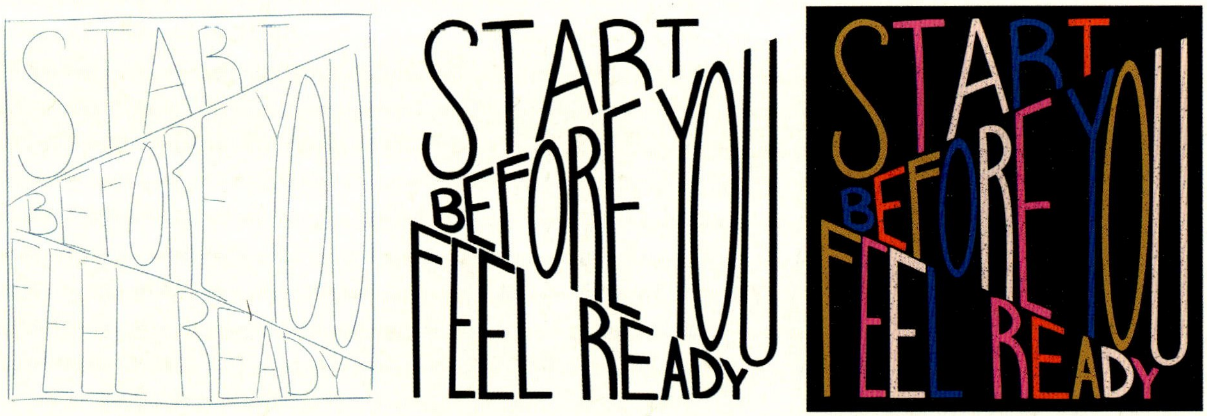

Now that you have a library of inspiring images and colors at your fingertips, it's time to get comfortable with the tools you'll use to create lettering projects. This chapter is your resource for all the important tools, finger gestures, and best practices for lettering in Procreate, so you may need to refer back to this chapter as you work through the projects in the book.

If you've already learned the basics of Procreate, you may prefer to skip this chapter or just refer to the sections you aren't sure about. We won't look at every tool in Procreate, just the ones that are crucial to the lettering process, so both novices and experienced Procreate users can pick up some helpful lettering-related tips.

I'll show you the basics of Procreate by taking you step-by-step through the creation of a finished composition, so I recommend getting out your stylus and following along with me as you read through the chapter to learn Procreate in the best way possible—through hands-on experience!

Creating a Canvas: Image Size and DPI

You already know from chapter 2 that you can tap the + symbol and then tap the **Custom Size** icon to create a new document, but you may be wondering about some of the other options on the document creation page.

You'll be using the default settings throughout the book, but as you start working on more complex projects, you may find some of the advanced settings helpful. Let's take a look at some of the things to consider when creating a new document.

1. Measurements and Image Sizes

You can work in any of the listed units of measurement, but it's important to always keep the pixel dimensions in mind. In general, 300 DPI (dots/pixels per inch) is considered the lowest acceptable DPI for printing onto paper. For example, if you create a 10″ × 10″ lettering project, it should be at least 3000 × 3000 pixels (that is 300 pixels for each inch of the document). If I was designing a 5″ × 7″ greeting card, I could either set my document to 5″ × 7″ at 300 DPI, or I could set it to 1500 × 2100 pixels. Both documents would be the same size with the same DPI, but are expressed using different units of measurement.

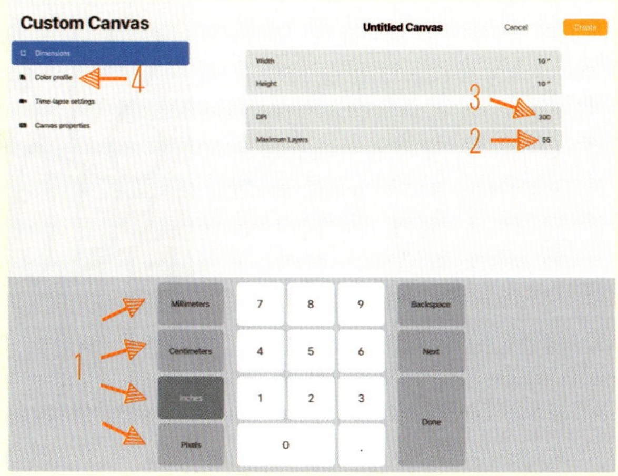

There are a few things to think about every time you create a new document: image size, maximum layers, DPI, and color space.

The first thing to consider before creating a new document is what the final use of your image will be. Knowing this will help you choose the correct pixel dimensions for your new document. Throughout the book, I give suggested image sizes for each type of project, but you can feel free to work at whatever size you'd like.

> Tip: One important rule about images made in Procreate is that it's okay to downsize, but it's never okay to upsize. Any time you increase the size of an image, it becomes blurry, so it's best to start your document at the size you need or larger.

2. Maximum Layers

You can see that changing the dimensions of your document will cause the number of maximum layers to change as well. This is because iPads are relatively small devices that have less processing power than laptops or desktop computers. To keep the app running smoothly, Procreate limits the number of layers you can use based on the size of the image. As a result, larger images can have fewer layers, and smaller images can have more. The number of layers for each size will depend on the iPad model you have, so the best way to test this feature is to choose different image sizes and observe how the maximum layers number changes.

3. DPI

The DPI of an image should be at least 300 for printing on paper; however, there may be cases when you need a different DPI. For example, some print-on-demand companies, or certain client projects, might require a specific DPI. If you're working on a project for a client and they haven't requested a specific DPI, you may want to work in 400 or 500 DPI to ensure a high resolution, which would be suitable for a wide variety of final uses.

Keep in mind that even though increasing the DPI also increases the image quality, there is a point at which the image quality may be increased to a level beyond what the human eye can detect. Therefore, 1000 DPI is not necessarily better than 400 DPI because the increase in DPI will have an imperceptible effect on image quality while significantly increasing the file size and decreasing the maximum number of layers.

4. Color Profile

This field describes the "color profile," which determines how color is translated by websites, applications, and printers. The default option is **sRGB**, which is the most commonly used color profile for most projects (websites, social media, and print-on-demand). If you are working on a project that requires a different color space, you can adjust it here.

You'll also see options for Time-lapse settings, which allow you to change the video size and quality for the recording of your drawing process. We'll talk more about Time-lapses later in the book.

To explore the rest of the tools, we'll need a new document. So let's get started with a 10″ × 10″ document at 300 DPI. Once you open the document, you'll notice an array of symbols along the top of the screen. Each of these symbols represents a menu, and each menu contains a selection of tools. Take a look at the figure on the right to see what type of task each menu performs and then tap on each menu along the top of the page to see what tools each menu contains. (Note that the Move tool won't work until we have actually drawn something to move.)

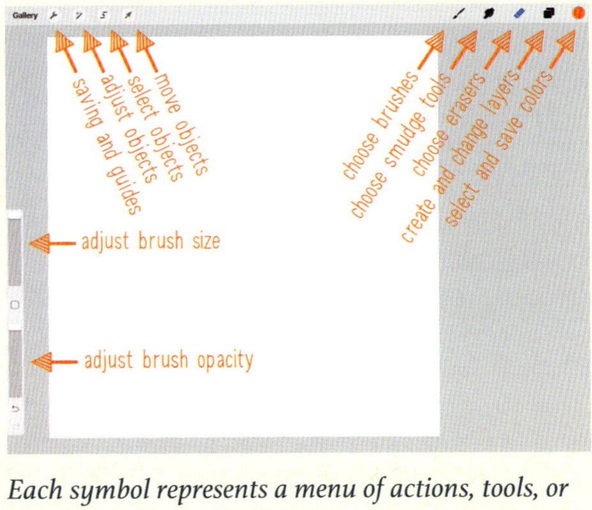

Each symbol represents a menu of actions, tools, or functions.

Here is the same screen with the names of the menus. I'll use these names throughout the book, so if you ever have trouble finding a menu or a specific tool within that menu, just refer back to this image.

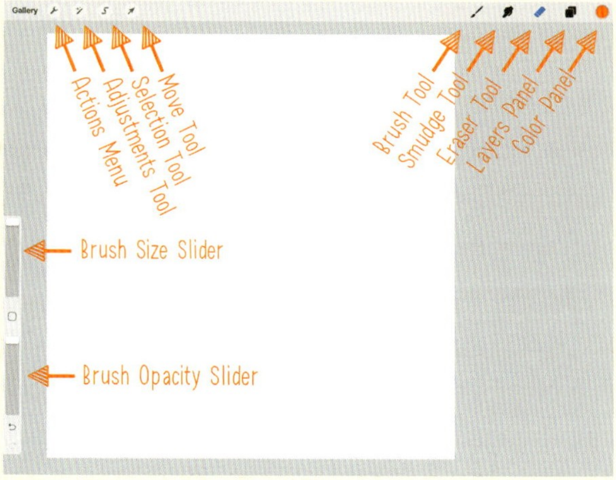

The name of each tool we'll be using throughout the book.

Essential Tools: Brushes, Smudgers, and Erasers

One of the best things about Procreate is the versatility of the brushes. You can use Procreate's built-in set of brushes, buy new brushes, or even make your own! Unlike physical paintbrushes, digital brushes are extremely versatile and can be used for a wide variety of tasks, which include laying down color (like a traditional paintbrush or pencil), erasing (imagine erasing a gritty texture out of a word drawn in blue to reveal the white background behind it), or blending/smudging (imagine putting two colors beside each other and blending them together like you would with an oil pastel).

Later in the book we'll use the brushes in the Hand Lettering set, but for now let's just play with one of the brush sets that come with Procreate. We'll use this same set of brushes for painting, blending, and erasing so you can get a feel for all three tools.

Follow these steps to get started:

STEP 1: Select a color by tapping the **Colors panel** and choosing a color.

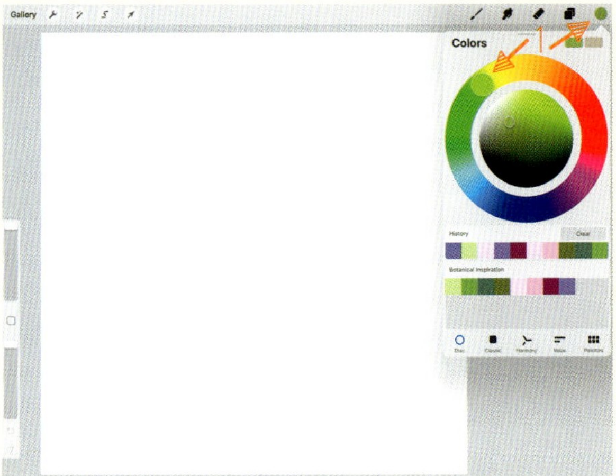

STEP 2: Tap on the **Brush** tool to open the **Brush Library**, then scroll down the menu and tap one of the brush sets. I suggest trying the **Calligraphy** set since these brushes are perfect for lettering projects.

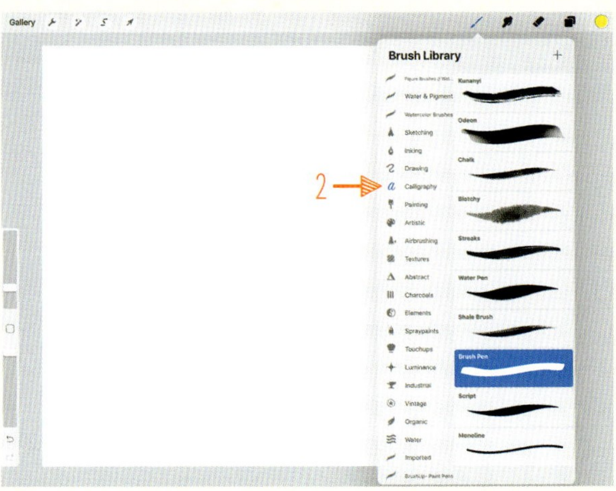

STEP 3: Make a long brush stroke with each brush in the set, changing colors after each stroke. You may need to adjust the size of a brush using the top slider on the left. (Remember, the top slider adjusts size and the bottom slider adjusts opacity.) Your canvas should look something like this when you're finished.

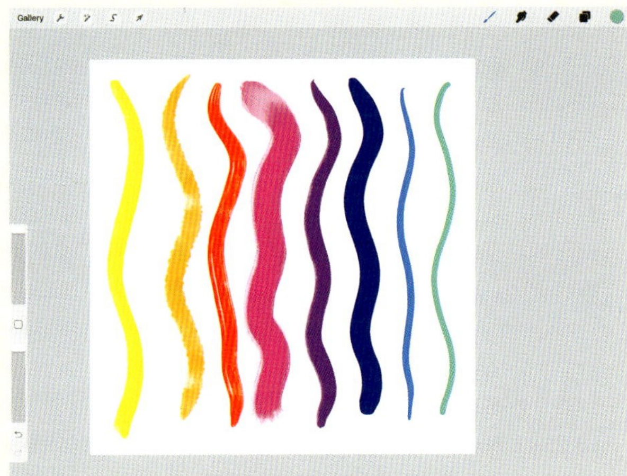

STEP 4: Tap the **Smudge** tool, and then find the same brush set you used for painting.

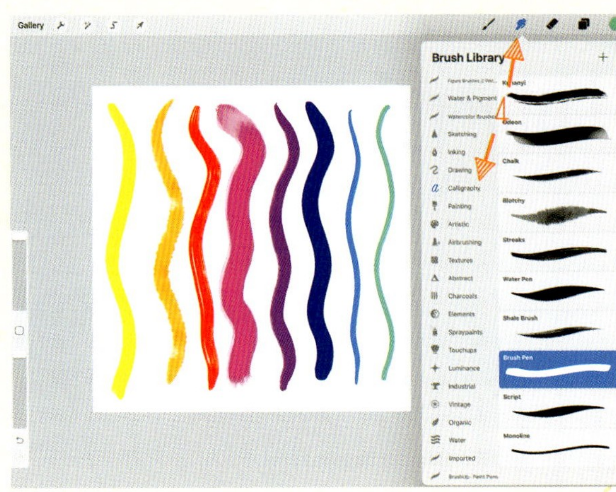

STEP 5: Make long strokes that run through each of the painted lines, changing brushes after each stroke. Your canvas should look something like this.

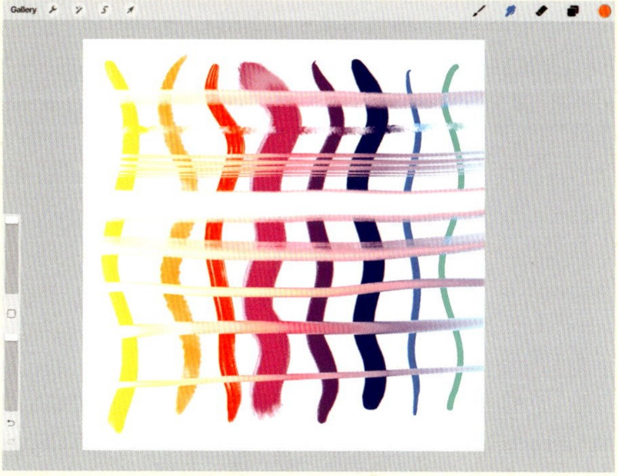

STEP 6: Follow the same process with the **Eraser** tool, running each brush diagonally through your lines. You can see that while the **Smudge** tool pulls colors together to create a new blended color, the **Eraser** tool removes color. You'll notice that some brushes erase all the color, while others erase only part of the color, so some eraser brushes will be more helpful than others depending on your project.

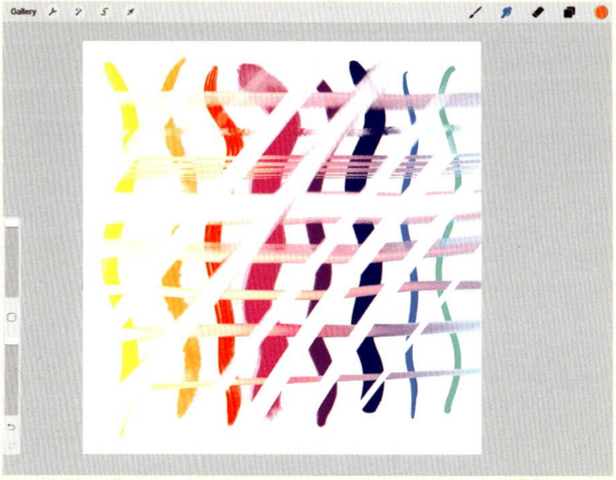

STEP 7: Take a few minutes to experiment with this process using a few different brush sets found in the **Brush Library** to get a feel for how diverse and versatile the brushes are.

Finger Gestures

Zoom In and Out

You may have already noticed that you can pinch to zoom in and reverse pinch (placing two fingers on the canvas and then spreading them apart) to zoom out. During the lettering process, I zoom in closely to each letter as I work on it, then I zoom out to see how it looks in the composition as a whole.

Undo and Redo

These finger gestures will save you time (and keep your frustration level low!) every single time you work in Procreate. Any time you make a mistake, or just want to step back, tap two fingers on the screen. Conversely, if you want to step forward (redo a step you just undid), then tap three fingers.

One thing to keep in mind with these finger gestures is that once you tap Gallery to go back to the app's home screen, you lose the drawing history of the document, so you can't reopen the document and start two-finger tapping to step back. This is why it is so essential to keep each of your colors and line styles separated into layers (we'll discuss layers in the next section).

Copy and Paste

You can drag three fingers down the canvas any time you have something selected (we'll practice this later in the chapter). When you use this finger gesture, you'll see the options to **Cut**, **Copy**, **Cut & Paste**, and **Copy & Paste**. For example, if you draw a beautiful **R** and want to duplicate it and place the copy elsewhere in your composition, you can select the letter and then drag three fingers down to copy and paste the letter somewhere else on your canvas. If you want to paste that same **R** into a different lettering project, you would select it, tap **Copy**, switch to the other document, slide three fingers down, and tap **Paste**.

While it may feel strange to use finger gestures at first, you'll be using them like a pro in no time. Don't be surprised if you accidentally do a two-finger tap on a piece of real paper after working in Procreate for a while!

Working in Layers

Layers are like pieces of transparent tracing paper. You can draw on one layer, then create a new layer and still see the first one. So as you're creating layers (and dragging and dropping them into order) imagine that your drawing is made up of overlapping sheets of transparent paper.

There are a few important things to keep in mind when you work with layers:

- You can affect only the layer that is currently selected. If you're trying to erase or draw on a layer and it isn't working, go back to the Layers panel and make sure the layer you want to work on is highlighted in blue. Blue indicates the active layer.
- Keep every color and line style that you experiment with on different layers to preserve the option to edit each one separately. Creating a document will look something like this: Sketch something, create a new layer, sketch over your sketch, create a new layer, ink your sketch, create a new layer, add some color, create a new layer, add some texture, create a new layer, and so on.

The easiest way to understand how using layers can save you time and frustration is by jumping right in and beginning a real lettering project. Let's start by choosing a short three- to five-word phrase. I'll use the phrase, "start before you feel ready." If you aren't sure what phrase to use, feel free to copy mine while you follow along with these steps:

STEP 1: Tap the **Layers** panel and swipe left on the layer, then tap **Clear** so that you can start with a blank canvas.

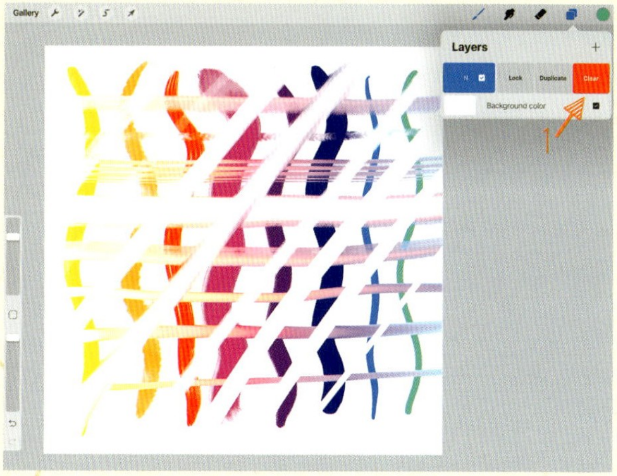

STEP 2: Choose a color (I'll be using blue), and then select the **Sketching Pencil** from the **Hand Lettering** brush set.

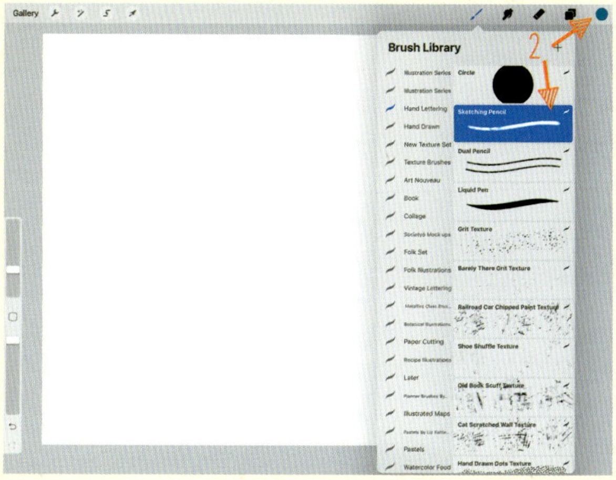

STEP 3: Sketch some lines where your letters will rest. I am using an angled format, but you could draw straight lines, curved lines, or whatever shape you want to use. I also like to add in some borders to help keep my lettering away from the edge of the canvas. Loosely sketch your phrase on the canvas. This is just a sketch to help you get a feel for the framework of your project, so don't worry about making it perfect.

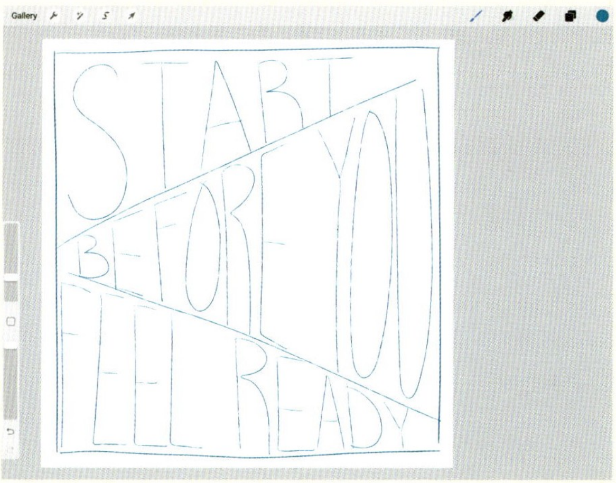

STEP 4: Tap the **Layers panel**, and then reduce the opacity of that layer by tapping on the **N** symbol on the layer and moving the opacity slider to the left. I like to reduce mine to about 40% so I can still see the layer but it isn't distracting.

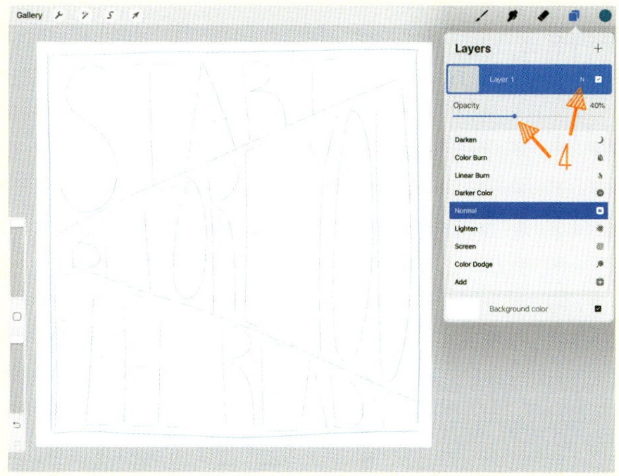

STEP 5: Create a new layer by tapping the + sign. This layer will be where we create our perfectly straight lines.

Quickline and Symmetry

To create two perfectly straight lines that are mirror images of each other on the top and bottom, we need help from two of Procreate's tools: the **Quickline** tool and the **Symmetry** tool. To see how the Quickline tool works, just draw a line, but don't pick up your stylus at the end of the line. While you are holding the stylus down, the line will snap to become straight, and if you drag your stylus around the canvas, the line moves with you.

Before you pick up your stylus, place two fingers anywhere on the canvas using your other hand. This lets you adjust the angle of your line in perfect 15-degree increments. These features will really come in handy as we start making grids and guides for our lettering projects. Play around with the Quickline tool until you feel comfortable making straight lines, and then tap two fingers to step back until you've removed the lines you created.

Next, I want to create two straight lines that are mirror images of each other, so I need to activate Procreate's **Symmetry** tool. Do so by following these steps:

STEP 6: First, double-check that you've created a new layer, and then tap on the **Actions** menu.

STEP 7: Tap **Canvas.**

STEP 8: Turn on the **Drawing Guide.**

STEP 9: Tap **Edit Drawing Guide.**

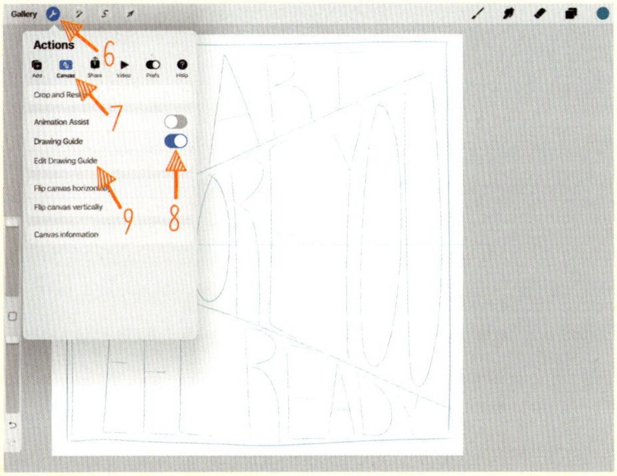

STEP 10: On the bottom of the screen, tap **Symmetry.**

STEP 11: Tap the **Options** button, and then tap **Horizontal.** This will cause anything you do on the top half of the canvas to be duplicated on the bottom half. (You'll see some other symmetry options on the options bar, so feel free to take some time and play with these to get a feel for how they work.)

STEP 12: You'll notice the colorful bar at the top of the page, which allows you to change the colors of the guides, and you will see the **Opacity** and **Thickness** sliders at the bottom of the page. You can adjust these now if you want your guidelines to be a different thickness or opacity. When you're finished, tap **Done** on the top right. Now your Symmetry tool is set.

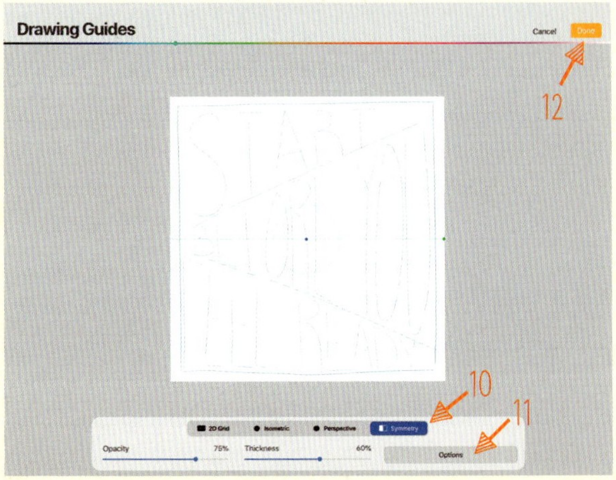

STEP 13 Now that the current layer is set to draw symmetrically, anything you draw on the top or bottom half of the screen will be repeated on the other half. As a test, draw something on the top then tap two fingers to step back (but not too many steps back or you'll undo the Symmetry tool).

> Tip: You can check to see if the Symmetry tool is activated by tapping on your Layers panel and checking for the word *Assisted* on that layer.

STEP 14: Choose a new color, and draw your lines on the top half of the canvas and use **Quickline** to make a straight line.

STEP 15: At this point, you may want to name your layers to help you stay organized. To do this, just tap on a layer in the **Layers** panel and tap **Rename**.

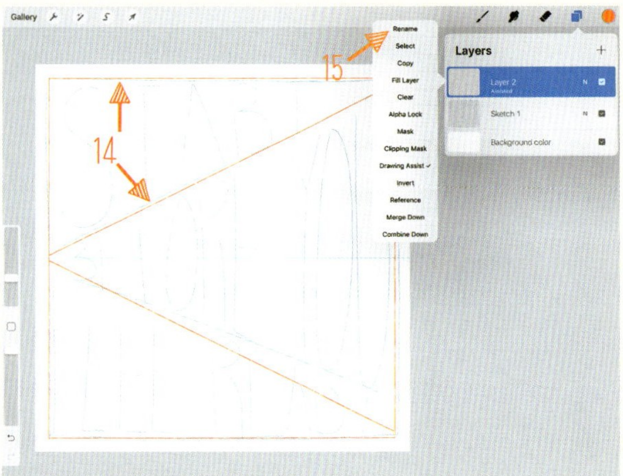

STEP 16 Create a new layer, and name it *Sketch 2*. Draw a more refined sketch of your text using your new straight lines as guides.

> Tip: For O shapes you can use *Quickshape* to get a more even circle. Do this by drawing a circle and then wait a moment before lifting your stylus off of the screen (similar to the Quickline tool). For the straight lines in your letters you can use Quickline.

STEP 17 Now you can make your first sketch layer invisible by opening the **Layers** panel, then tapping the check symbol on the layers you want to hide. I recommend hiding them like this rather than deleting them, because you may need to refer back to a sketch layer later on.

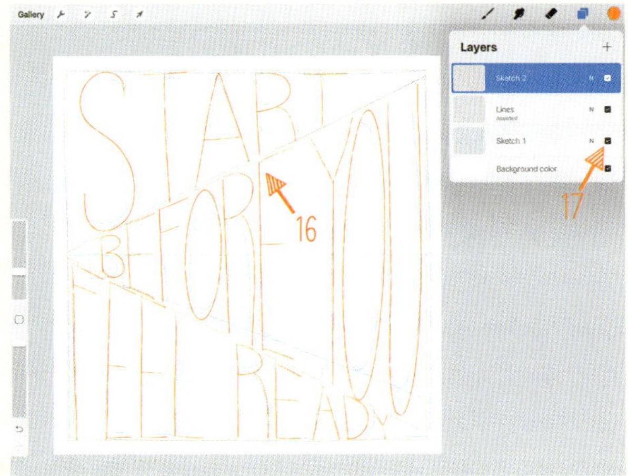

STEP 18 Reduce the **Opacity** of the lines layer in the *Sketch 2* layer we just created.

STEP 19 Create a new layer and name it *Dual Pencil*. Choose a new color and then select the **Dual Pencil** brush in the **Hand Lettering** brush set.

STEP 20 Adjust the brush size using the top slider on the left. You can use any size you'd like here. I used 30%. Zoom in on each letter by reverse pinching so you can easily see the sketch lines.

> Tip: Test your brush on the smallest letters on the canvas first. If it's too thick to work on the smallest letter, then reduce the brush size.

STEP 21 Trace each letter. Afterwards, reduce the opacity of your *Dual Pencil* layer and make the *Sketch 2* layer invisible so all you can see on your canvas are the Dual Pencil lines and straight lines.

Tip: Remember that Quickline works with any brush in Procreate, so if your lines look too wobbly feel free to use Quickline to straighten them. You may prefer the authentic look of an imperfect hand-drawn line, so go with whatever works for your personal style! One of your goals as you work your way through this book should be to start developing your personal style. Deciding when to use Quickline and Quickshape and when to sketch freehand is an important part of this process.

STEP 22: Create a new Layer, and name it *Ink*. This will be your inking layer. I always ink in black and then change the color later. Black is the easiest color to see on a white background, so working in black will help you see any errors as you work.

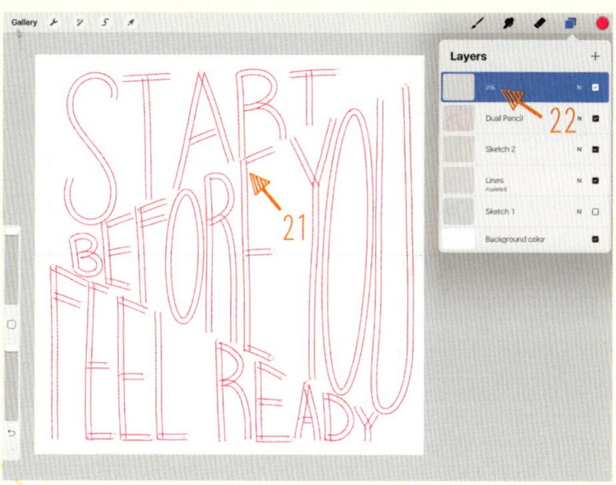

STEP 23: Select the **Liquid Pen** brush from the **Hand Lettering** brush set.

STEP 24: Start outlining the letters on your sketch layer. (Note: Make sure you completely close your letter shapes. In the next step we will automatically fill the shapes in using **Color Drop**, and if there is even a one pixel opening in the outline, the color will fill the whole canvas rather than filling just the letter.)

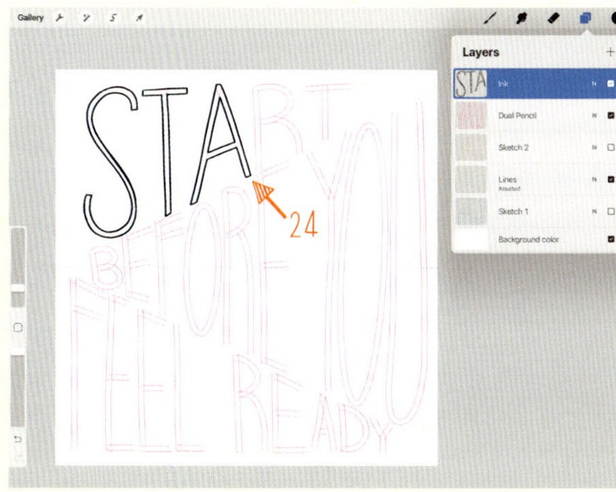

Color Drop

STEP 25 Put your stylus on the **Color dot** and without lifting, drag the dot over to the interior of the shape before lifting the stylus. This should seamlessly fill the shape with black.

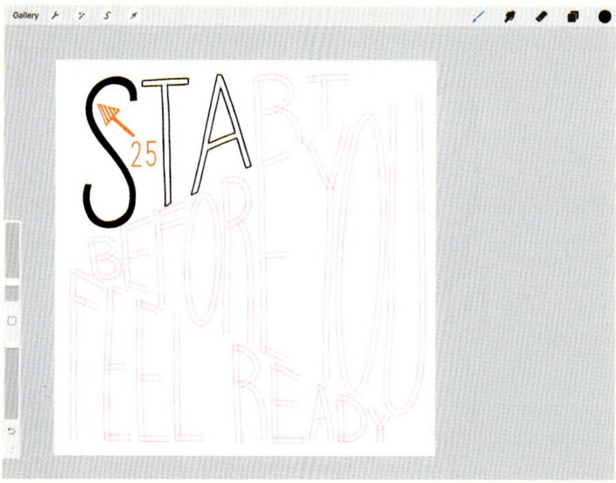

STEP 26: Repeat the Outline/Color Drop process with each letter in your composition, and then make all layers except your *Ink* layer invisible by unchecking the boxes next to them in the Layers panel.

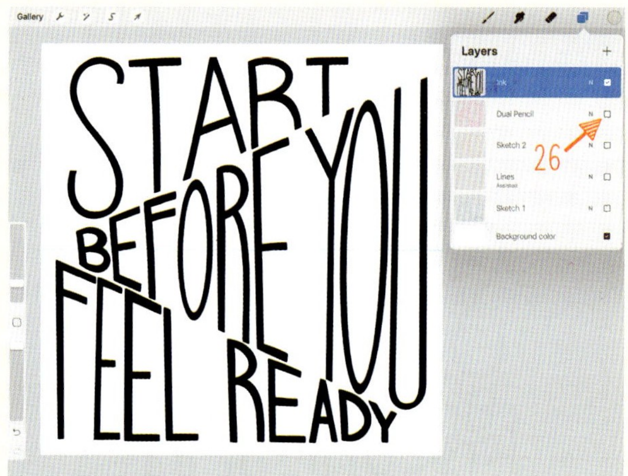

Troubleshooting: If you see a fine outline on your color drop area, the **Threshold** may be too low. **Threshold** decides how densely to fill the color drop area. To increase this density and eliminate any visible imperfections within the colored area, do a color drop, but before releasing your stylus, drag it to the right slightly. At the top of the screen you'll see the **Threshold** percentage change as you move the stylus to the right. Continue to drag the stylus to the right until it is set to around 99%. This is the default when you buy the app, but if you've already played around with Procreate a bit, it may have been adjusted at some point.

Freehand Selection Tool

You might find that you need to shift some things around as you work in order to improve the letter spacing.

To move elements, follow these steps:

STEP 27: Tap the **Selection** tool.

STEP 28: Tap **Freehand.**

STEP 29: Using your stylus, draw around the item you want to move.

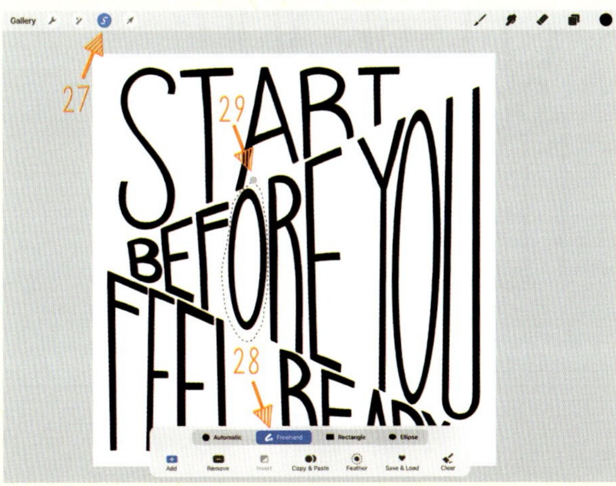

STEP 30: Tap the **Move** tool and turn off **Magnetics** in the **Snapping** section.

STEP 31: Use your finger or stylus to move the object.

STEP 32: Tap the **Move** tool again to set the placement.

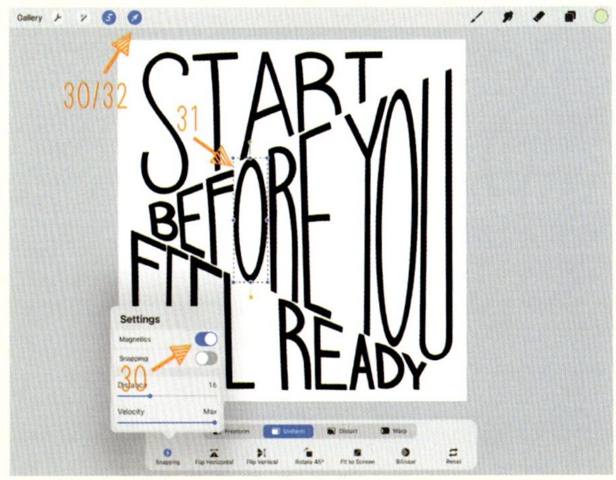

Tip: You can use this same process to resize or rotate anything on your canvas.

Move Tool

As you can see, the **Move** tool allows you to manipulate individual elements in your composition. If, for example, I thought the letter **O** would fit into the composition better if it was thinner, all I would have to do is select the **O** and resize it. (However, keep in mind that resizing also changes the thickness of the letter, so you may need to thicken a letter after making it smaller.)

Reduce the size of an element using the following steps:

STEP 33: Do a **Freehand Selection** using the steps above.

STEP 34: Then tap the **Move** tool, and use the blue dots to resize the letter, making it narrower. (Note: You may have to thicken some of your ink lines on letters that you made more narrow using the **Move** tool. This is because narrowing the whole letter narrows the lines as well.)

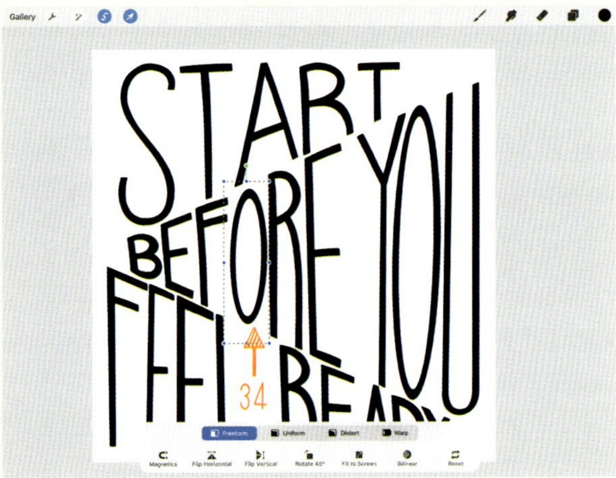

On that same **Move** tool menu you'll see an option called **Snapping**. **Snapping** is an extremely useful tool that we'll use throughout the book, so it's important to understand the basics before we continue. The **Snapping** menu contains two settings: **Magnetics** and **Snapping**. **Snapping** simply snaps the moved object to specific points on the canvas like the edges or in alignment with other objects. **Magnetics** does the following:

- It helps you move things around the canvas in a perfectly horizontal or vertical fashion, in case you want to move something on the page so it aligns perfectly with something above or beside it.
- It makes it difficult to make tiny adjustments in a freeform manner. So turn it off by tapping it if you just want to do a slight movement without any alignment help.

You'll also see the **Freeform** and **Uniform** options on that same settings menu. **Freeform** allows you to resize elements around the canvas with no constraints, whereas **Uniform** constrains the proportions of elements, so if you resize something, it will maintain the original proportions. You can also resize the whole drawing, so if you realize your artwork is too large, just tap on the layer in the **Layers** panel, tap the **Move** tool, turn on **Uniform**, and resize by dragging the blue corner dots.

When resizing always remember one important rule: you can always downsize, but you can't upsize. This is because upsizing stretches the pixels of an image and creates blurriness. For example, if you draw a letter and then realize it's too small, you have to redraw it. However, if you draw a letter and realize it's too big, you can just make it smaller using the Move tool.

To refine your drawing, follow these steps:

STEP 35: Once everything is in place just how you want it, it's clean up time! Make all layers except your black *Ink* layer invisible.

STEP 36: Zoom in closely to look at all the corners and edges of your letters. Switch between the **Eraser** tool with the **Liquid Pen** selected and the **Brush** tool with the **Liquid Pen** selected to clean up any stray marks, messy corners, or uneven lines.

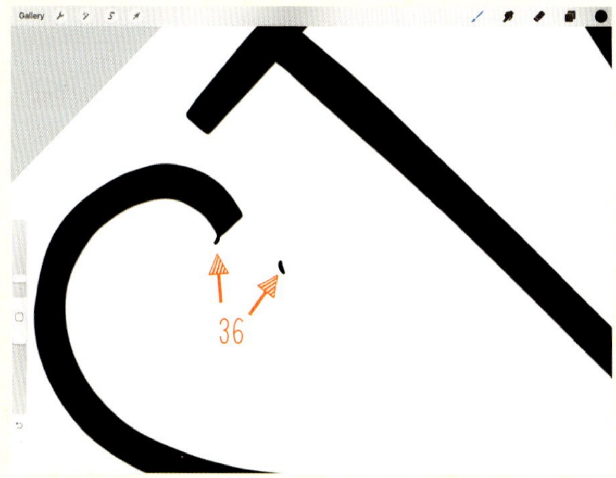

Color

Now that we have the structure of our lettering finished, it's time to start adding some color.

To add a background color, follow these steps:

STEP 37: Tap the bottom part of the **Layers** panel that says **Background Color.**

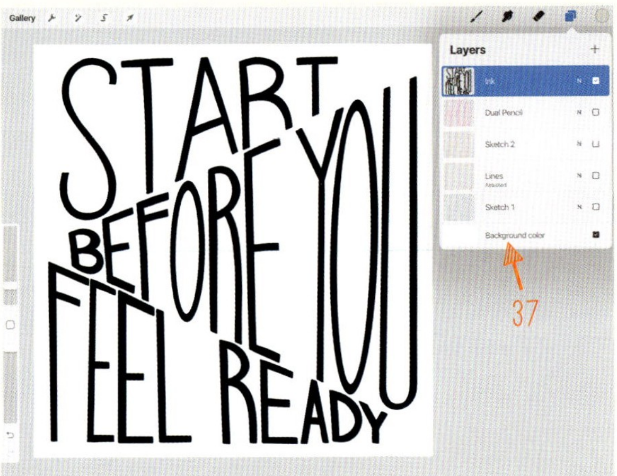

STEP 38: Choose a color. I chose a light gray from a palette I created using the steps in chapter 2

STEP 39 Tap **Done** to set the color.

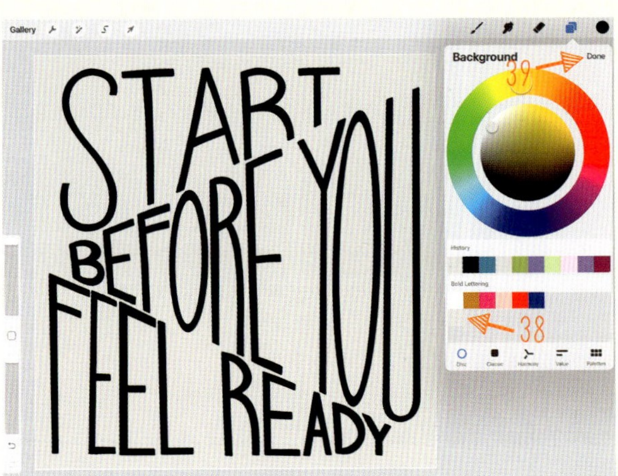

STEP 40: Select the layer with your ink lines. It should be highlighted in blue on the **Layers** panel.

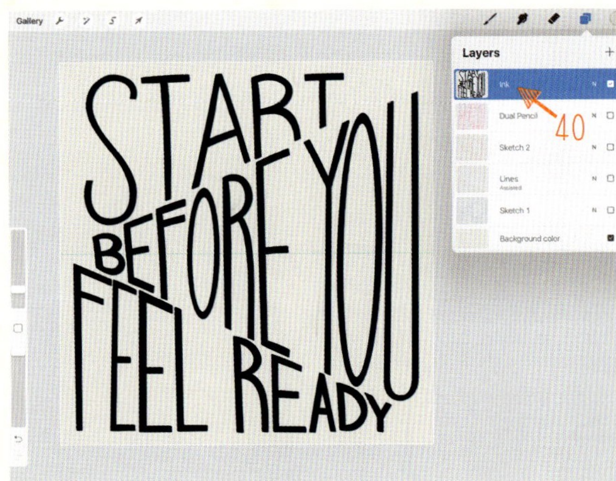

STEP 41: Select a color from the color wheel or a palette you created, and then do a **Color Drop** onto one or more of the letters. This is just like the Color Drop you did to fill these letters, but this time you're dropping onto a solid shape rather than the interior of an outlined shape.

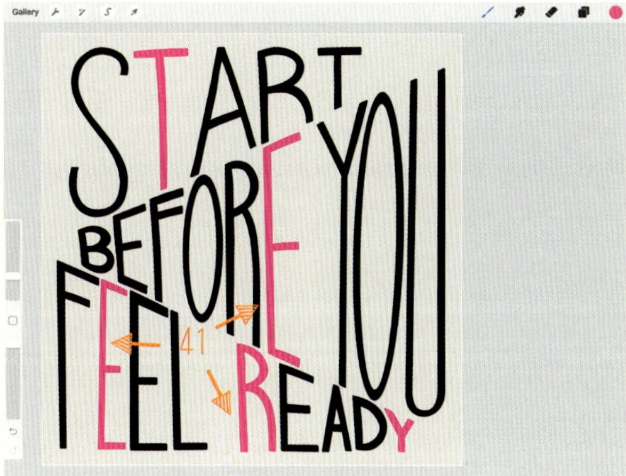

STEP 42: Repeat the same process using a variety colors.

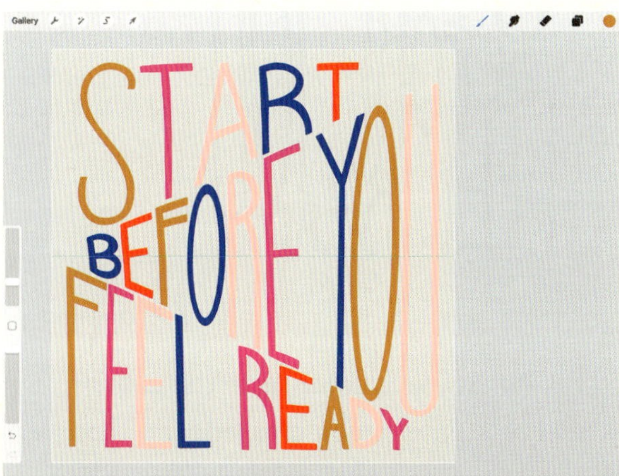

STEP 43: Now that your letters have some color, let's try a few different background color options. Tap on the **Background** layer, and and tap on different colors to see how each one looks with your letters. You will discover a lot of interesting combinations this way! The figures below show a few background color options I tried.

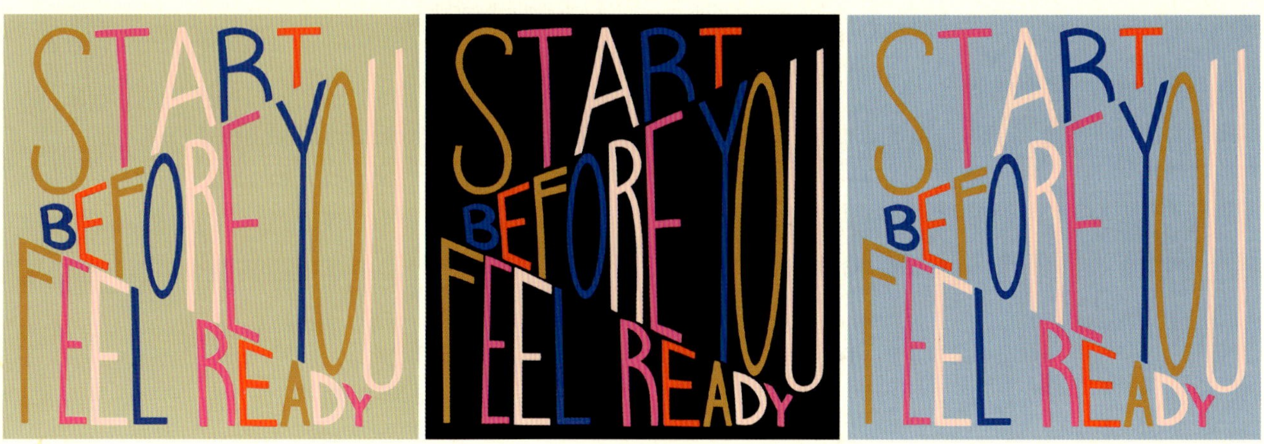

Changing the background color completely changes the mood of the composition.

Texture

After you've decided on a background color, it's time to add some texture. You don't have to add texture to every composition you create in Procreate, but sometimes it can really help add some depth and dimension to an otherwise flat-looking digital design.

Add texture with these steps:

STEP 44: Create a new layer for your textures. Tap one of the texture brushes in the **Hand Lettering** set. I'll use the **Barely There Grit Texture.** Try each of the 12 textures to see which ones fit your composition and personal style the best.

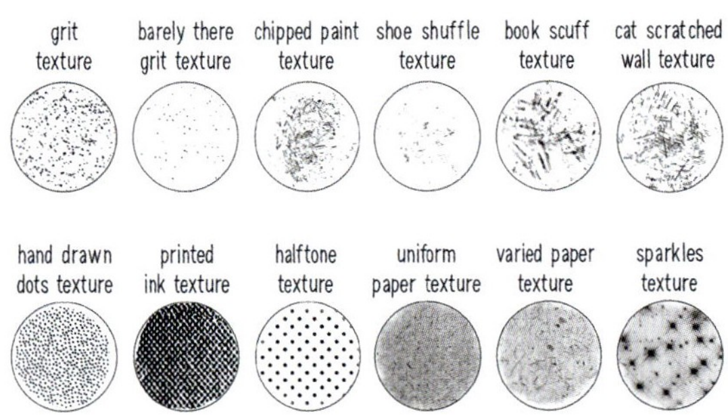

Twelve texture brushes from the Hand Lettering set can be used for painting, erasing, or smudging.

> Tip: The top row textures work better if you repeatedly tap your stylus on the canvas. The bottom row textures work better if you sweep your brush across the canvas without picking it up. You'll notice that each texture brush in Procreate has a different behavior, so when you encounter a new brush, try both tapping and sweeping to see which one works best.

STEP 45: Choose a color and start tapping around the canvas to add some texture to the composition. I'm using white as my color, but you could also use a darker or lighter version of your background color to create a subtle textured effect. Note that my texture layer is above all the other layers. If you don't want the texture to appear on top of your letters, just open the **Layers** panel and drag the *Texture* layer below the *Ink* layer.

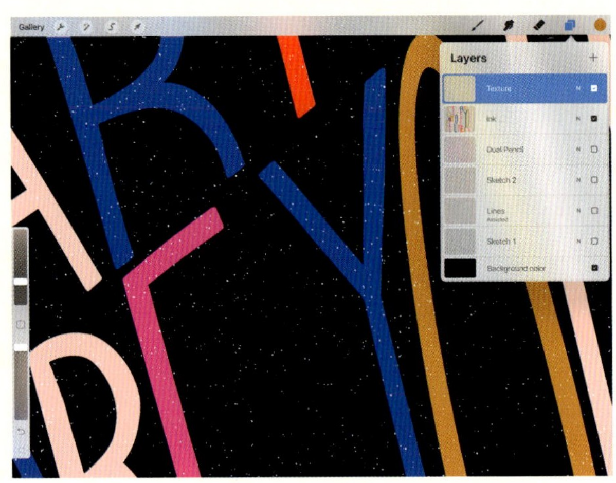

STEP 46: Try a lot of variations here by combining different textures and colors or by creating multiple texture layers and reducing the opacity of one or both.

Tip: If you don't like the size of a texture, tap on the brush to open the brush settings, tap **Grain** and adjust the scale of the texture. This allows you to make the textured bits larger or smaller.

You might even want to start erasing some textures out of your letters, but first let's save this image as a **Master Document** to avoid making permanent changes that we can't undo later.

Master Documents

Procreate automatically records every action you've taken during the current session, so there is no actual save function. However, once you close the canvas by tapping Gallery in the top left corner of the screen, Procreate will erase the entire history of the steps you took so you can't open an old canvas and start two-finger tapping to undo. Therefore, if you are happy with the artwork and want to save it as your final version, you should create a **Master Document.**

For example, let's say you are working on a lettering project like the one we did in this chapter. You've just finished your ink layer and want to see what it would look like if you used a texture eraser over the letters (imagine erasing a polka dot pattern out of the letters). You wouldn't want to permanently alter the letters with the texture eraser, because if you later change your mind, the next time you open the canvas you won't be able to step back to go back to solid letters. Your only option would be to completely redraw each letter.

For this reason, I always create a **Master Document** (aka a duplicated version) of my composition before I experiment with any permanent changes.

Follow these steps to create a Master Document:

STEP 47: Tap **Gallery** on the top left of the screen to close the document.

STEP 48: On the **Gallery** page, tap **Select**.

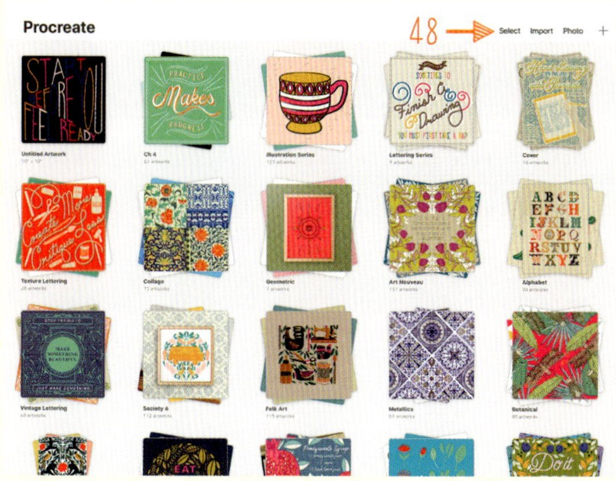

STEP 49: Tap the **canvas**, and then tap **Duplicate** three or four times so you create a few copies of your original.

STEP 50: Tap the **X** to close the selection menu.

STEP 51: Tap the title of one of the copies, and rename it to **Master Document**, which will serve as a reminder not to make permanent changes to this copy.

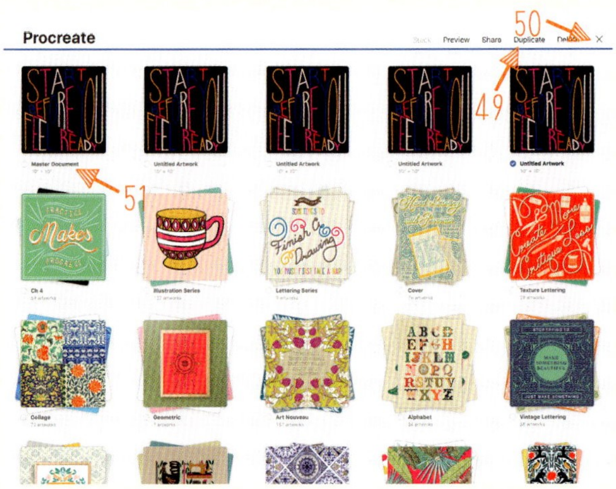

Now you can do whatever you want to the rest of the duplicated versions (like erasing parts of the words to create a textured effect or shrinking the words to create space for a decorative border) without losing your original drawing. I find that I'm much less likely to make bold, creative changes to a composition if I'm worried about damaging the original, so I always make color and texture changes on my copies rather than working on the original.

Stacks: Keeping Your Work Organized

You can organize your artwork into folders known as **Stacks** in Procreate. For example, after creating a few color versions of this lettering piece and saving one as a Master Document on the Gallery screen, I want to stack them so they are separate from all of my other projects.

You can easily stack documents by following these steps:

STEP 52: Tap **Select** on the top right of the **Gallery**, and then tap on each document you want to include, and then tap **Stack**.

STEP 53: Tap the **X** symbol to end the stacking process.

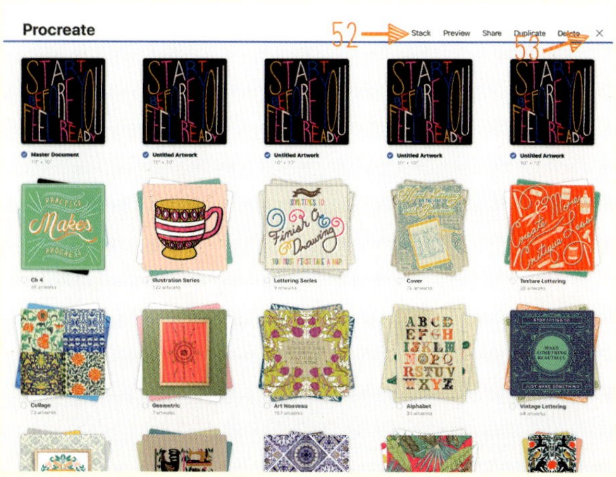

STEP 54: Name or rename a Stack by tapping on its name, and simply entering a new title. (This works for individual documents too!)

STEP 55: To open the Stack, just tap on it.

STEP 56: To go back to the main Gallery, tap the Stack name in the upper left-hand corner.

STEP 57: Now you can start creating some various color/texture versions of your project using a variety of features and tools such as Color Drop, texture brushes, and changing the background color. Try everything you can think of and feel free to duplicate your Master Document a few more times if you need more color versions!

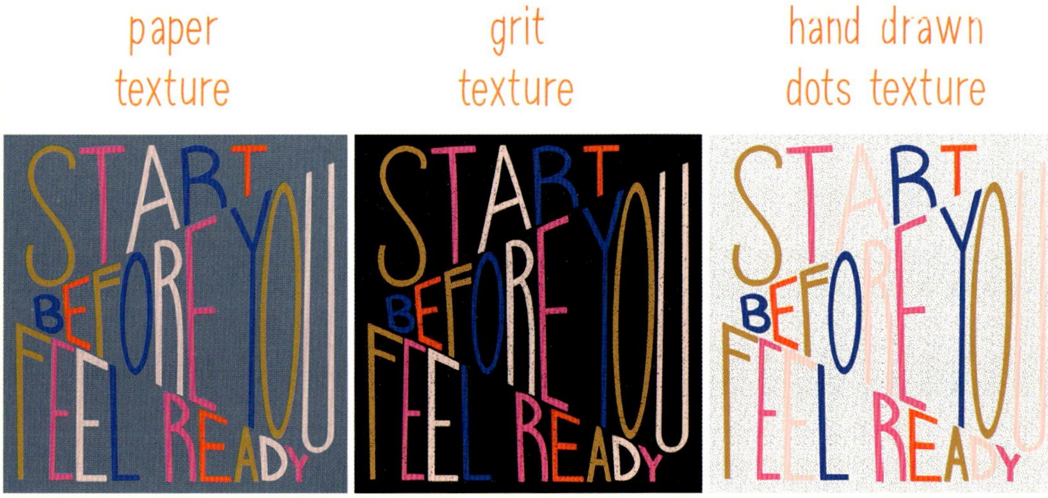

Three different texture and color combinations.

Above are few of the versions I created.

Once you have one or more versions you are happy with, it's time to share your work with the world.

Saving and Exporting Your Work

You can share your work from the Gallery screen by tapping **Select** like we did when creating a Master Document earlier in this chapter, selecting the documents you want to share, and then tapping **Share.** Alternatively, you can share individual projects from the document page by doing following:

STEP 58: Tap the **Actions** menu.

STEP 59: Tap **Share.**

STEP 60: Choose a file type.

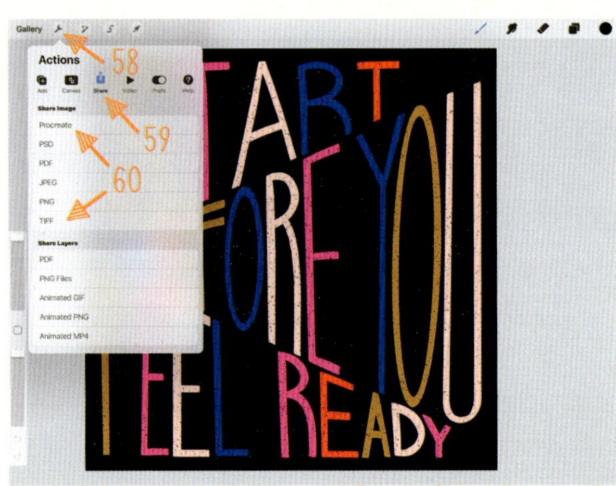

In most cases, I export **JPEG** files for social media and website uses and **PNG** files for print. If you'd like to go deeper, here are a few things to know about each file type:

- **Procreate:** Layered files that can be used only in Procreate. You could use this format to save Procreate files in cloud storage so you never lose the ability to alter layers and look at your Time-lapses for each composition.
- **PSD:** Layered Photoshop files that can be easily sent to Procreate through AirDrop or cloud storage.
- **PDF:** A universal format for anyone who needs to send images to customers or publishers.
- **JPEG:** A smaller (more compressed) file than the other types, which makes it great for sharing on social media or your website. This is a so-called "lossy" file format, which means some quality is lost each time a file is saved as a JPEG.
- **PNG:** A "lossless" file format (meaning you don't lose quality when you save it), which is ideal for sending to printers or for creating high-resolution images for your portfolio.
- **TIFF:** A "lossless" file format that works well for certain programs that require TIFF files.

STEP 61: After you have chosen a file type, you'll see the option to choose a location to save the image. I recommend signing up for a free cloud storage option, such as Google Drive, Dropbox, iCloud, or a similar service. Some Procreate files will be too large to send by email, so that may not be an option. You will also see the option to share straight to any social media apps that you have downloaded on your iPad.

Time-lapses

Time-lapses are the recorded history of your drawing in video form. They are great for sharing online, but are also helpful for reminding you of your process of making a composition. Let's say you drank way too much coffee and went into a creative whirlwind resulting in a beautiful drawing with 50 layers. Now you want to create a similar piece but you can't remember the steps you took to create the first one. Your Time-lapse video will show you exactly how you created the piece from start to finish!

To see your Time-lapse video, follow these steps:

STEP 62: Tap **Video** in the **Actions** menu.

STEP 63: Tap **Time-lapse Replay.**

STEP 64: If you want to share your Time-lapse, you can export it. Tap **Export Time-lapse video** to export to an app or cloud storage.

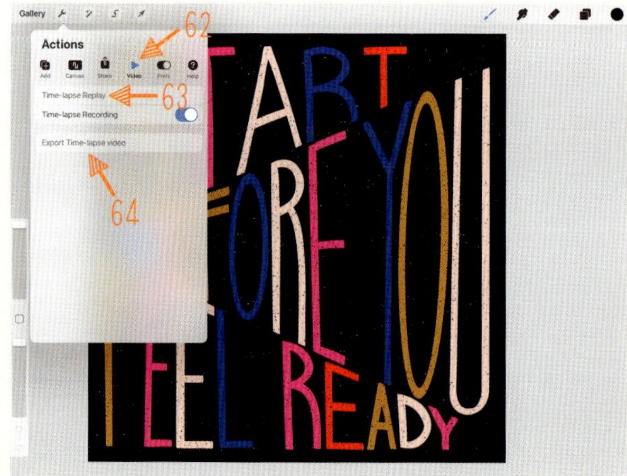

We'll go deeper into sharing your work later in the book, but if you're ready to try some interesting ways to share your work now, jump ahead to chapter 9 to see more options.

If you feel like you need a little more practice with Procreate why not create another lettering composition? More practice will never hurt! It's also helpful to create different versions of the same piece in order to explore subtle stylistic differences.

For example, in the first piece I created I didn't use Quickline very much to build my letters because I wanted it to have a hand-drawn feel. In this composition though (right) I used Quickline to create all of my horizontal and vertical lines before adding in the curves. You can see this resulted in a less playful, but more unified composition in terms of directional linework.

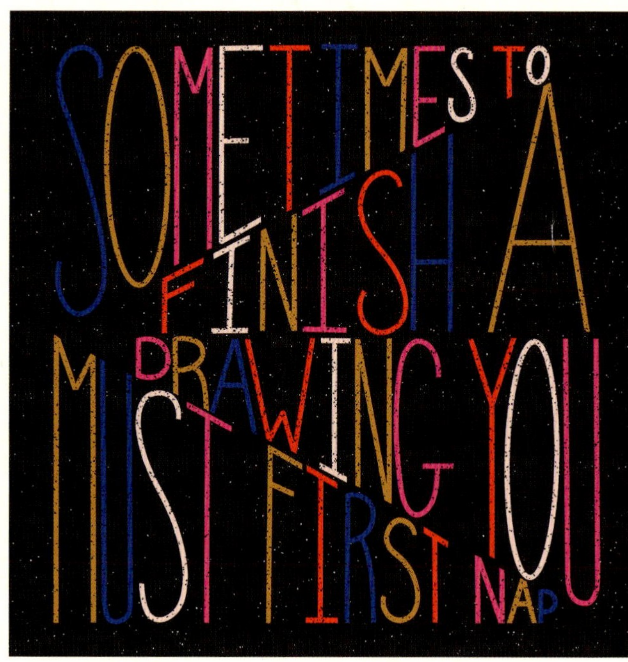

I used Quickline on all the straight lines in this composition.

Now that you understand the basics of Procreate, let's dive into the structure and styles of lettering, so you can start building your lettering skills and developing your own lettering style!

CHAPTER 4

Letterforms and Guides

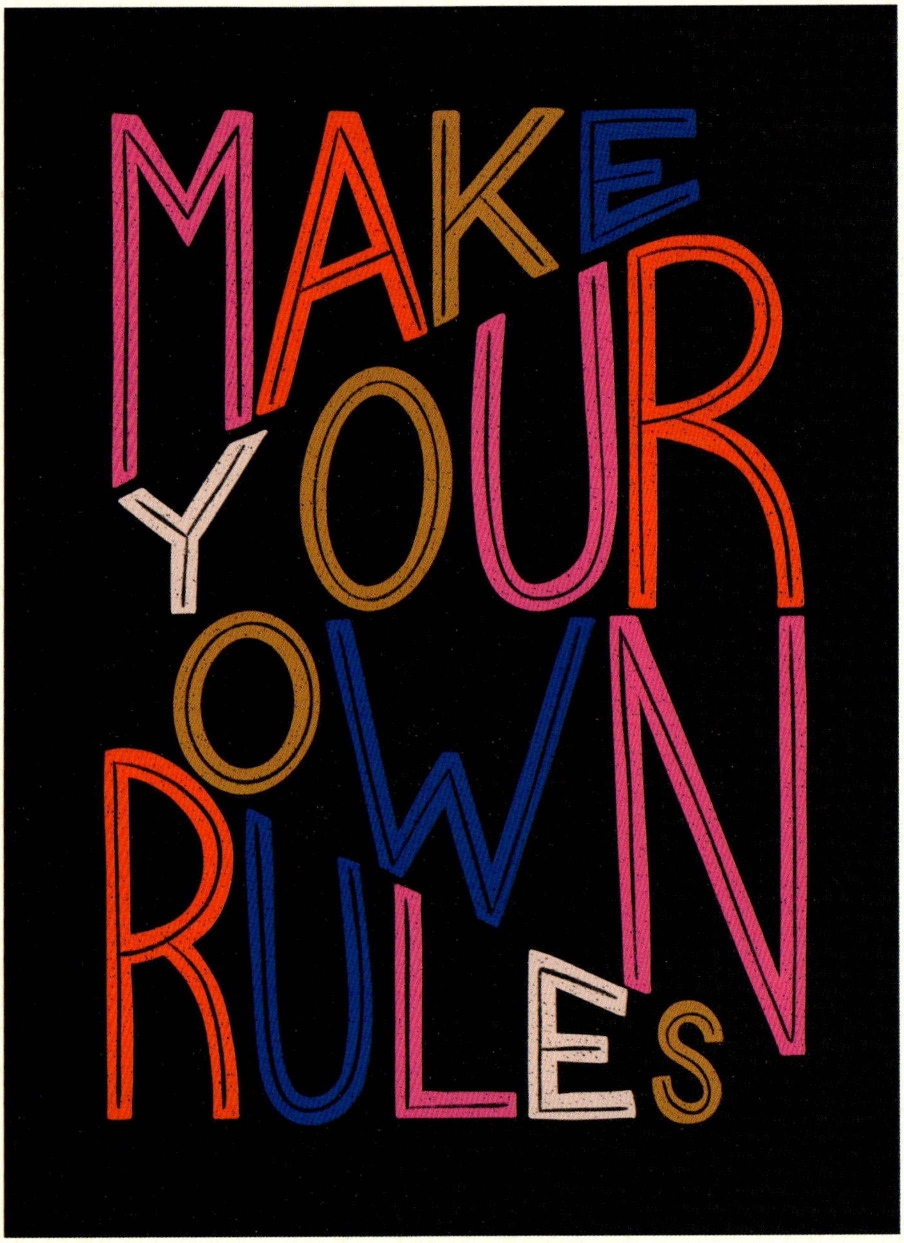

Learning rules, making rules, and breaking rules are essential parts of the lettering process. In this chapter, we'll look at the rules that dictate how letters are traditionally formed and we'll talk about how you can develop your own unique set of lettering rules without sacrificing legibility.

In the previous chapter we used one type of rule: guides. We created angled guides and made a rule that our letters would always stay within those guides to conform to a particular overall shape. There are lots of other rules you can choose to apply to each lettering project, but of course, you don't have to use *all* of them in every lettering project!

One type of rule that contributes to the cohesion and style of a composition is the letterform, or the style of letters. Let's take a look at the most common types of letterforms: serif, sans serif, script, slab, and creative lettering.

I've included only a few examples of serifs (the decorative marks on the ends of letters), but we'll explore many other options in the next chapter.

Next, let's look at some basic rules for designing letters. Keep in mind as we look at these that all letterforms are different, so don't feel like you have to memorize every rule to be a great letterer. Think of the rules merely as suggestions to help you create lettering projects that are legible and cohesive.

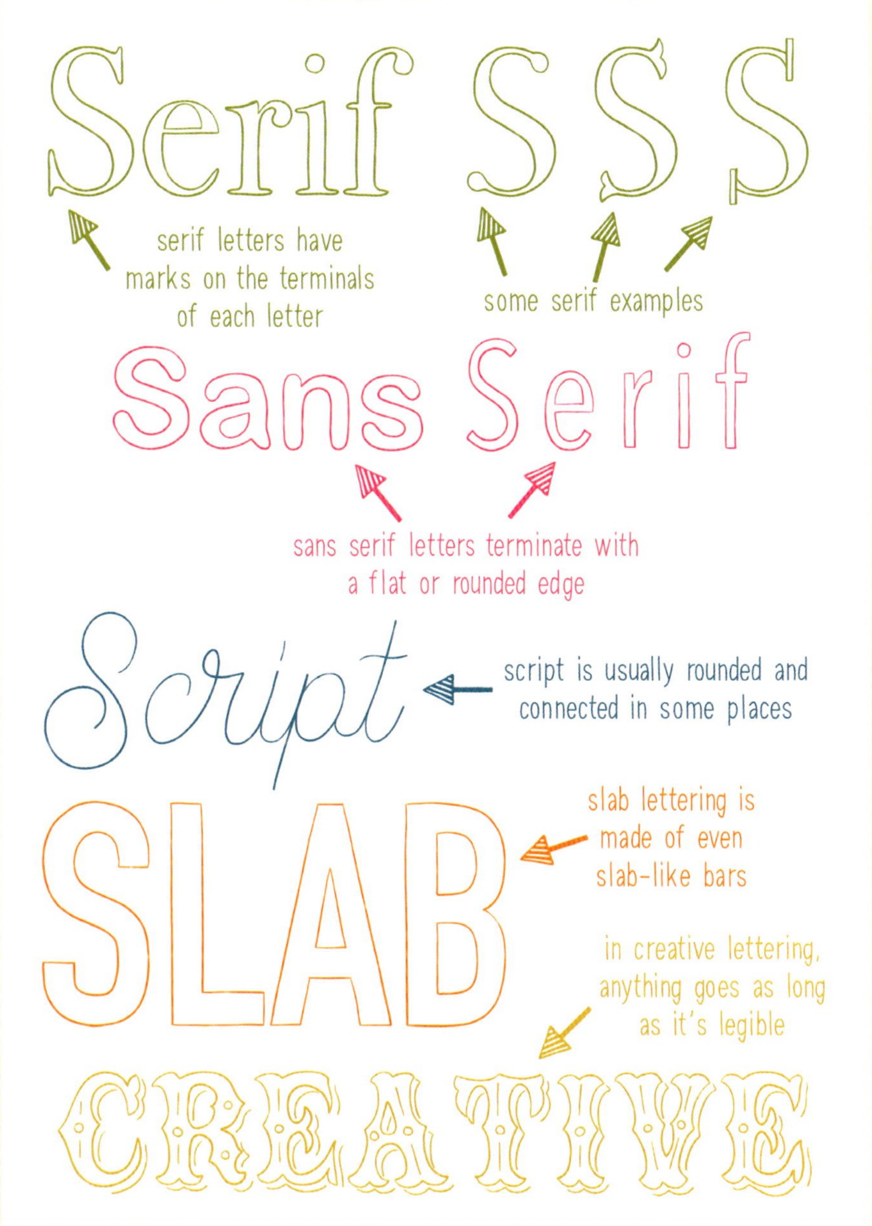

These are the most common types of letterforms used in hand lettering.

Let's try to answer the seemingly simple question, "How wide should each letter I create be?" by examining the chart below.

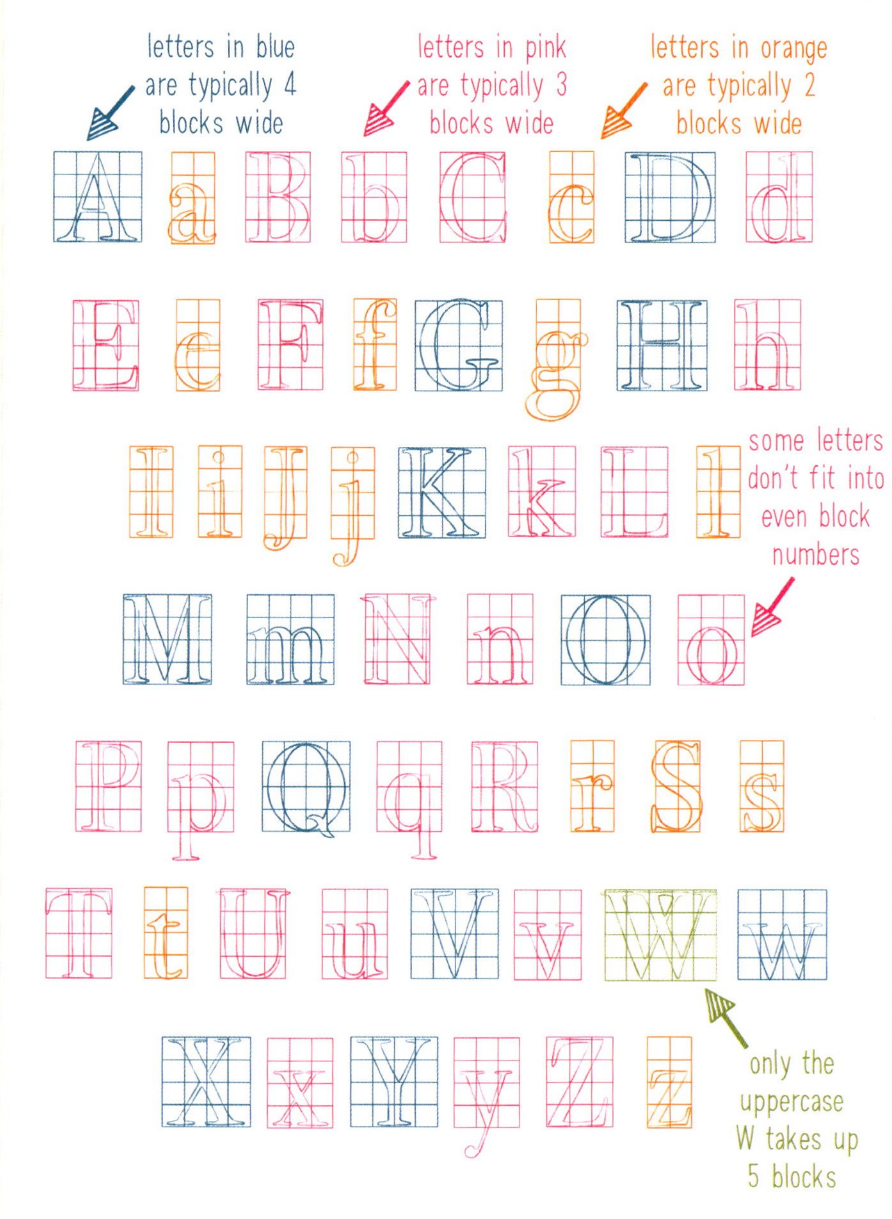

This chart shows the widths of letters in a typical serif alphabet.

As you can see, the answer is not so simple! Each letter has its own peculiarities, but following are a few helpful rules we can take from this chart:

- The **W** is wider than all other letters.
- Uppercase letters are typically wider than their lowercase counterparts.
- Rounded uppercase letters (like **D**, **G**, **O**, and **Q**) and letters with V shapes in them (like **A**, **K**, **M**, **V**, **X**, **W**, and **Y**) are typically wider than letters with straight vertical lines (like **B**, **E**, **F**, **P**, **R**, **T**, and **U**).

Next, let's revisit a rule you learned about in the last chapter: use of guides to help give form to a composition. You can think of guides as the basic framework, or structure, of a lettering project. Each time you create a new lettering project, you can start by creating some guidelines that keep your letters aligned with each other along straight or curved lines.

Typically, letterers use three essential lines (and a few optional ones) to keep their lettering consistent and cohesive.

The essential lines include the following:

- **Cap height**: The "ceiling" line or uppermost limit for capital letters. This is also the height of tall lowercase letters like **b**, **d**, **f**, and **h**, in certain letterform styles like the one to the right.
- **X-height**: The uppermost limit for the letter **x** and many other lowercase letters and crossbars (the horizontal lines in the middle of some letters, such as **E**, **F**, **G**, and **P**).
- **Baseline**: The "floor" line where the bottom of every letter rests.

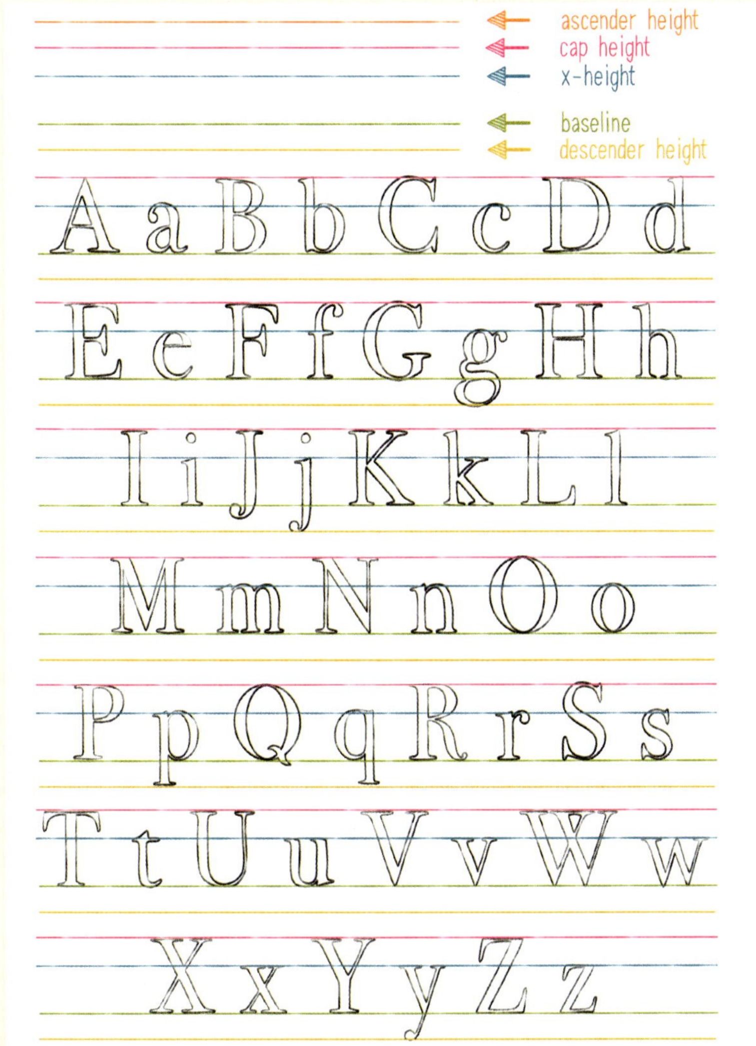

The optional lines include:

- **Descender height**: The lowermost limit for lowercase letters that hang below the baseline, such as **g**, **j**, **p**, **q**, and **y**. (This line is optional because not every project will include lowercase letters.)
- **Ascender height**: The uppermost limit for lowercase letters in certain letter styles where the lowercase letters are actually taller than the capital letters. You'll notice that the letter style above doesn't need an ascender guide because it simply uses the cap height line for both capital letters and tall lowercase letters (like **b**, **d**, **f**, **h**, etc.).

Guidelines are the framework of every lettering project.

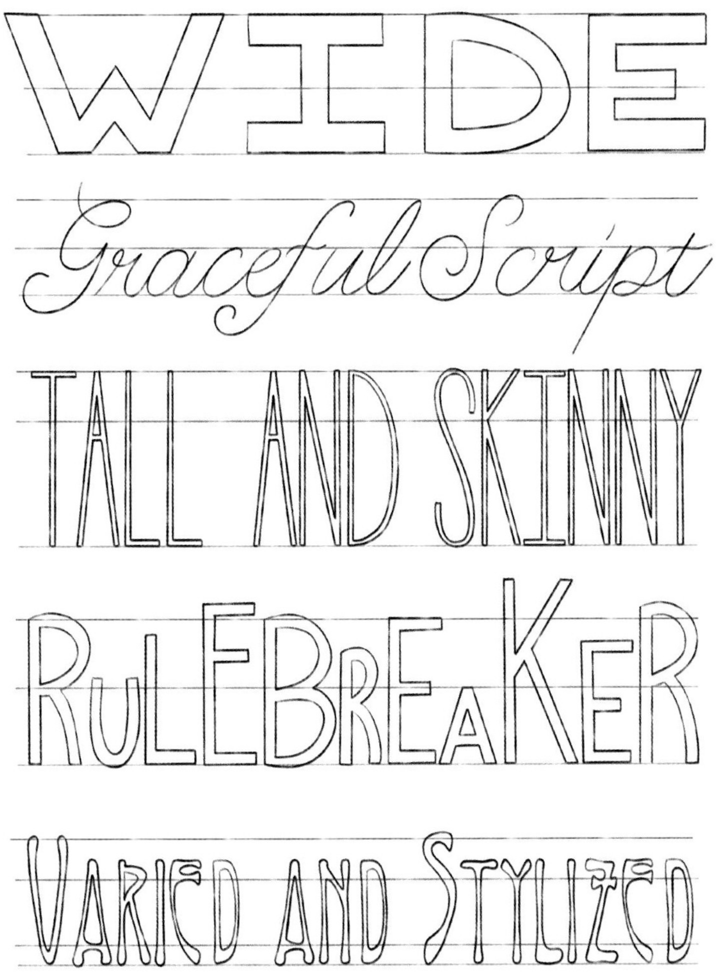

Changing the letter width, style, and guides can completely change the feel of a lettering composition! Take a look at the examples on this page.

Guides and letterform styles set the mood and feeling for a project.

You can see what an important role these rules play in both the stylistic character of your letters and the feelings they evoke. Therefore, when you start a new composition, your first thought should be what feeling you want to communicate to your viewers (e.g., playful, formal, or wacky), and then determine the rules for the anatomy of your letters accordingly.

Common Beginner Mistakes

Before we start lettering, let's look at a few common beginner mistakes. Remember that even though you are the rule-maker (and occasional rule-breaker) in your lettering world, there are some rules that exist to prevent your letters from appearing unbalanced or unreadable. Therefore, keep the following common errors in mind as you create your letters:

- **Rs**: The leg of the **R** comes from the right or middle of the bowl, not the corner where the bowl and bar meet.

- **Space:** Imagine pouring a cup full of sand into the space between each letter. The same amount of sand should fit into each space.
- **The letter A's X-height:** The horizontal bar on the uppercase A is lower than on the other letters, which keeps the triangle from looking too small.
- **Round shapes:** Round letters (like **C, G, O, Q, E,** and **S**) and pointed letters (like **A, V,** and **W**) will often be slightly taller than letters that fit in a box shape (like **H, E,** and **I**). This is because square shapes take up more visual real estate than rounded or pointed ones. To make them appear the same size, we have to make the non-square shapes a bit bigger. This isn't true in all letterforms though!

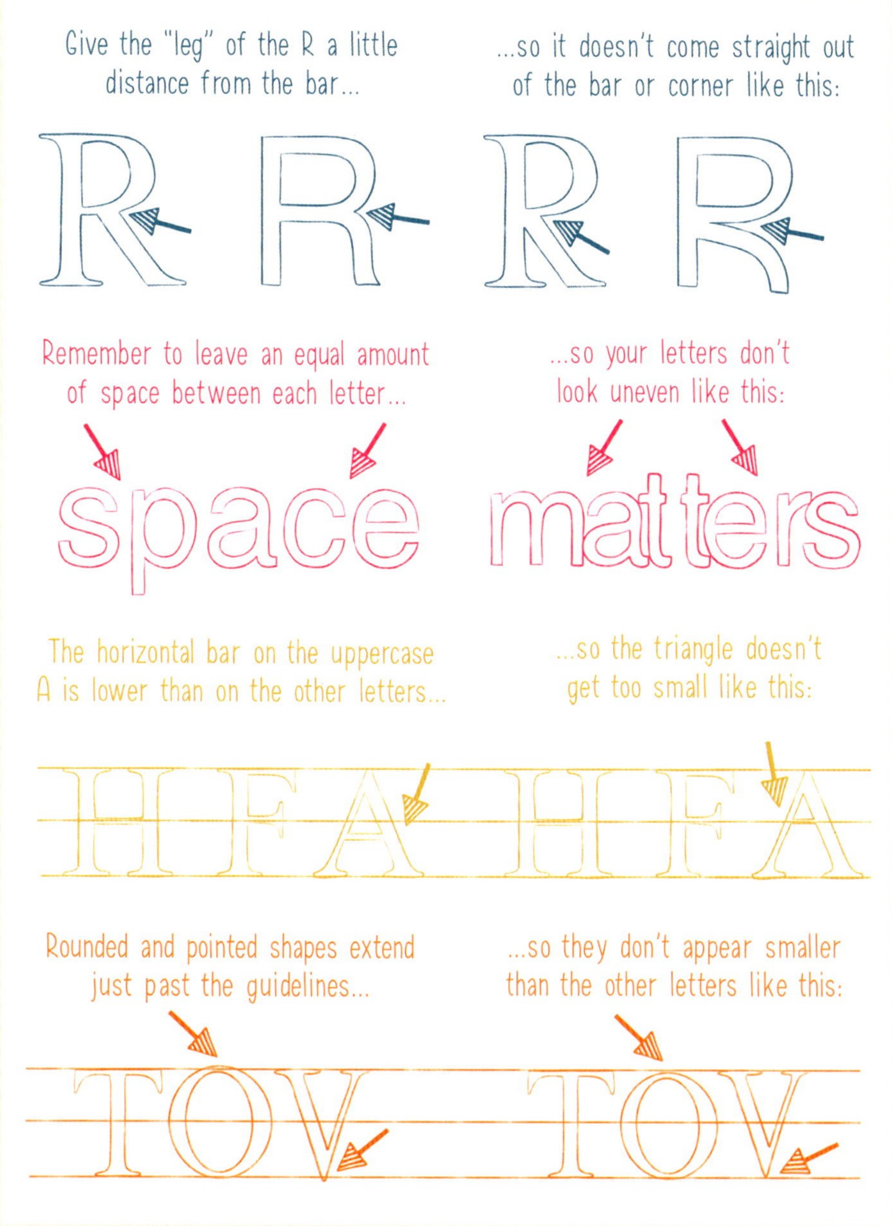

These common beginner mistakes are easy to avoid once you are aware of them.

Let's Start Lettering!

The best way to become comfortable with drawing letters is to—you guessed it—practice! Let's start with some practice sheets that will help you get used to drawing letters. You can download the sheets using the instructions in chapter 1.

Practice Sheet 1 (below) contains slab-style lettering. This is the easiest and simplest form of lettering and is a great foundation before starting on more complex letterforms. I recommend starting with *Practice Sheet 1* if you are a complete beginner and *Practice Sheet 2* if you have done some lettering in the past.

Practice Sheet 2 contains a serif alphabet. Anytime you add serifs to your letters, you're introducing more complexity into your piece, therefore if you're new to lettering, it's probably better to start with slab-style letters and work your way up from there.

Practice Sheet 1

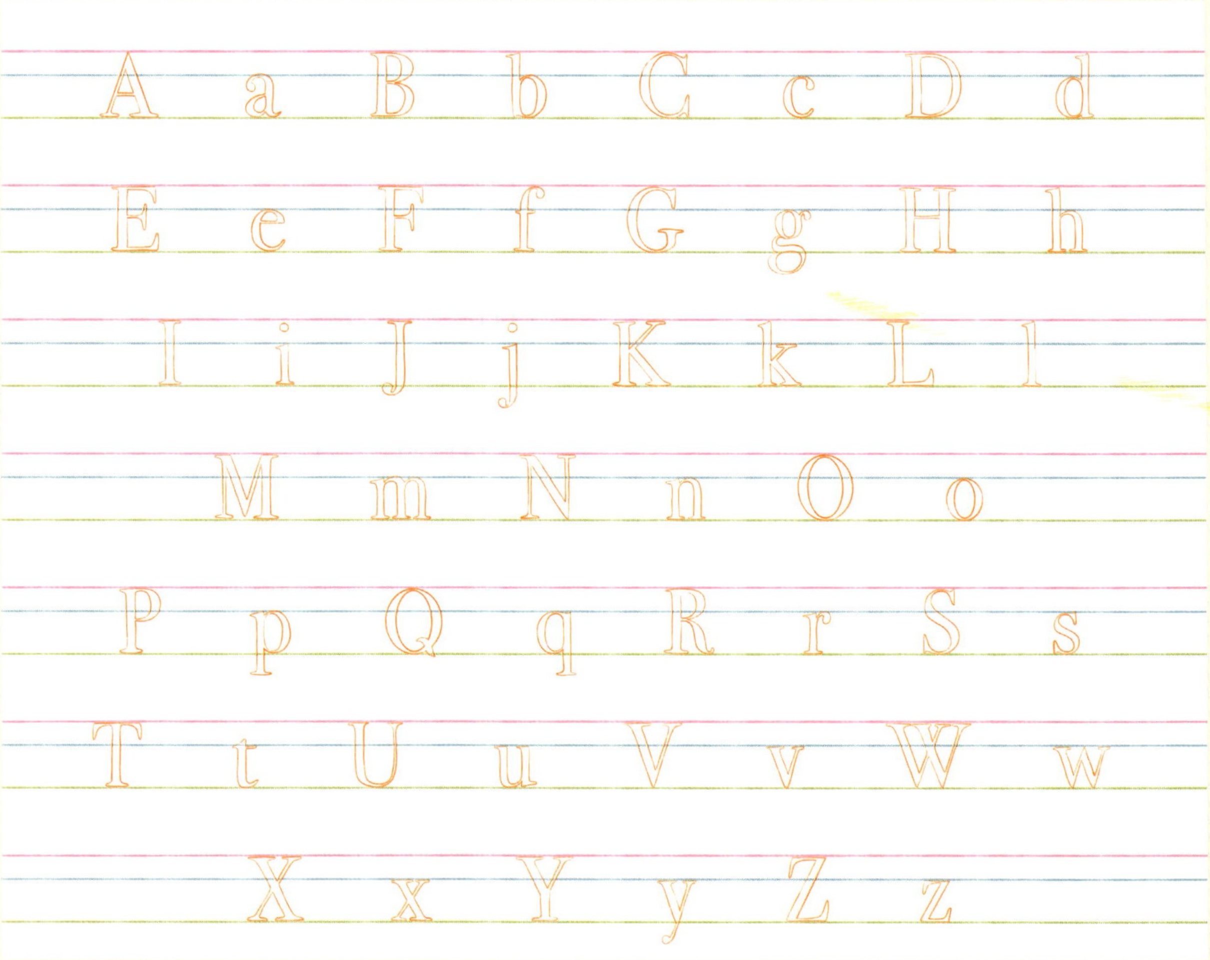

Practice Sheet 2

Note: If you've already had a lot of practice drawing letterforms, you may want to skip ahead to the next project where you'll learn how to create your own practice sheets for letterforms that fit your personal style.

Using the Practice Sheets

Follow these steps to get started with the practice sheets:

STEP 1: Download the practice sheets from the resources using the instructions found in chapter 1. When prompted to choose an app to open the sheets, select Procreate. Alternatively, you can save the practice sheet to your photo library or cloud storage, then open Procreate, tap **Import**, and locate the saved sheets.

STEP 2: Once you have opened *Practice Sheet 1*, create a new layer and select the **Dual Pencil.**

STEP 3: Redraw the letter A, and then use the **Sketching Pencil** to close the open spaces at the top and bottom of the letter.

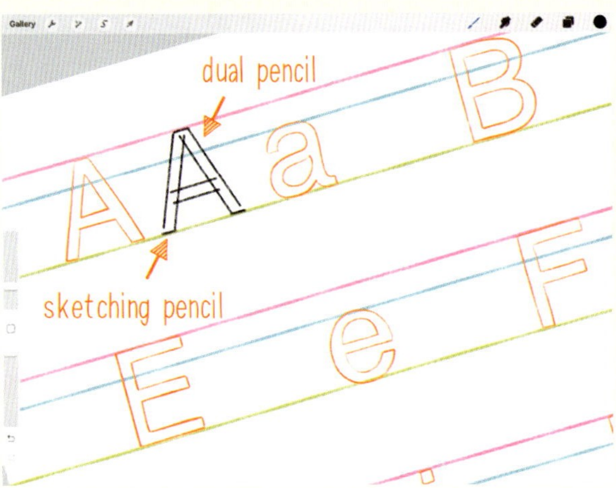

STEP 4: Reduce the opacity of that layer, then create a new layer and redraw the letter with the **Sketching Pencil,** being careful to fully close off the corners. You can use **Quickline** here to keep your lines straight, and also **Quickline** with two fingers on the canvas to get a perfectly horizontal line.

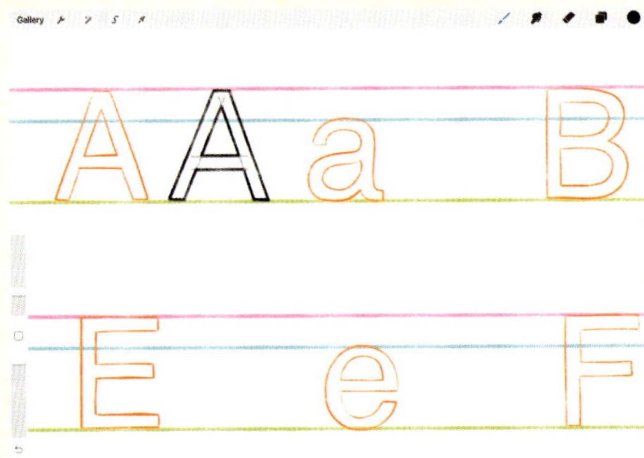

STEP 5: Repeat the process for every letter while keeping an eye on how each one conforms to the guidelines.

STEP 6: Follow the same process with *Practice Sheet 2*.

Drawing serif letters follows the same basic process outlined above. The only difference is that once you switch to your Sketching Pencil in step 3 to close the open spaces around the letter, you draw serifs instead of straight lines. I prefer to draw all of my Dual Pencil lines first and then add the serifs all at once instead of completing one letter at a time. I find this makes it easier to keep the size and shape of my serifs consistent. Feel free to add a guideline to help keep all your serifs the same height.

Tip: You can use these practice sheets as many times as you'd like. Just make your sketch layers invisible, create a new layer, and start lettering.

Making Your Own Practice Sheet

Once you feel comfortable with drawing the slab and serif letter styles on the practice sheets, it's time to take the first step toward creating a letterform that fits your personal style (i.e., something you love to look at!). First, use the resources mentioned in chapter 1 to find a letterform that suits your style. I recommend starting with a serif, sans serif, creative, or slab letterform. Scripts can bring some additional challenges to the table, so we'll wait until later in the book to dig deeper into script lettering.

As you'll see when you start studying different letterforms, each one has its own rules set by the creator. When you're studying a vintage letterform your job is to discover the rules, and apply them to your own work while also setting some of your own rules to bring your personal style into the mix.

Let's create your first practice sheet using the following steps:

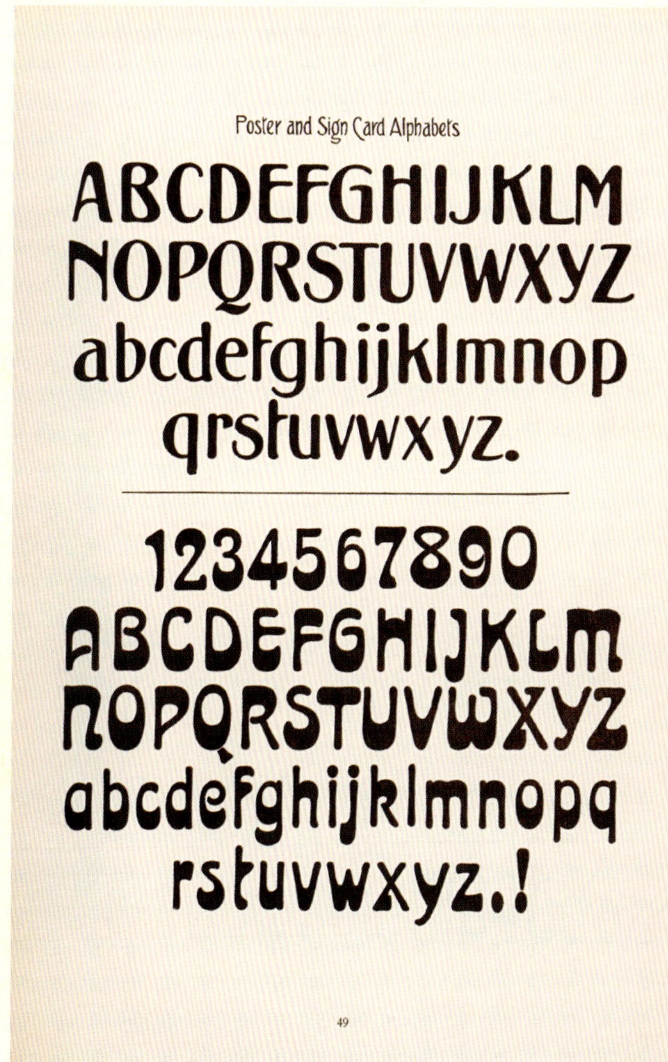

A page from the 1914 book Art Alphabets and Lettering *by John Mauritz Bergling*

STEP 1: Save or take a screenshot of your resource image. I'll be using a page from the 1914 *Art Alphabets and Lettering* by John Mauritz Bergling (opposite). (Note that this book is over 100 years old, so the letterform is in the creative commons. Even though we're only going to be using these resources for inspiration, not copying them, I still would not recommend following this process with a recently created letterform, font, or any resource with an unknown copyright status.)

STEP 2: Create a new document that is 11″ × 6″ at 300 DPI.

STEP 3: Insert your letter inspiration image by tapping the **Actions** menu.

STEP 4: Tap **Add**.

STEP 5: Select **Insert a Photo**.

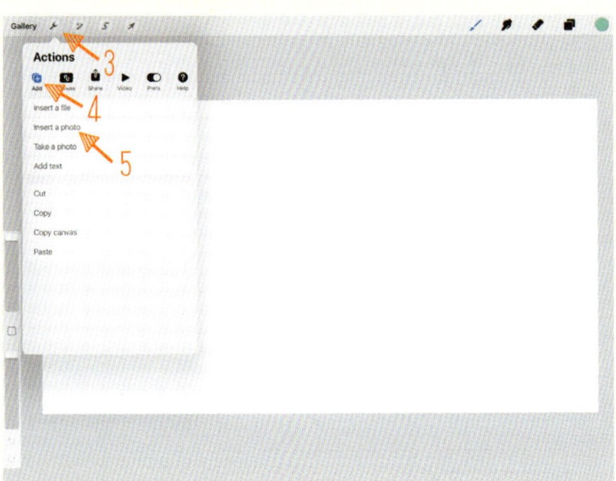

STEP 6: Move the image to the left side of the canvas if you're right-handed, or the right side of the canvas if you're left-handed.

STEP 7: Create a new layer, and make three guidelines on the first line of letters using **Quickline** and two fingers to get perfectly horizontal lines. Put each guideline on its own layer so you can easily adjust them independently using the **Move** tool.

STEP 8: Once your guidelines are set, merge all three lines onto one layer by pinching the three layers together on the **Layers** panel.

STEP 9: Swipe left on the **Guidelines** layer, and tap **Duplicate**.

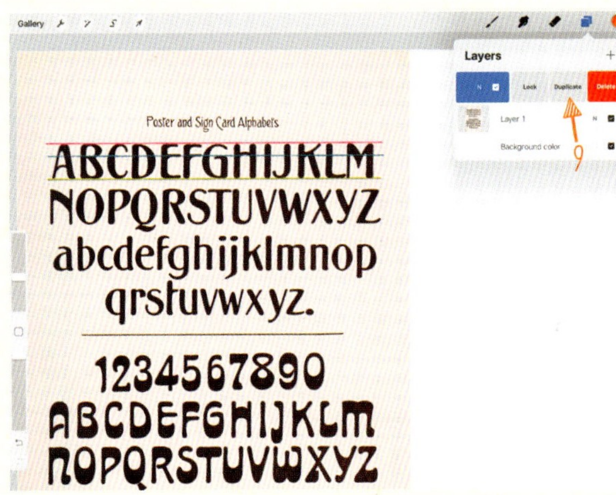

STEP 10: Tap the **Move** tool, and move the new **Guidelines** layer to the next line of text. (You may need to do this multiple times depending on the layout of the resource image you're using.) Repeat the same process with the lowercase letters. Your practice sheet and **Layers** panel should look similar to mine.

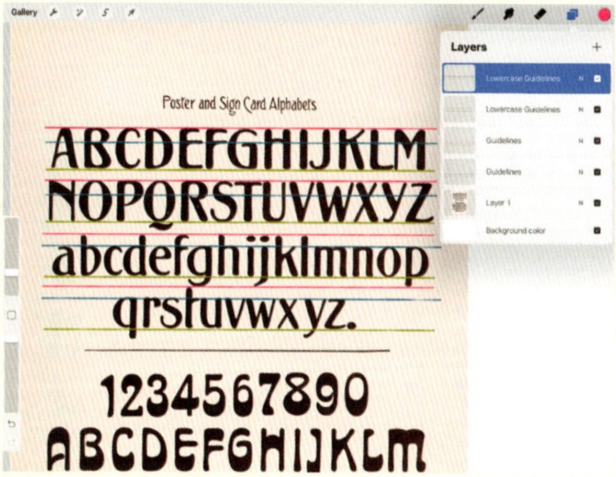

Create a baseline, X-height, and cap height line on top of your resource image.

STEP 11: Now merge all of your guidelines onto one layer by pinching them together, then swipe left on that layer and tap **Duplicate.**

STEP 12: Tap the **Move** tool, make sure **Magnetics** is on, and move the guideline duplicate beside your lettering resource. Tap the **Move** tool again to set the placement.

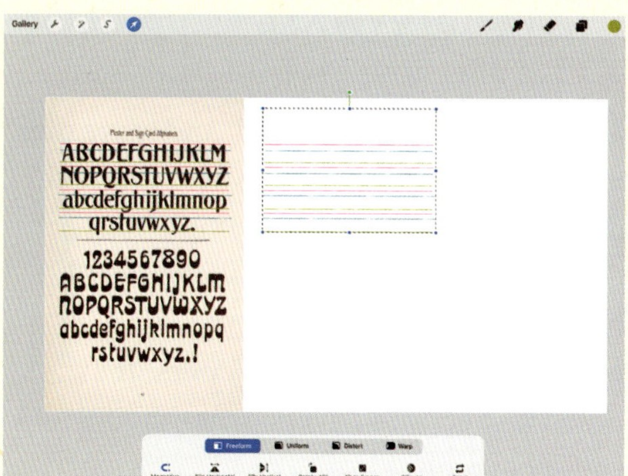

STEP 13: At this point, you might realize that your canvas is too wide (or not wide enough). You can easily resize your canvas by tapping the **Actions** menu.

STEP 14: Tap **Canvas.**

STEP 15: Select **Crop and Resize.**

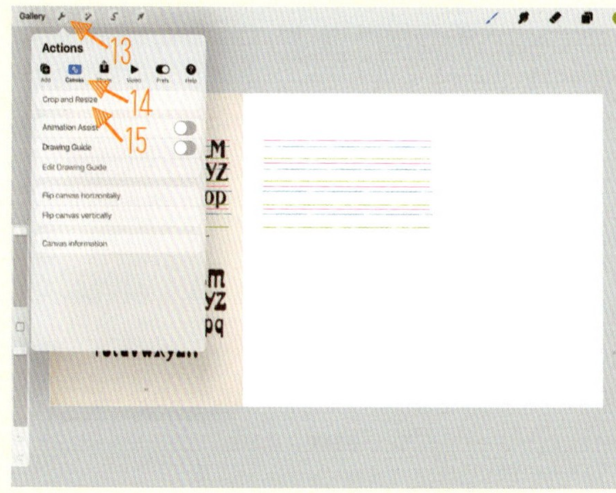

STEP 16: Drag the crop bars to resize your image.

STEP 17: Tap **Done** to set the crop.

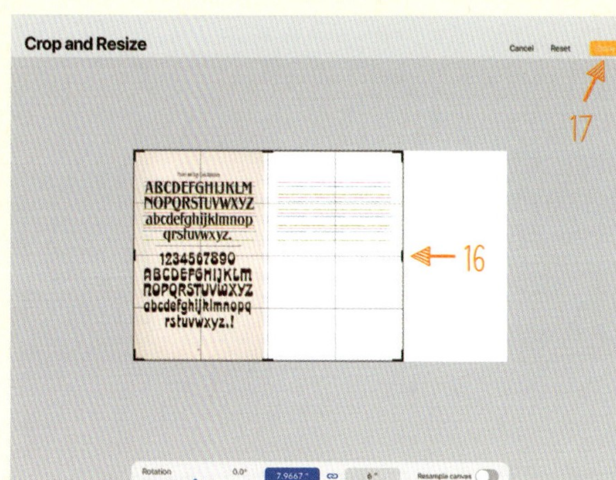

STEP 18: Create a new layer, and start sketching the letters using the **Sketching Pencil.** I like to start with a simple single-line sketch just to get the placement and overall shape of each letter.

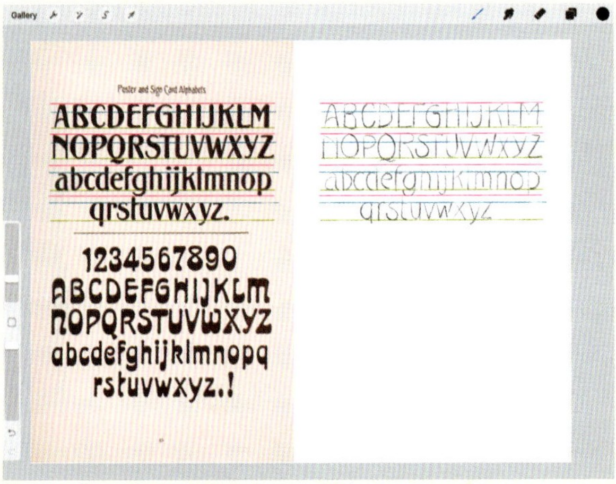

STEP 19: Reduce the opacity of that layer, and create a more precise sketch of each letter. This doesn't have to be perfect, just start getting the thick and thin portions of the letters in place. Feel free to use the **Dual Pencil** in some areas to help maintain the same thickness throughout the letter.

> Tip: There is no correct number of sketch layers to use before moving on to the more refined layers. Always use as many layers as you need in order to get the shapes right!

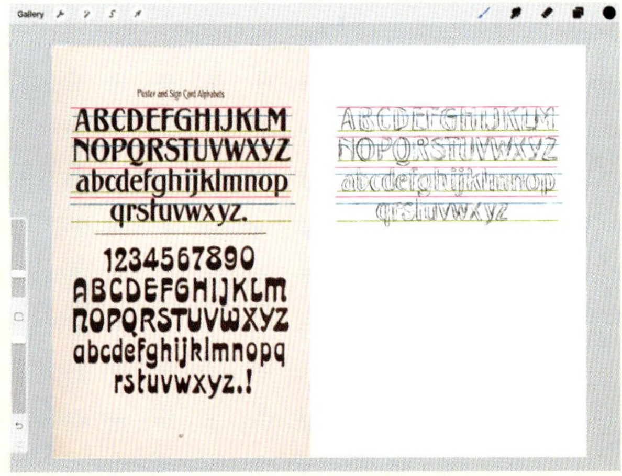

STEP 20: Reduce the opacity of that new sketch layer, and start drawing the final letters, keeping an eye on your resource image for guidance. It doesn't have to be perfect! This is an exercise to help you get comfortable with the process of building letters, but don't worry if your letters don't look exactly like the resource image. The differences between your work and your resource images are where you'll find your style!

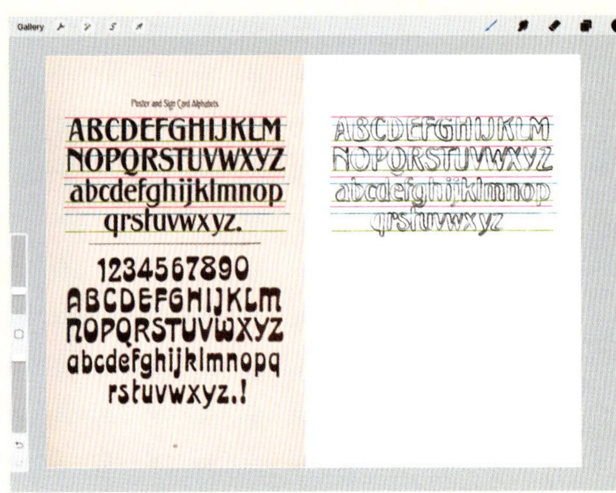

STEP 21: Repeat this same process with any other letterform you want to practice.

Working From an Incomplete Alphabet

Often, when you're working from an inspiration image, you don't have access to the entire alphabet. Let's say you see a beautiful letterform in a vintage magazine and want to use it to letter a quote, but some of the letters you'll need in your quote aren't present on the ad. In this case, you have to rely on the information you have to piece together the puzzle of the letterform. This is another example of why developing an instinct for seeing the "rules" of a letterform can be an invaluable skill. If you understand the rules, then you can make accurate assumptions about how any missing letters would be drawn by the original creator.

Let's take this vintage ad from the 1880 *San Francisco, Oakland and Alameda Business Directory* for example.

This has only a few letters of the alphabet, but it is enough to help me determine how any letter of the alphabet would look in this style. The process is similar to putting a puzzle together: Start with what you know, and use that as a guide to fill in the spaces you don't know.

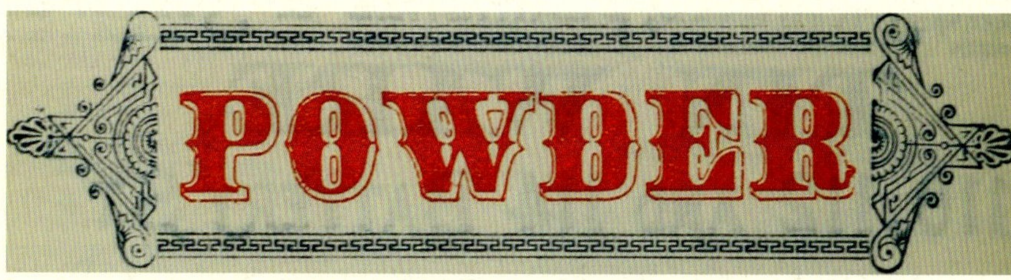

A vintage advertisement from an 1880 business directory

First, we'll create a set of guidelines using the process from the previous section. Then we'll add the letters that we have, using the sketching and drawing process we used to create customized practice pages. Can you identify some of the missing letters that would be easy to determine right off the bat?

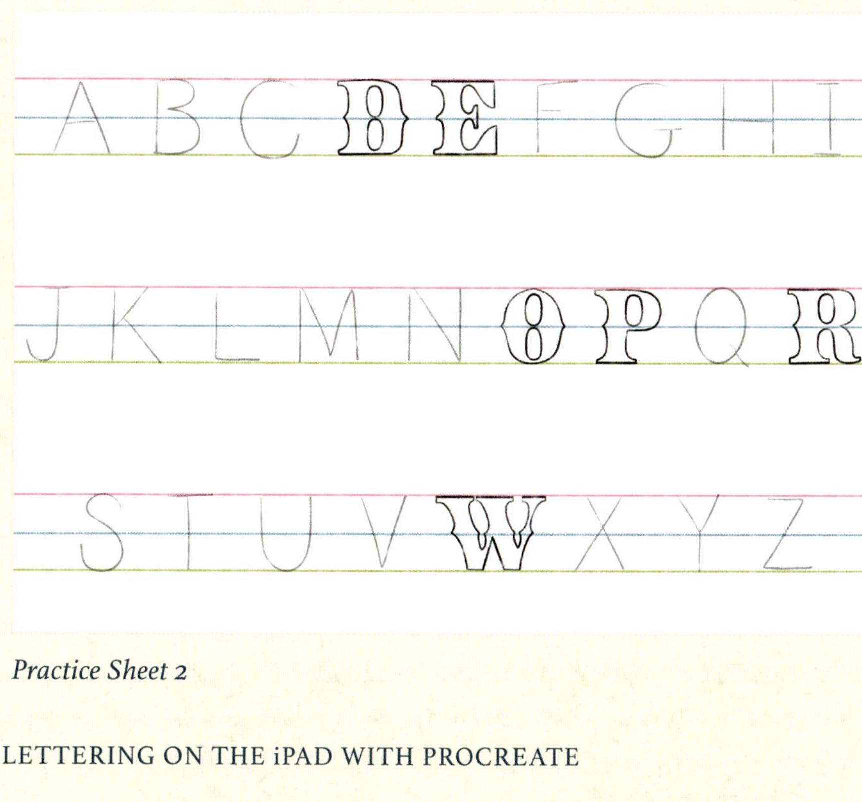

Practice Sheet 2

STEP 1: Start by creating some guidelines and placing the letters you have on the lines.

Anything with a straight vertical bar will copy the bar of the **E**, **P**, and **R**, so I can go through my alphabet and fill in the letters with horizontal bars. To accomplish this, I could either redraw each bar or I could make a Freehand Selection around the part I want to copy, drag three fingers down the screen, and tap **Copy and Paste**. This copies and pastes the selected portion onto a new layer. Then I can use the **Move** tool to put it into place.

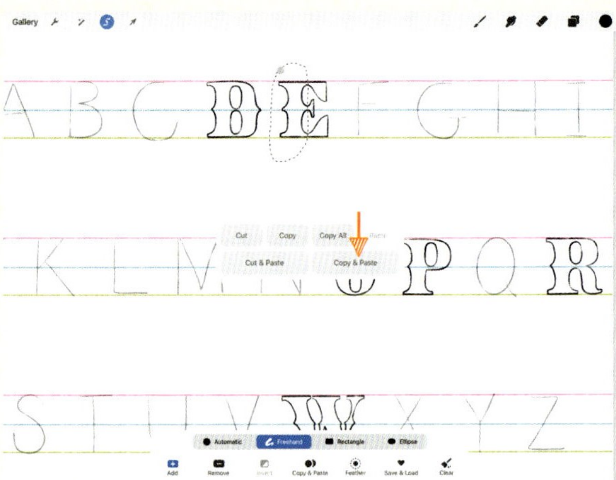

STEP 2: Next, repeat the same process with any letters that have straight bars, and use the **Eraser** tool to remove any parts you don't need (such as the top part of the **Y** and the bottom part of the **J**).

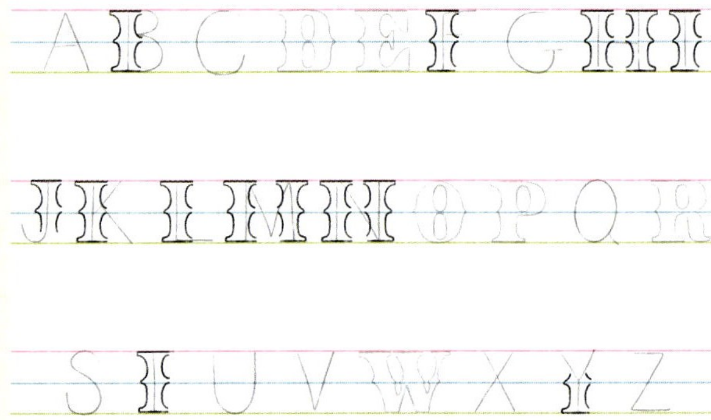

STEP 3: Use the vertical bars from one letter to fill in all the others.

Next, I used the **O** shape to help me get the rounded shape of the **C**, **G**, and **Q**.

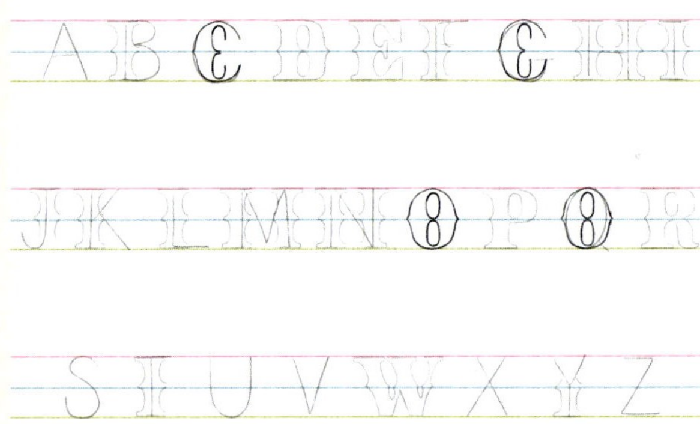

STEP 4: Copy the O shape for rounded letters.

If you need some help with building a letter, look at parts of the existing letters for clues. For example, I used the curve in the **E** as inspiration for the **F**, **T**, and **Z**.

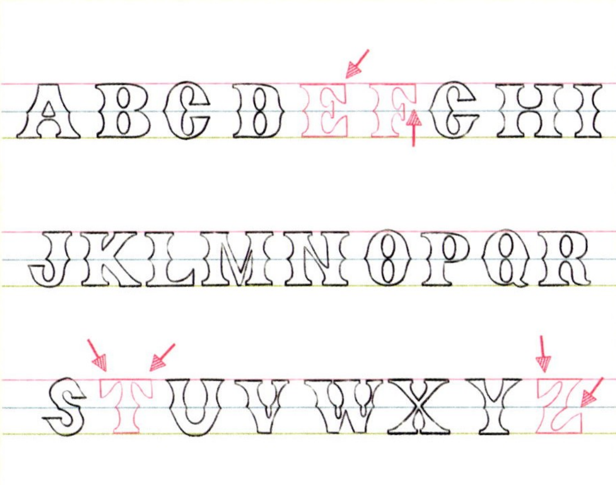

Take cues from the letters you have to create the letters you're missing!

I also used elements from the original letters to help make the set cohesive. See the pointed marks (in pink) and the angled serifs (in yellow) on each letter? Those elements help make the letters appear as if they belong together, so I wanted every letter to contain at least one of those elements (below).

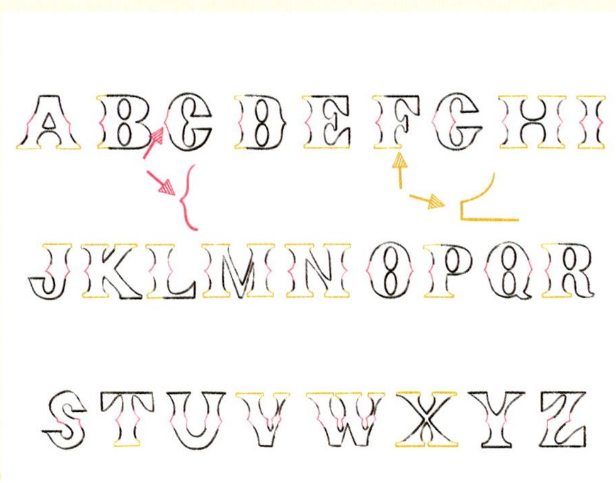

Identify the elements that make the letters unique in order to create a cohesive set.

Of course, when you're using an inspiration image, you don't have to create the whole alphabet. Just recreate the letters you need for your lettering project (unless of course you love the challenge of piecing together the puzzle of an alphabet!).

If you'd like a little practice with this process, download the ***Letter Puzzle*** sheets and try to fill in the missing letters of these alphabets. You might want to start with *Letter Puzzle 1* first, which includes suggestions on what letters to use for guidance (below).

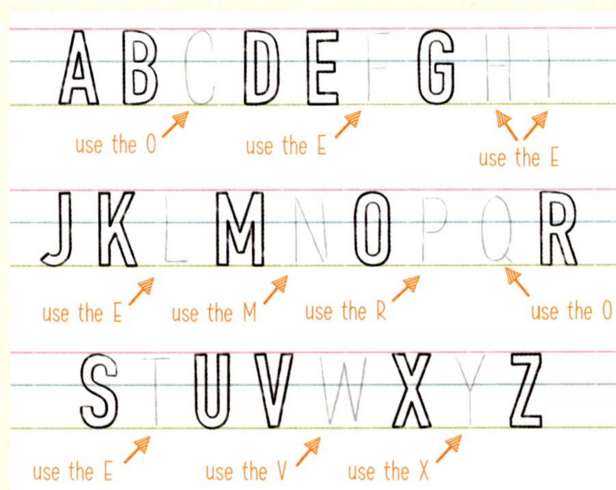

Letter Puzzle 1

If you'd like a bit more of a challenge, try *Letter Puzzle 2*, where you have to figure out which letters of the alphabet to use for inspiration (below).

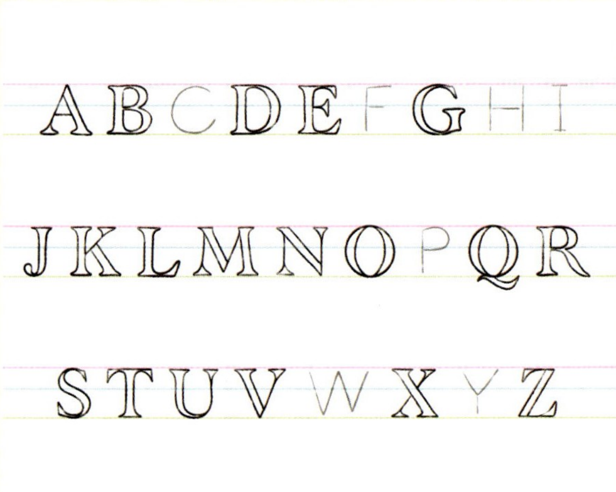

Letter Puzzle 2

Then move on to *Letter Puzzle 3*, where you'll find a more challenging letterform with ornate serifs.

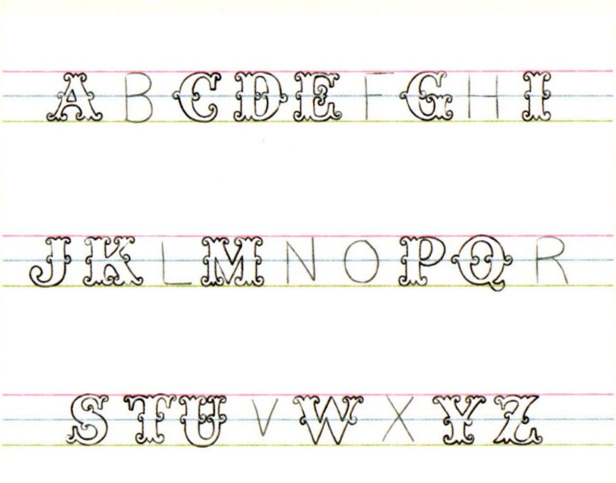

Letter Puzzle 3

Of course, the greatest challenge is to find an old letterform that speaks to your personal artistic style, and then make your own practice sheet to recreate that alphabet. Add a simple border using the **Symmetry** tool and it becomes a great shareable image that lets you share your progress with the world!

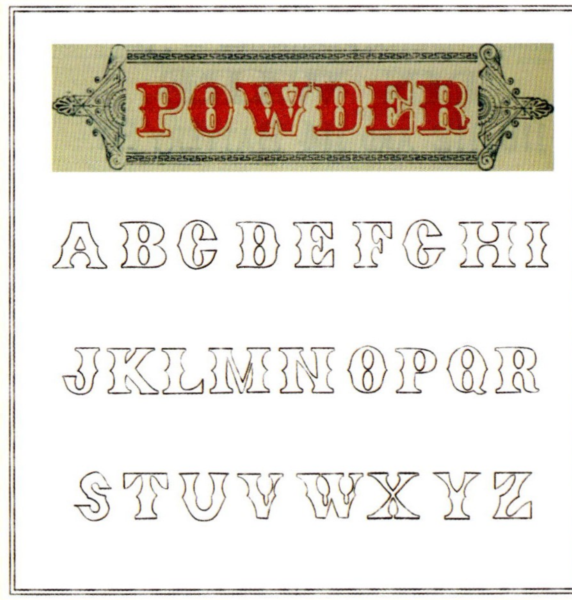

Combine your vintage resource with your finished letters to share online.

Think Outside the Grid

Now that you've gotten comfortable with drawing letters, let's take your letters to the next level by placing them on angled and curved guidelines. Here are a few interesting shapes you can try. You can download these *Guide Sheets* from the **Downloads and Resources** page as described in chapter 1.

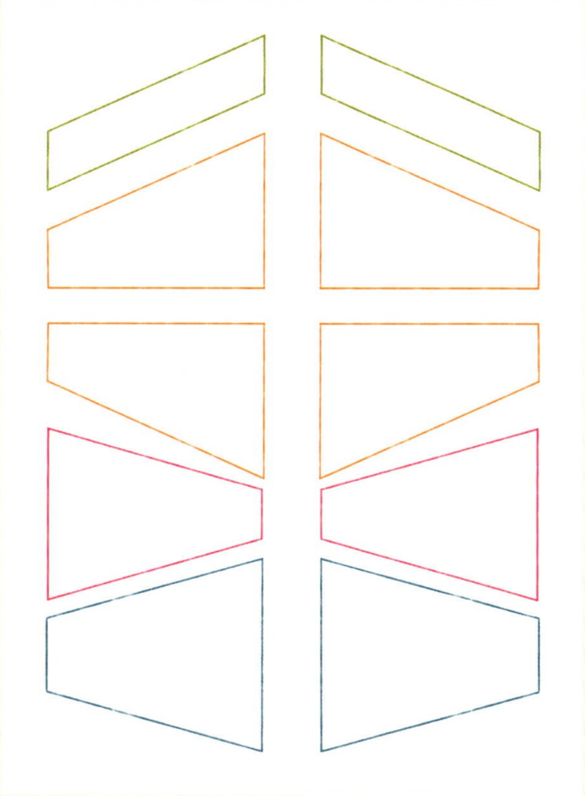

Guide Sheet 1

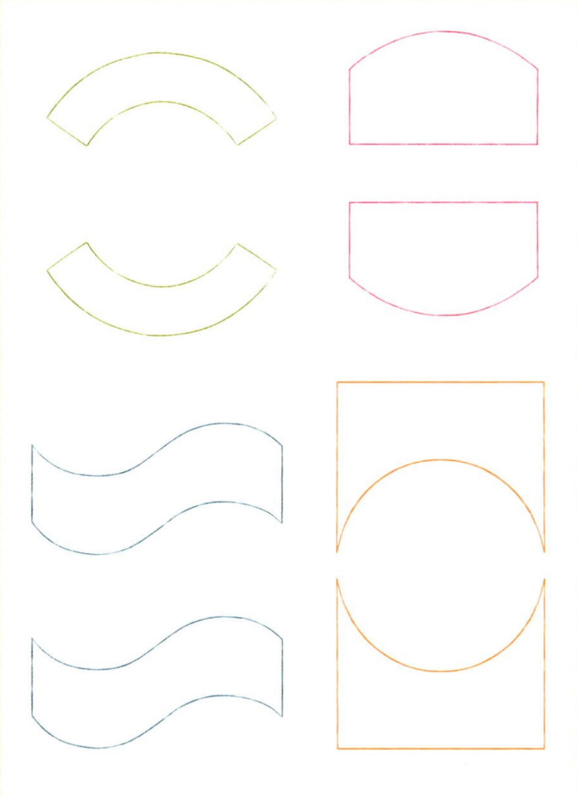

Guide Sheet 2

STEP 1: Choose a word that you don't mind lettering a few times over. (Remember that chapter 2 has a long list of word ideas.)

STEP 2: Open one of the **Guide Sheets** in Procreate, and create a new layer.

STEP 3: Choose the **Sketching Pencil** as your brush and turn on some guides to help keep your letters straight by tapping the **Actions** menu, tap **Canvas**, turn on **Drawing Guides**, and tap **Edit Drawing Guides**.

STEP 4: Adjust the **Grid Size** down so there are at least 10 to 15 squares across each guide. Remember, you can adjust the grid color, thickness, and opacity on this page too.

Tap **Done** to set your grid.

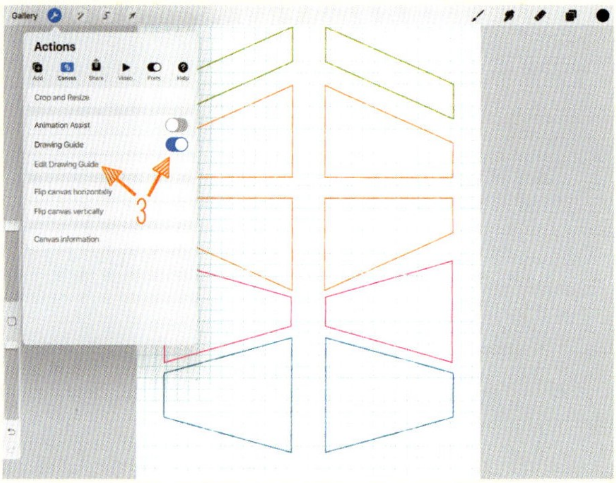

STEP 5: Create an X-height for your letters on a new layer by drawing a line along the baseline, and then move the line up to the middle of the box. Drawing it along the baseline ensures that the X-height is placed at the same angle as the box.

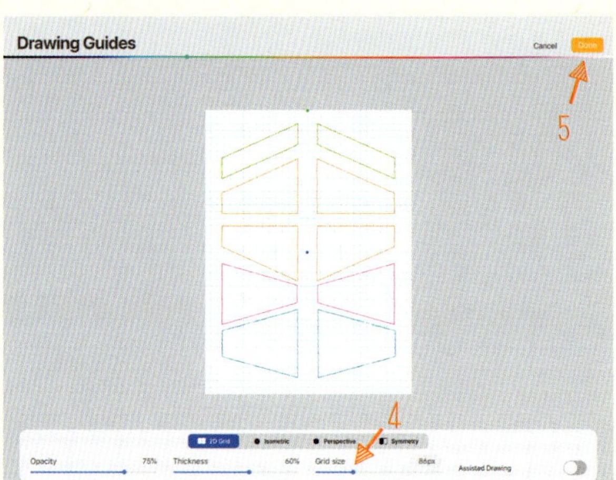

STEP 6: On a new layer, make a rough sketch of the word using the **Sketching Pencil.** Use the blue guides to help keep the vertical bars straight up and down.

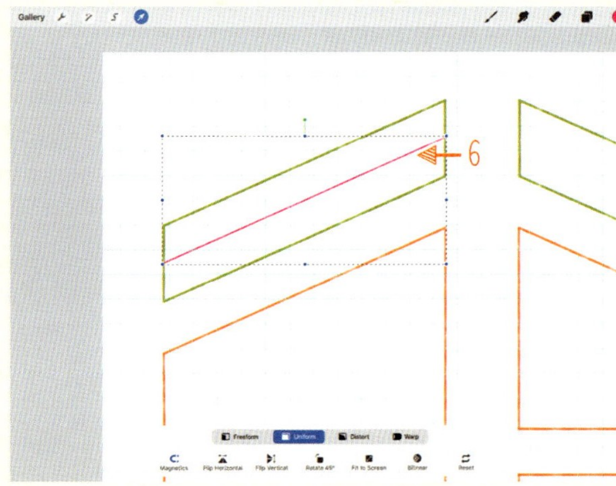

STEP 7: Reduce the opacity of that layer, then create a new layer and use the **Dual Pencil** and the **Sketching Pencil** to sketch your text. Note that the horizontal lines should match up with the baseline and X-height guides.

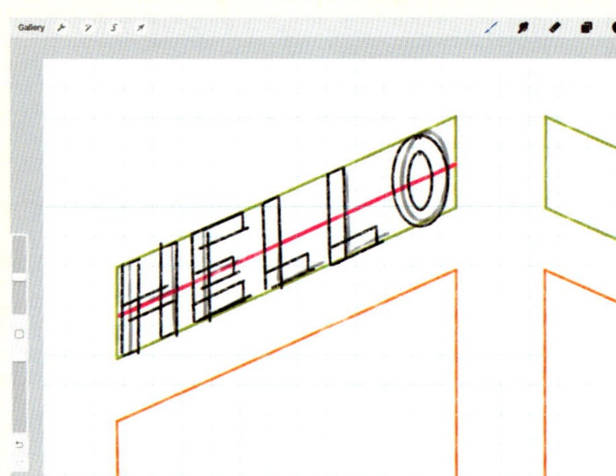

STEP 8: Last, use the **Sketching Pencil** to outline the letters. Remember, if your spacing is off, you can use the **Freehand** selection method shown in the previous chapter to move individual letters.

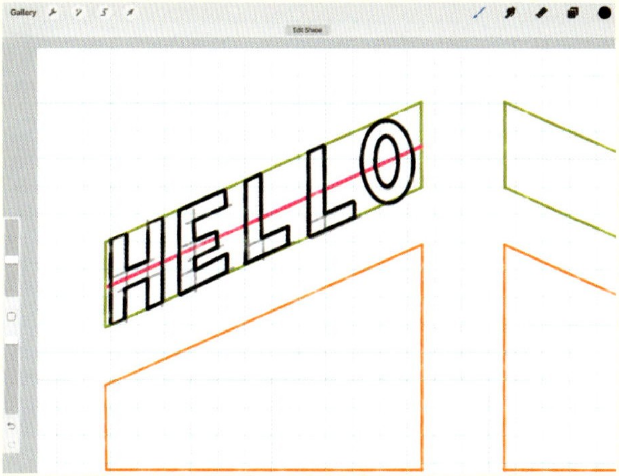

You may want to use the same style of text for all of the guides, or try a different style on each guide.

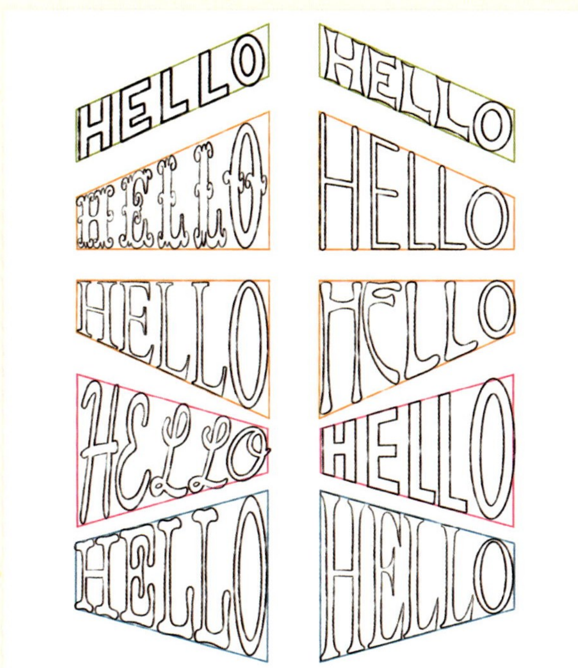

Note that some of the curved guides like the one in green shown below (taken from *Guide Sheet 2*), will require a different type of grid to help you keep the vertical bars of your letters straight. To create this grid, first draw two lines (the pink lines) that overlap the outer edges of the curved guide (below). Use the point where those two lines intersect to add the lines for the rest of the grid.

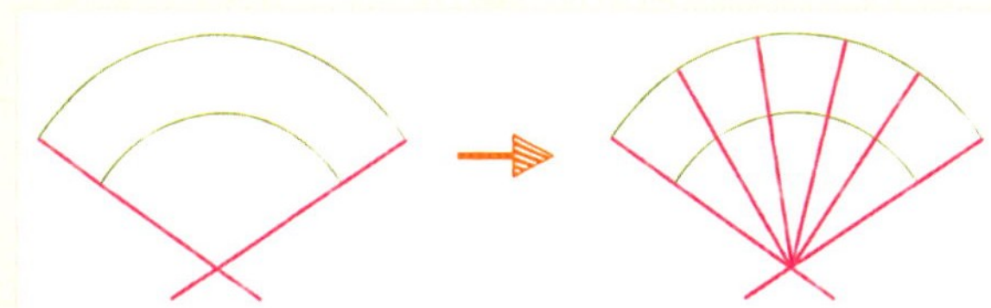

Create circle guides from the outside in.

One Letterform at a Time

When you realize how many beautiful letterforms are out there just waiting to be learned, it can be a bit overwhelming. The most effective way to build your lettering skills is focused practice on just a few letterforms at a time. I suggest choosing a few letterforms that you like and practicing them until they feel easy and familiar, then introduce a couple more into your repertoire. When it comes to getting the most out of your lettering practice, it is better to focus on becoming a master of a few letterforms than to be an amateur of hundreds!

Now that you know the basics of Procreate and how to build guides and letters, let's start practicing drawing letterforms in context by building some finished compositions.

In the next chapter, we'll create eye-catching lettering compositions by combining letterforms with interesting layouts, texture, and decorative elements. We'll also experiment further with color versions and illustrative elements so you can take the next step in developing your own signature lettering style.

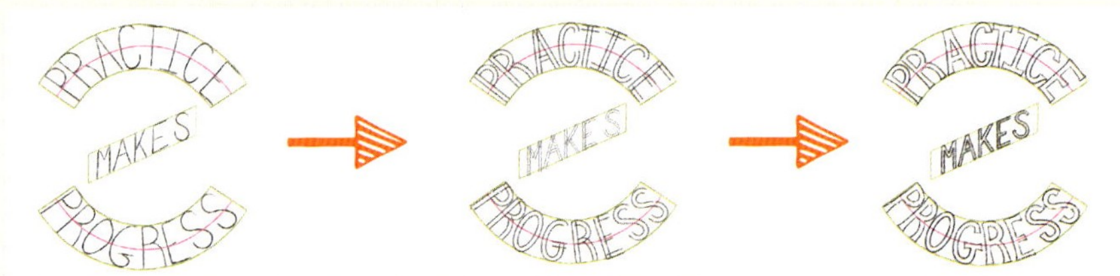

Building a lettering composition

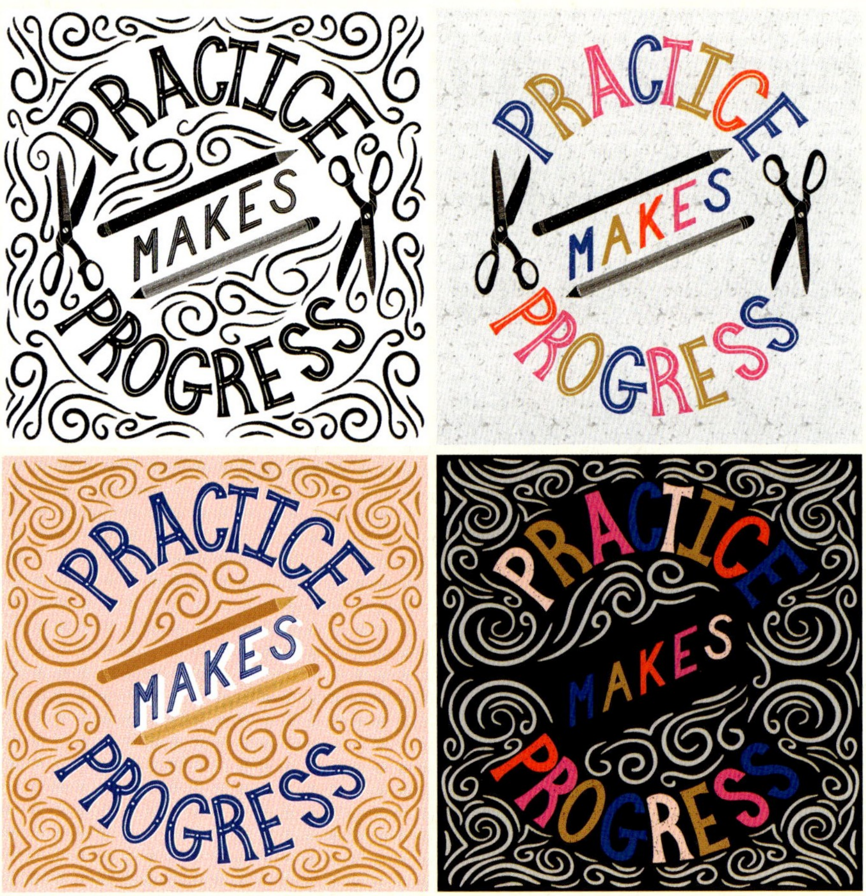

Four ways to finish a lettering composition

CHAPTER 5

Serif and Sans Serif Lettering

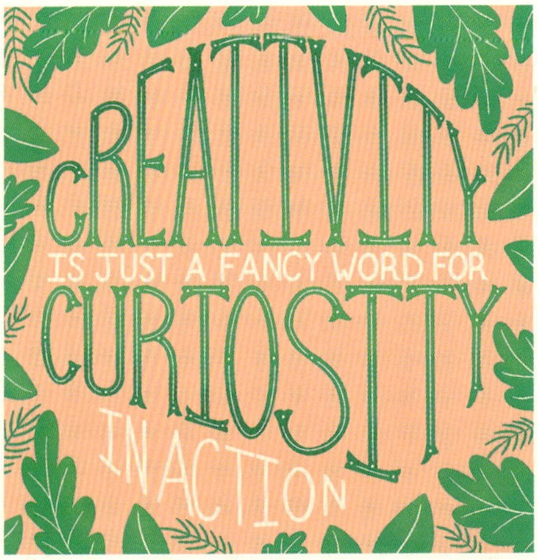

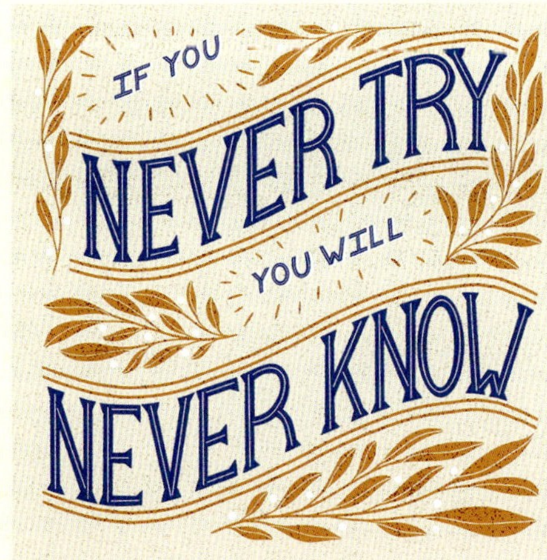

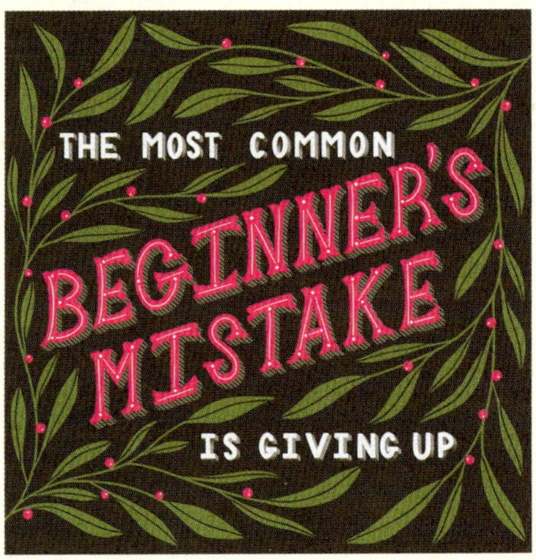

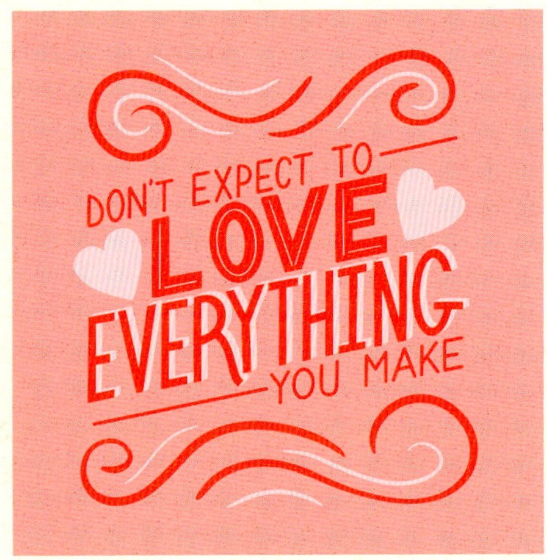

Now that you know the basics of how to build letterforms, let's look at how to style them with serifs, decorative elements, and interesting layouts. We'll look at every step of the lettering process from sketching your design and choosing letter shapes to creating depth using shadows and perspective.

Serifs

If you've perused the resources described in chapter 2, you already know there are a seemingly endless number of serif shapes to choose from. Serifs can include decorative elements on the top, middle, or bottom of the letter. In the image below, which displays a few typical serif styles, you can see how much the serif affects the mood and feel of the letters. A tiny change in the serif can take it from a serious, ornate Gothic style to a whimsical, modern style.

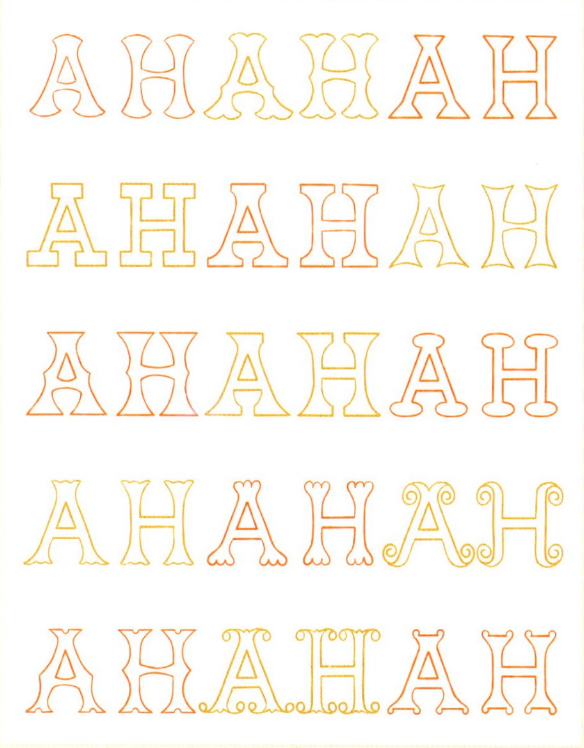

Notice how I used the serifs on the top and bottom as inspiration for the crossbars and sides on some letters.

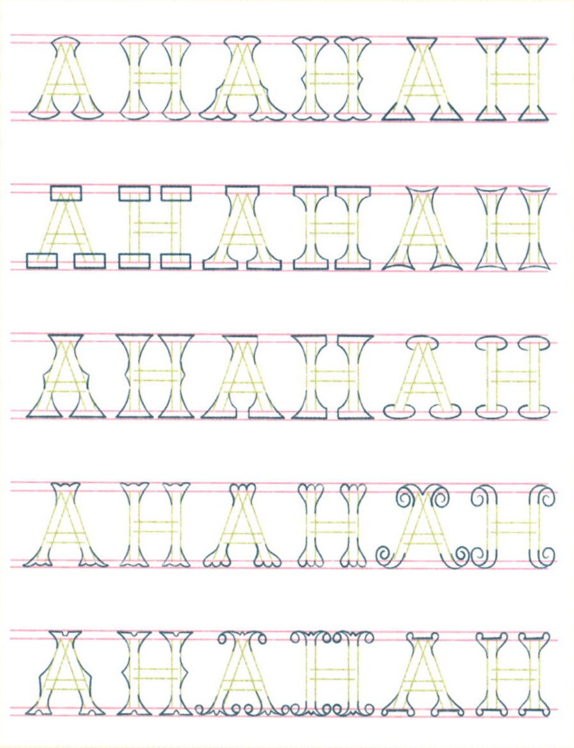

Serif Practice Sheet

In this example, I used the same letter width for each of these styles so you can see how much of a difference the serif makes on a single width. Of course, you can try each serif with wider or thinner base shapes in order to change the feel of the letter.

Try It!

Download the *Serif Practice Sheet* (above, right) to practice drawing a few common serifs. You can refer back to this image (above, left) if you'd like to copy the serifs I used, or you could pull inspiration from letters you find on the **Downloads and Resources** page mentioned in chapter 1.

You'll see in the following steps that I draw the serif shape once, then I copy and paste that serif in order to reuse it for all the others. This helps to keep the shapes cohesive and proportional.

Follow these steps to create serifs:

STEP 1: Download the **Serif Practice Sheet** from the **Downloads and Resources** page described in chapter 1.

STEP 2: Open the download in Procreate.

STEP 3: Create a new layer.

STEP 4: Draw the first serif on the bottom-left part of the A using the **Sketching Pencil.**

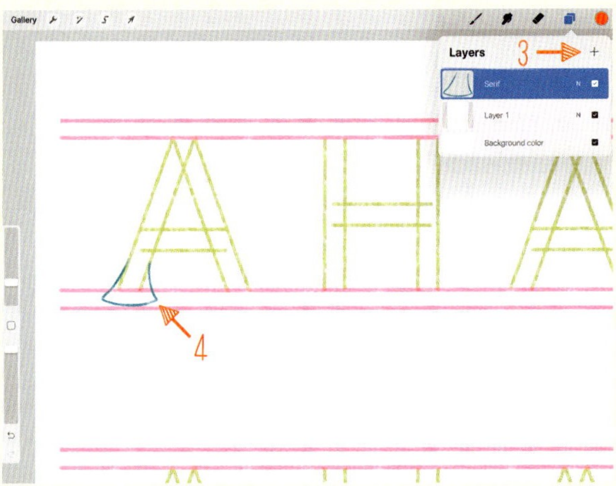

STEP 5: Swipe left on that layer, and tap **Duplicate.**

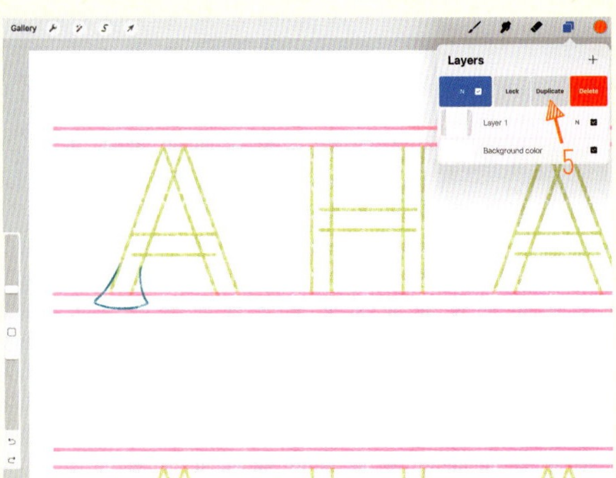

STEP 6: Tap the **Move** tool.

STEP 7: Tap **Flip Horizontal.**

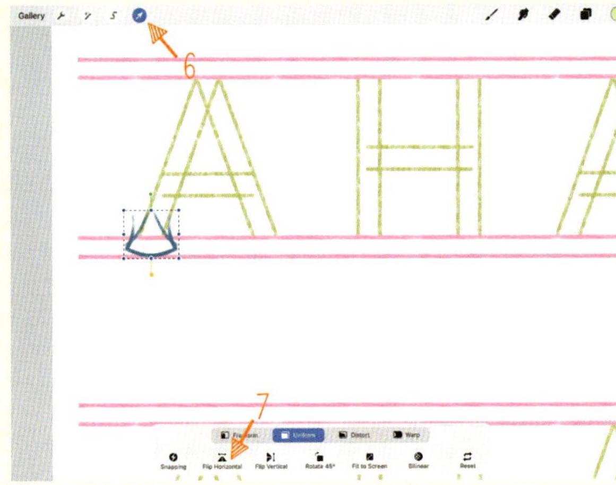

STEP 8: Make sure **Magnetics** is on, and move the serif over to the right side of the **A.** Now you should have the two bottom serifs on the **A** completed.

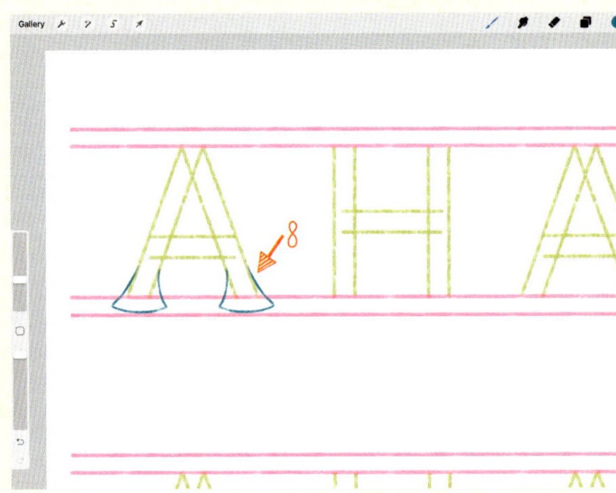

STEP 9: Duplicate one of the serif layers, then tap the **Move** tool. Tap **Rotate** four times, and move the serif to the top of the **A.** You can see it doesn't exactly fit, but we're going to use it as a guide to make the top serifs similar to the bottom ones.

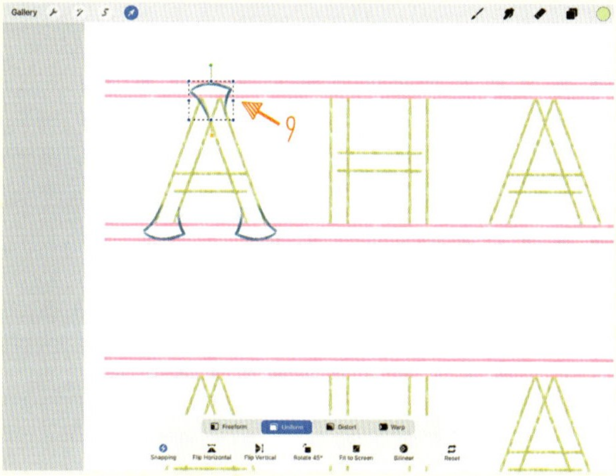

STEP 10: Reduce the opacity of that layer, then create a new layer and draw one half of the serif.

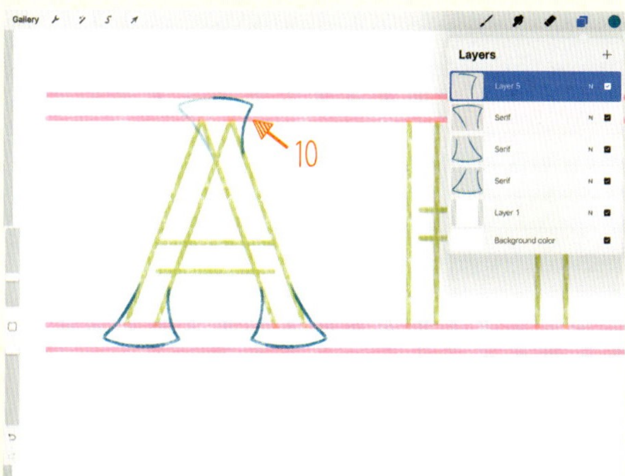

STEP 11: Duplicate that layer, tap the **Move** tool, tap **Flip Horizontal**, and then move the serif to the other side of the letter.

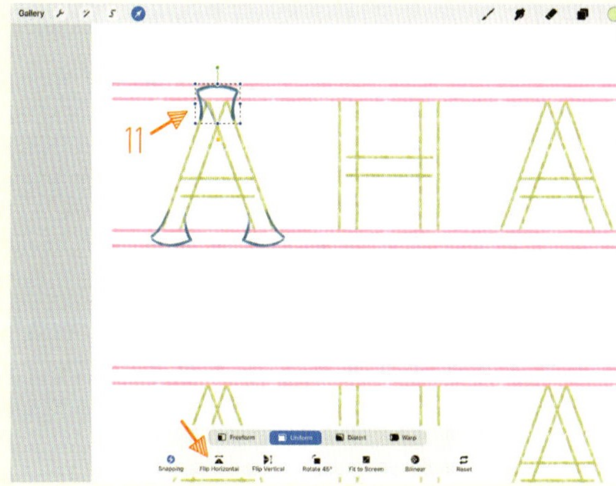

STEP 12: Merge both sides of the serif by pinching the layers together.

STEP 13: Delete the serif that you used as a guide.

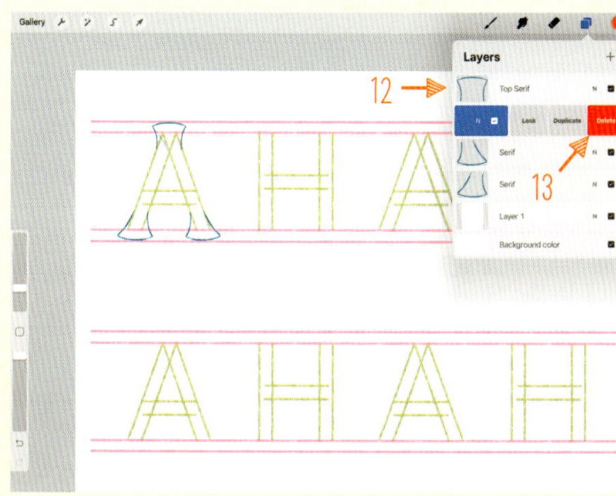

STEP 14: Duplicate the serif on the top of the A, and move it over to the top left side of the H.

STEP 15: On a new layer, redraw the serif to fit the shape of the **H** using the same process you used for the top of the **A.**

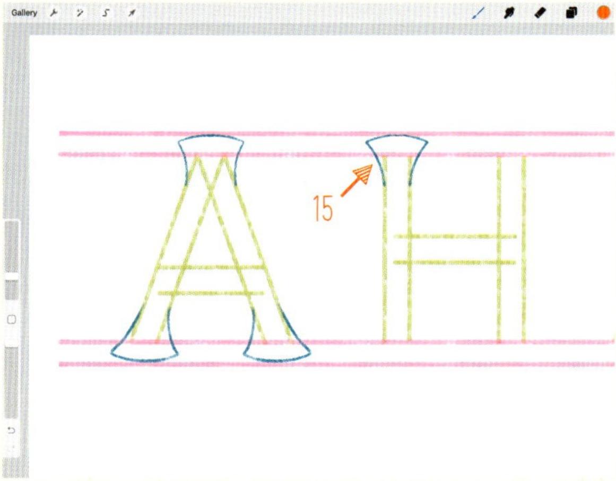

STEP 16: Duplicate that layer and move it over to the right side of the **H.**

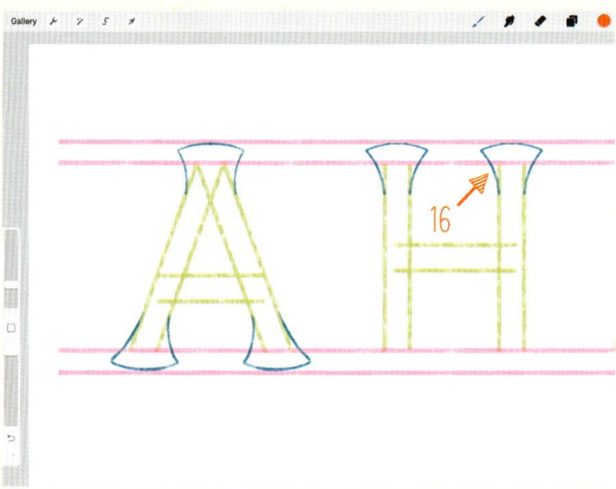

STEP 17: Merge those two layers together, tap **Duplicate,** tap the **Move** tool, and then tap **Flip Vertical.**

STEP 18: Move the new layer down to the bottom part of the **H.**

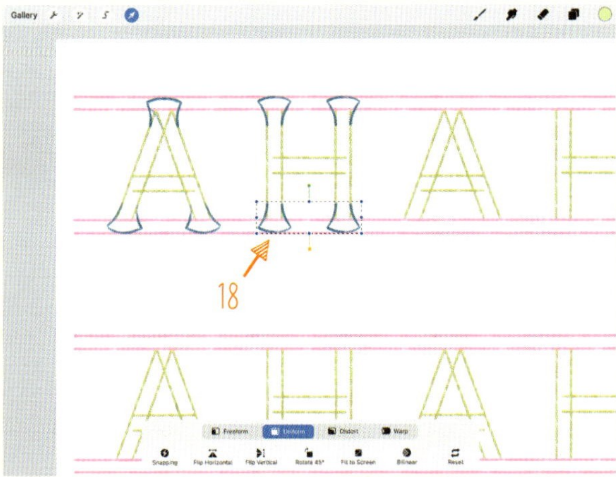

STEP 19: Merge all your serifs onto one layer by pinching them together. Then reduce the opacity of that layer, create a new layer, and trace over your colored lines.

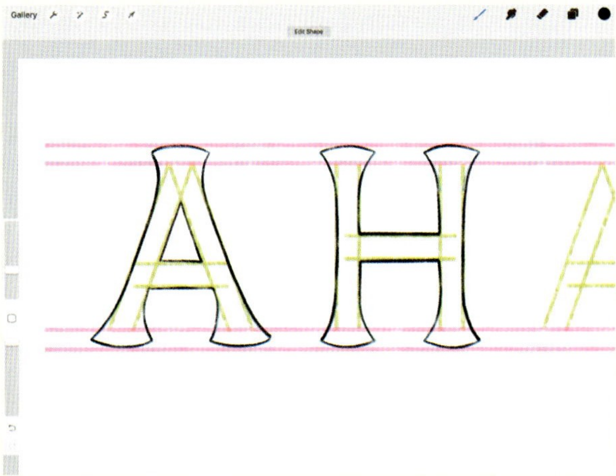

STEP 20: Repeat the same process with each serif type or draw the serifs by hand rather than copying and pasting in order to get a hand-drawn look.

Now that you know how to add any kind of serif to your letters, let's start the process of planning a finished lettering project by getting to know some common lettering layouts.

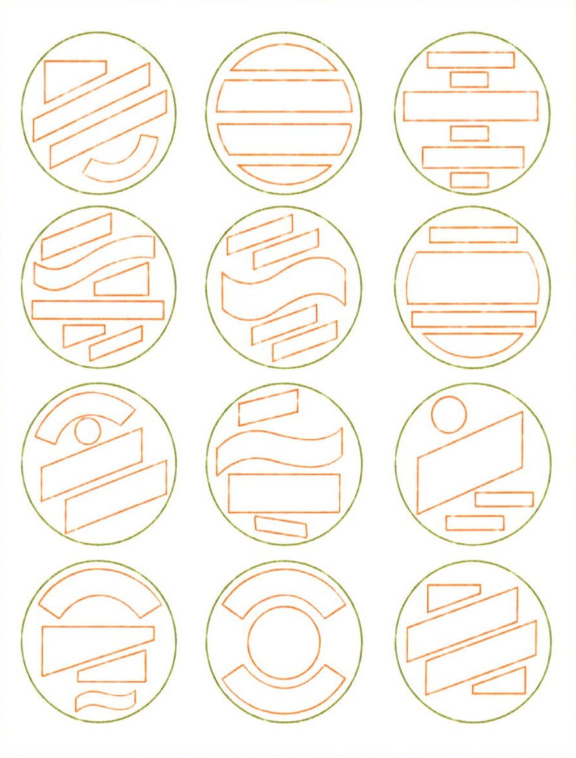

Layouts

Let's start by looking at three common composition shapes: circles, squares, and rectangles. Within those outer shapes (in green) you can fit a variety of guide shapes (in orange), which could include circles, rectangles, angled boxes, curved banners, or any shape you can dream up. Of course, you'll come up with a variety of layouts on

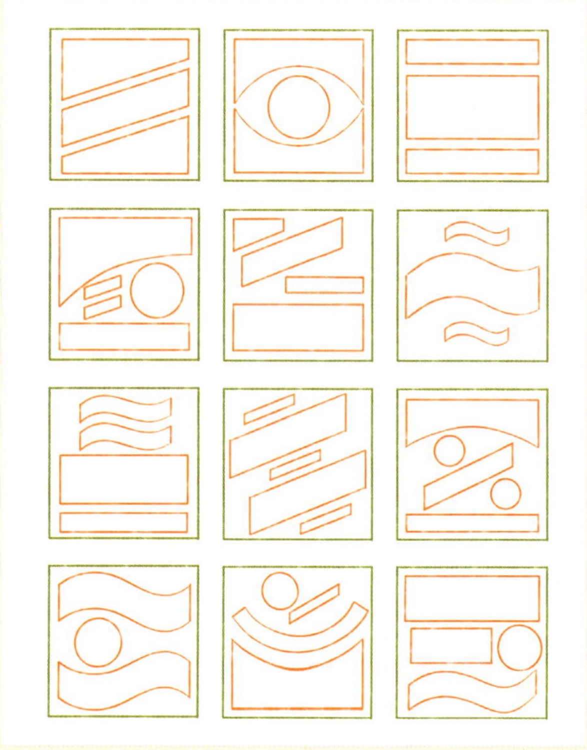

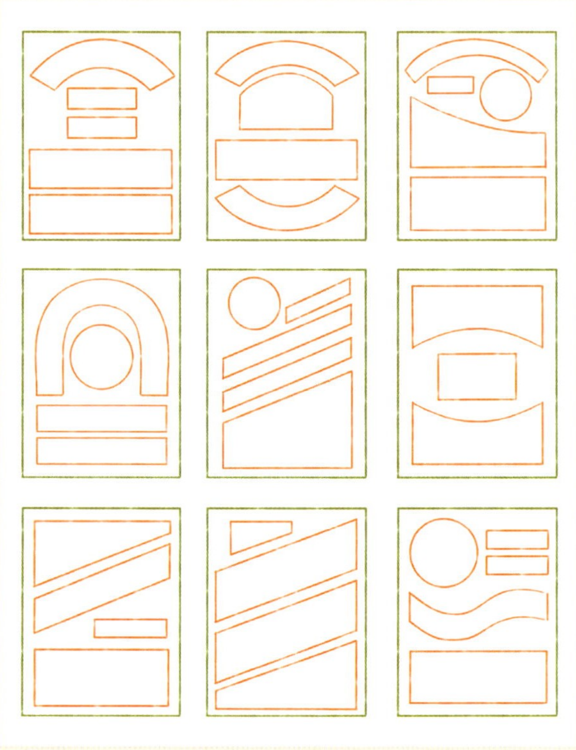

your own, so these examples are really just a starting point for finding a layout that works well with the phrase you choose to letter.

To create these layouts all you need are straight lines and circles, so chapter 4 has already covered all the skills you need to build these layouts. You'll also find a set of guide stamps in the **Hand Lettering** brush set so you can just select one of those, create a new layer, and then tap once on your canvas to immediately have a ready-to-use guide on your canvas.

Now that you have a toolbox full of letter styles and layout ideas, let's combine them to create a finished composition. The first step in starting a new lettering project is to choose a phrase to letter (see chapter 2 for ideas). The next step is figuring out the best way to fit your phrase into a composition. But how in the world do you know which way is "best"? To help answer this question, we will look to the principles of design.

Principles of Design for Letterers

Let's take a look at some of the tried-and-true conventions of design that are especially helpful in building lettering compositions that are both clear and aesthetically pleasing.

The basic principles include the following:

- **Contrast:** The juxtaposition of elements that differ in some way in order to highlight the most important elements (e.g., wide text beside thin text or a dark color beside a light color).
- **Emphasis:** Special attention given to a part of a composition in order to highlight it as important (e.g., one large word in hot pink surrounded by small words in light green).
- **Balance:** A systematic arrangement of colors, shapes, or words to create the impression of equal weight (e.g., decorating the space around your letters with red berries that are spread throughout the canvas rather than concentrated in one area).
- **Scale:** The relationship between objects with respect to size or visual weight (e.g., making the most important words three times the size of the less important words).
- **Harmony:** The arrangement of elements in a balanced and cohesive way that gives each element the feeling of being part of a whole (e.g., using colors and shapes that complement each other, or using the same texture on each element).

With these design principles in mind, let's start sketching some ideas for our composition.

Thumbnails

Thumbnails are quick, tiny sketches of a composition that help you work out the basic layout of your design before you start putting much effort into refining your letters. Sketching thumbnails is kind of like choosing a recipe before you start cooking instead of making it up as you go: It's not a requirement, but will probably lead to a much better outcome! You can create as many thumbnails as you'd like, but I tend to use nine to start with because I find it takes that many sketches to get into the groove.

As you create your thumbnails, think about the principles of design in relation to your phrase. For example, I'm going to letter the phrase, "The most common beginner's mistake is giving up." I want the words "beginner's mistake" to stand out, so as I create my thumbnails I'm going to use the design principles of **scale** and **emphasis** to draw the viewer's attention to those words.

Create your thumbnail sketching page as follows:

STEP 1: Create a new canvas that is 10″ × 10″ at 300 DPI (I'll use a square canvas, but feel free to use a rectangular canvas if you'd like).

STEP 2: Use the **Sketching Pencil** and **Quickline** to draw the top of a square, remembering to put two fingers down on the canvas to make the line perfectly horizontal.

STEP 3: Duplicate the layer.

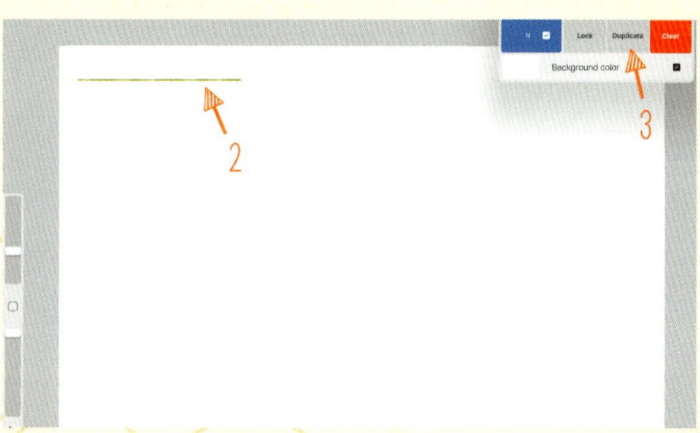

STEP 4: Tap the **Move** tool. Tap **Rotate 45 Degrees** twice, and then move the line to the left of the original line to form the first two sides of a square.

STEP 5: Merge those two layers together by pinching them, and then duplicate that layer.

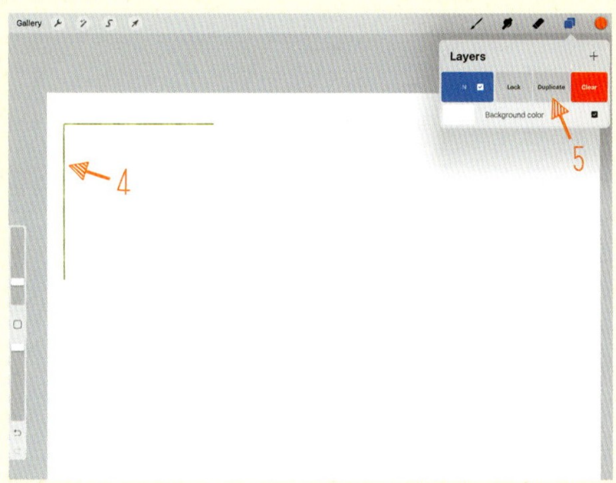

STEP 6: Tap the **Move** tool, and then tap **Rotate 45 Degrees** four times to complete your square.

STEP 7: Merge those two layers together.

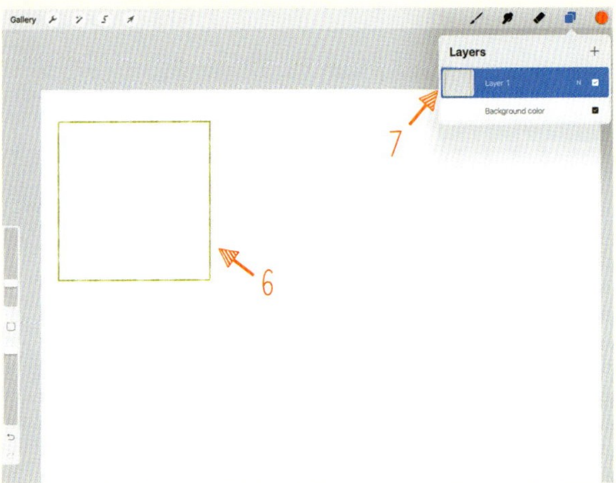

STEP 8: Duplicate the square layer twice, and move each one into place. Before doing this, make sure **Magnetics** is turned on to keep your alignment straight. (Don't worry about perfect spacing here. These are just sketches that no one will ever see.)

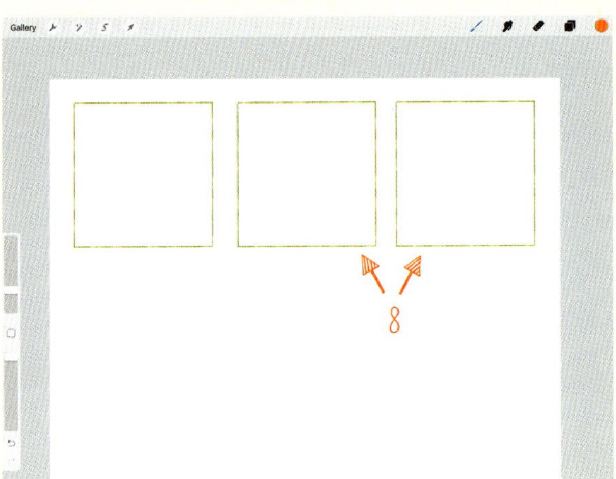

STEP 9: Merge the three squares together into a single layer, then duplicate them and move them down the canvas. Repeat that step once more to create nine squares.

STEP 10: Start sketching! Organize your phrase in as many different ways as possible. This process will help you organize your thoughts on the page and create a well balanced composition.

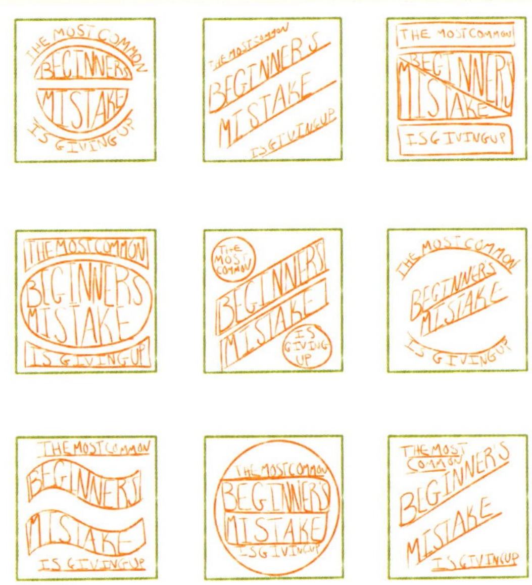

You can see in my thumbnails that I focused on **emphasis** (making the phrase "beginner's mistake" prominent); I considered **balance** (organizing the top and bottom text in a similar way); and I paid attention to **scale** (making the middle text about double the size of the top and bottom text). The other principles of design will come into play later when we start choosing widths, serifs, and colors.

My favorite layout is the final thumbnail, so I will work on that one as an example project, but feel free to use any of the layouts on my thumbnails page if you'd like to follow along with my steps before completing your own composition.

Now that we have a layout plan, let's start sketching the composition and adding guides to help keep the lettering straight.

Start by following along using these steps:

STEP 1: Make your **Thumbnails** layer invisible, and start sketching the layout on your canvas. Remember, you can use the **Freehand Selection** tool with the **Move** tool to move or resize elements of your sketches.

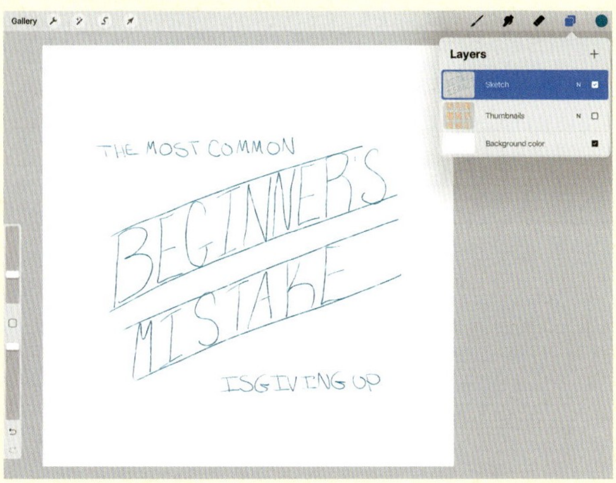

STEP 2: At this point, think about what kind of decorative elements fit your composition. For example, I've decided to surround my quote with some vines and leaves, so for now I'm just going to sketch the vines to be sure they fit around my lettering.

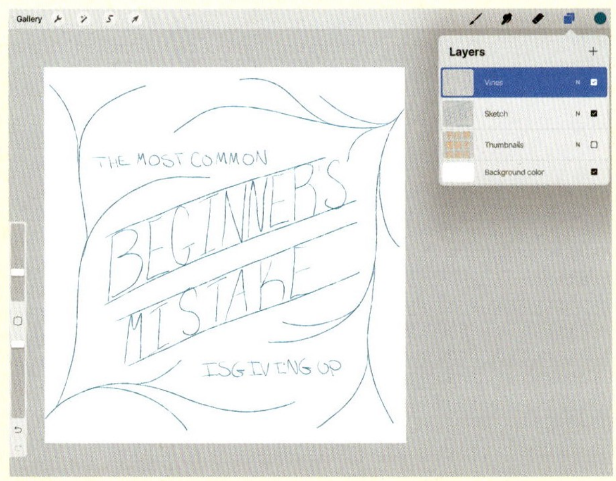

STEP 3: On a new layer, create your guides using **Quickline** to ensure the lines are straight. You can make rectangular guides using the same technique we used to make the boxes on the Thumbnails layer, by first creating two sides, then duplicating and flipping the shape. You can also duplicate a guide to use in different parts of your composition if they are to be the same (like the top and bottom portions of my quote).

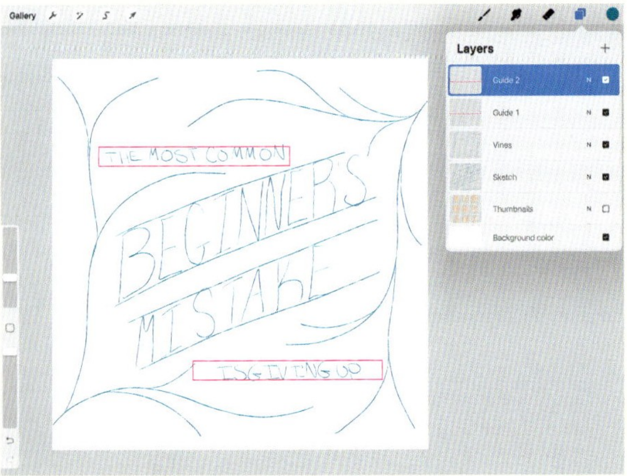

STEP 4: For the diagonal guides, I like to draw the top and right sides of the guide on a new layer, duplicate, and then flip the new layer both vertically and horizontally. This insures that the top and bottom line angles are the same.

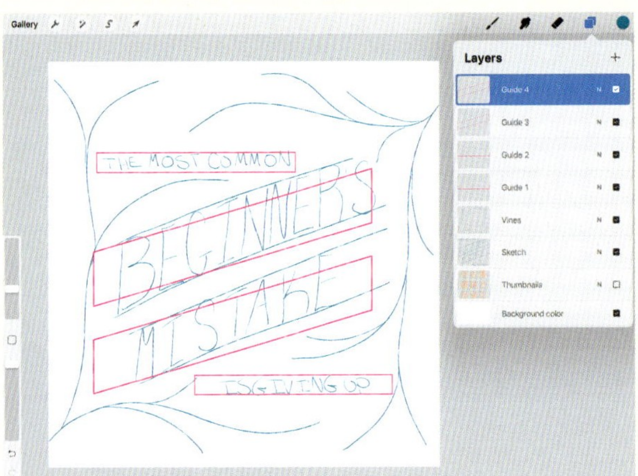

> Tip: For curved guides, use the *Circle* brush in the ***Hand Lettering*** brush set to get nice rounded curves. You can make the circle bigger or smaller to change the curve's shape, but make sure ***Magnetics*** is on before resizing to avoid distorting the circle shape.

STEP 5: Before going further, it's a good idea to take a step back and make sure your composition is balanced. You'll put a lot of work into the letters after this point, so it's important to be sure everything is arranged exactly the way you want it. For example, I realized that I needed to make the guide box for the word "beginner's" wider, so I duplicated it and moved the duplicate to the end of the first one, and then I erased the lines where the two guides overlapped.

STEP 6: Reduce the opacity of the sketch layer, and draw a more refined sketch, using your guides for help with alignment. Space your letters out more than you do with your handwriting, because there are two things that need to fit into this space: 1.) the thickness of the letters and 2.) the serifs [if you're using them].

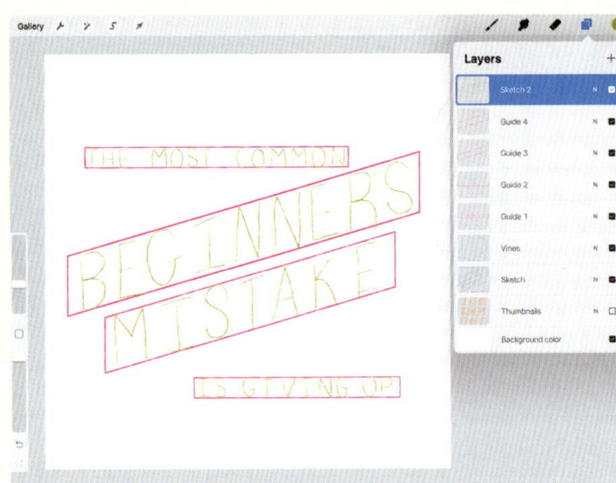

STEP 7: Once you are happy with your new sketch, make the original sketch invisible, and reduce the opacity of your guides and new sketch layer.

STEP 8: Select the **Dual Pencil** from the brush set and choose a width for the letters, remembering that **contrast** and **scale** can help add visual interest to your composition. For example, I'm choosing a width for the smaller letters that is about half that of the larger letters.

STEP 9: Put a grid on the canvas by tapping the **Actions** menu, tap **Canvas**, turn on the **Drawing Guide**, and then tap **Edit Drawing Guide** to adjust the grid size. (Note: I like to reduce the opacity of the grid so it isn't too distracting on the canvas.)

STEP 10: Tap **Done** to set the grid.

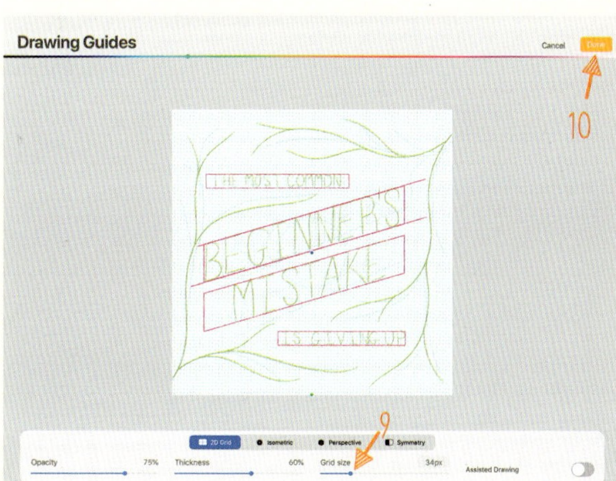

STEP 11: Draw all of your **Dual Pencil** lines, then make all of your sketch layers invisible so you can only see your Dual Pencil lines and guides. This is a good time to use the **Freehand Selection** tool on the **Dual Pencil Lines** layer to adjust the spacing between your letters.

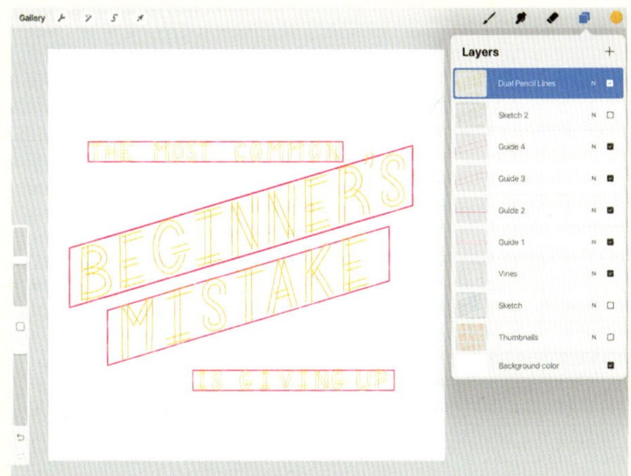

STEP 12: Add serifs to your letters using the process we followed at the beginning of this chapter. It's a little tricky to add serifs on an angle, so you may want to sketch your serifs on one layer and then create a new layer to refine your sketch.

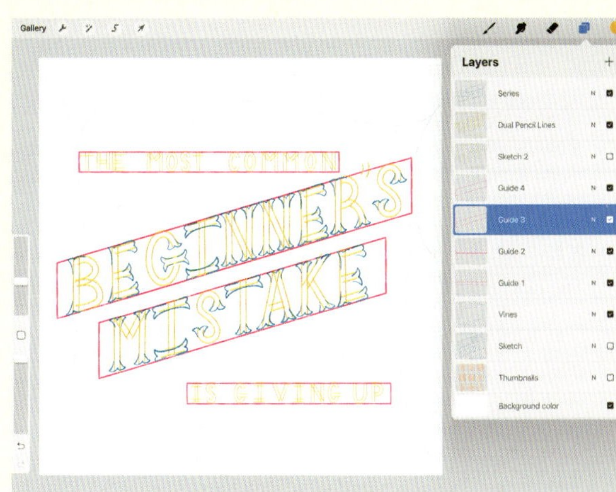

Tip: Remember in chapter 4 when we recreated a whole alphabet from a few letters in a vintage advertisement? You can do the same thing with your own letters. For example, if you draw an E that you like, you can use that shape to create your F by copying and pasting the E onto a new layer and then erasing the bottom horizontal bar.

STEP 13: Create a new layer, and ink your letters using the **Liquid Pen** or any brush of your choosing (e.g., I sometimes use the **Colored Pencil** brush from the **Hand Lettering** brush set to fill my letters when I want to create a rough texture). Keep letters that will be in the same style on the same layer. For example, I put "**the most common**" and "**is giving up**" on one layer, and "**beginner's mistake**" on a different layer.

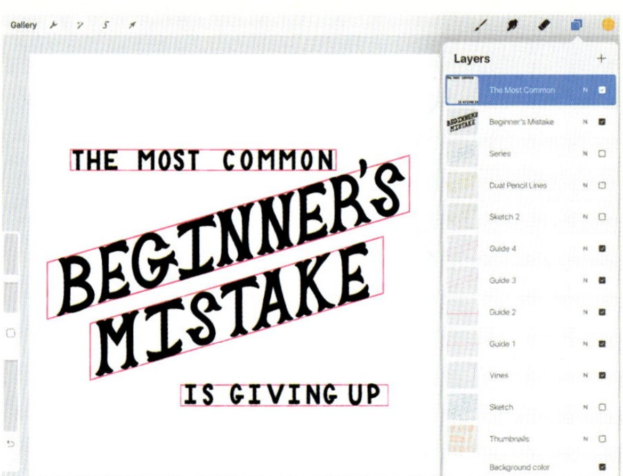

Tip: You can copy and paste inked letters so you don't have to redraw them each time. For example, I drew the letter I in the phrase "**is giving up**" once, I then used the **Freehand Selection** tool to circle the letter, and then I dragged three fingers down the canvas to get the **Copy/Paste** menu.

STEP 14: At this point I usually create a Master Document as described in chapter 3. (Go to the gallery, select the document, tap **Duplicate**, and then open the duplicate document.) This way you can delete all the sketch layers while still saving them in a separate document. This keeps your layers panel tidy, and helps you avoid hitting your layer limit. You can delete layers by swiping left on the layer, then tapping Delete.

STEP 15: Next I'm going to ink my vines, so I know exactly where they'll be on the canvas. This will help me determine how much space I have left on the canvas for things like shadows, texture, and filler elements. If you're using vines or some other decoration in the background, this is a good time to at least lay down the basic shapes on a new layer.

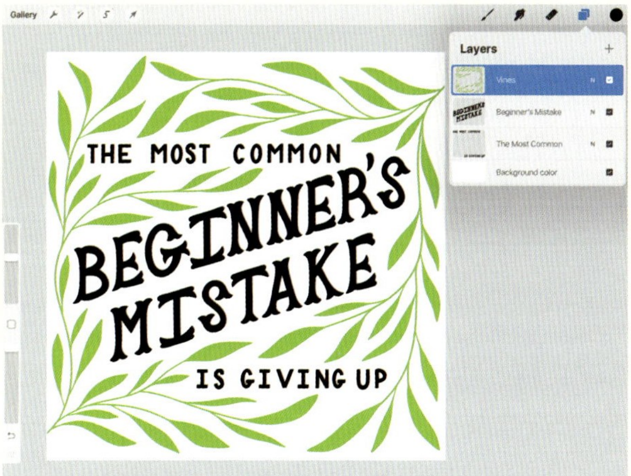

STEP 16: Add some color to your background by tapping the **Background** layer and choosing a color just like we did in chapter 3.

STEP 17: To add color to your letters, first select a color from the **Colors** menu. Then tap on the layer that contains your letters on the layers panel twice to reveal the flyout menu. Tap **Alpha Lock**, then tap **Fill.** Now your letters should be filled with the selected color.

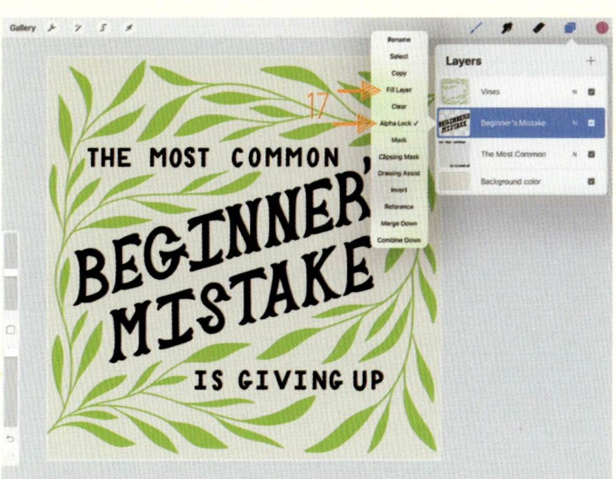

STEP 18: You can repeat this process with multiple colors, but this time you only need to choose a color and tap **Fill** on the layer flyout menu. (We'll talk about the function of the **Alpha Lock** setting in Chapter 6.)

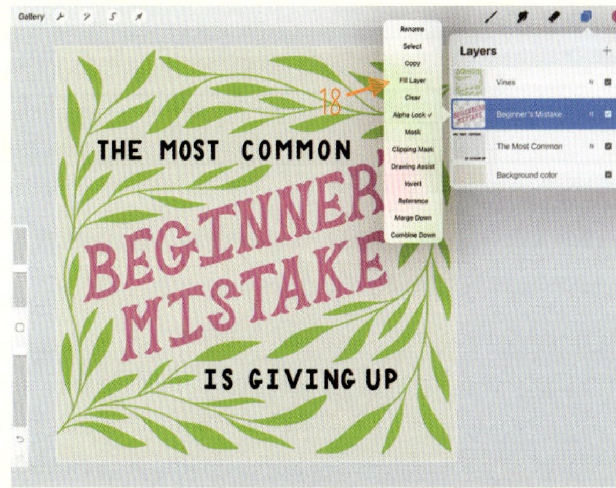

Tip: There are several ways to change the color of objects in Procreate. The **Alpha Lock/Fill** method that we just used is most helpful when you need to change everything that has a certain color on the same layer. Whereas the Color Drop that we used in chapter 3 is better for coloring individual objects one at a time.

Adding Depth: Perspective, Shadows, and Layers

There are three ways to add depth to your lettering in Procreate: perspective, shadows, and layers. You can use just one, or any combination of them! First, let's look at the process for basic perspective lettering, then I'll show you a bunch of options so you can choose the style that best fits your composition.

Let's add these elements using the following steps:

> Tip: Before adding any shading or perspective layers, make sure your letters are evenly spaced. You can adjust the spacing by circling a letter with the **Freehand Selection** tool and then use the **Move** tool to adjust its location.

STEP 19: Duplicate the text layer on which you want to give some shadow or perspective by swiping left on the layer and tapping **Duplicate.** Then, make the duplicate layer a different color than your original letters using the **Alpha Lock/Fill** method from step 17. I usually use a color that is lighter or darker than my original color.

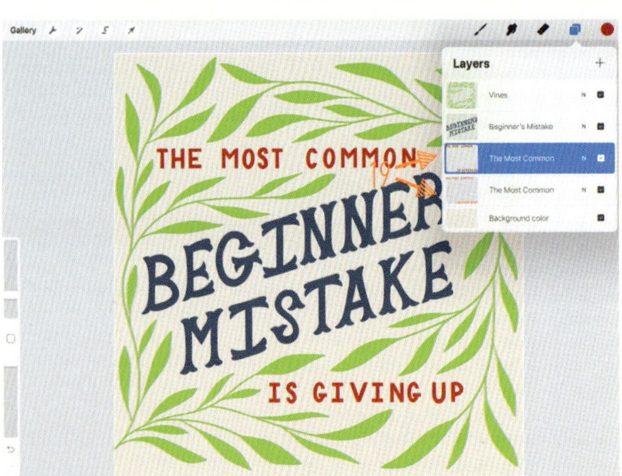

> Tip: Don't worry about choosing the perfect colors at this stage as you can always change colors later. For now, just choose shades that are easy to see.

STEP 20: Drag the duplicated layer (I named this the "Perspective Layer") below the original in the Layers panel.

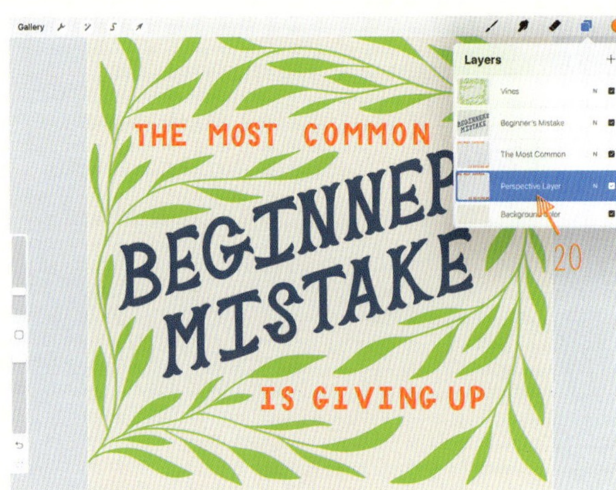

STEP 21: Tap the **Move** tool, and move the Perspective Layer to the left or right of the letter making it slightly offset. You can move it as far as you like, but be aware of

how it interacts with the letters on the top layer. For example, you don't want to leave only a tiny edge of the **Perspective Layer** peeking out from behind a letter because it might look like a mistake. Instead, choose a position that looks intentional and clear.

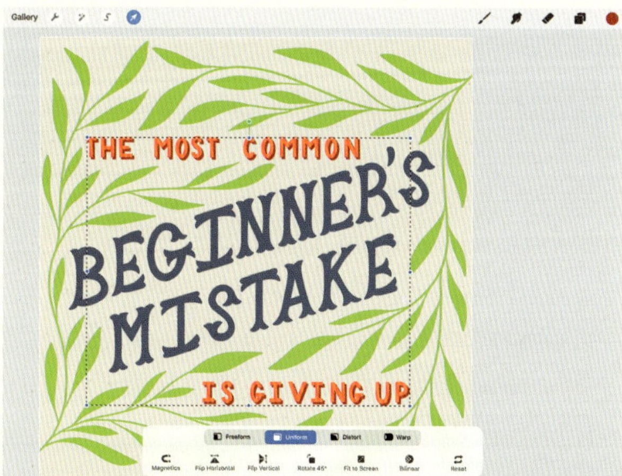

STEP 22: Zoom in closely to the first letter, and connect the corners of the Perspective Layer to the original using the **Monoline** brush, being sure you are drawing on your **Perspective Layer.** You might want to reduce the opacity of the top text layer so you can easily see any corners that are hidden behind the top layer.

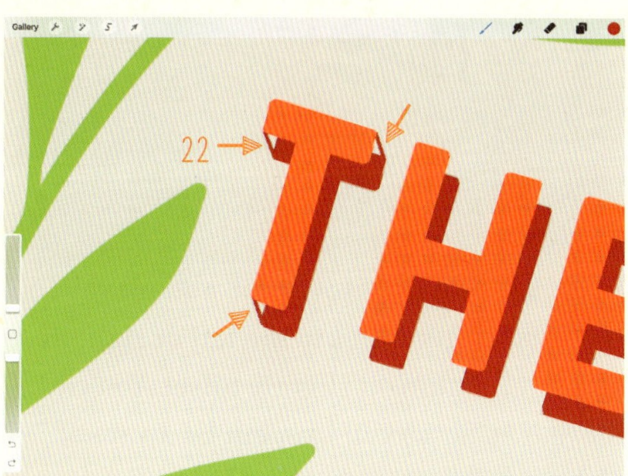

Tip: Use the **Monoline** brush when you want a perfectly straight line, and use the **Liquid Pen** when you want some fluidity and variation to your line.

STEP 23: Once you connect the shapes on all the letters, make your brush size larger and fill in the interior shapes with color.

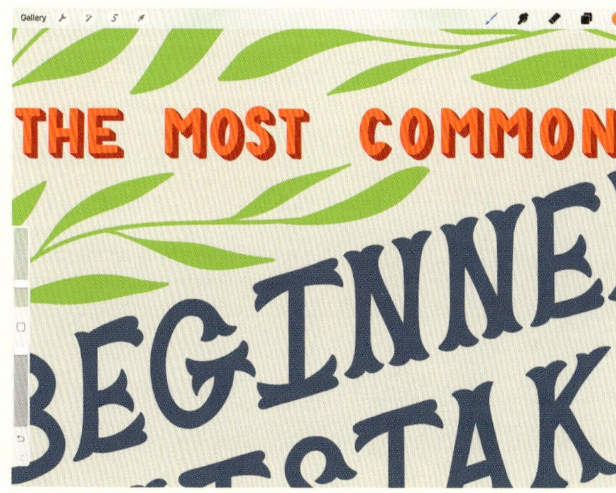

STEP 24: Now let's add some shadow. I used the **Gritty Shading** brush from the **Hand Lettering** brush set, but there are a lot of brushes that come with Procreate that would also work well for adding shadows. To make the brush more or less gritty, tap on the brush twice to see the **Brush** menu, then tap **Grain.**

STEP 25: Increase or decrease the **Scale** to your liking. You can see how it will look in the brush preview on the right side of the screen.

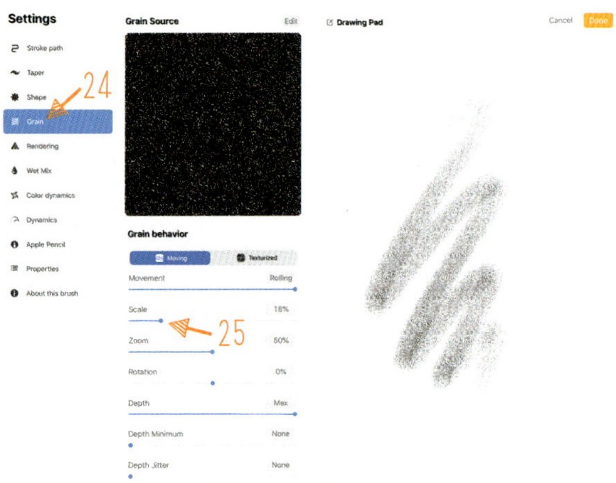

STEP 26: Create a new layer and then drag it above the **Perspective Layer**, so it's between the original text and the perspective text. Tap the layer one time and on the flyout menu that appears, tap **Clipping Mask**. Now when you draw, the color will appear only in the areas where there is ink on the perspective layer.

A Clipping Mask layer uses whatever layer is below it like a stencil, so you can freely draw on the Clipping Mask layer without worrying about getting ink on your background or other letters. Test it out by selecting a dark color and painting over your letters and then tap two fingers to step back to undo your test.

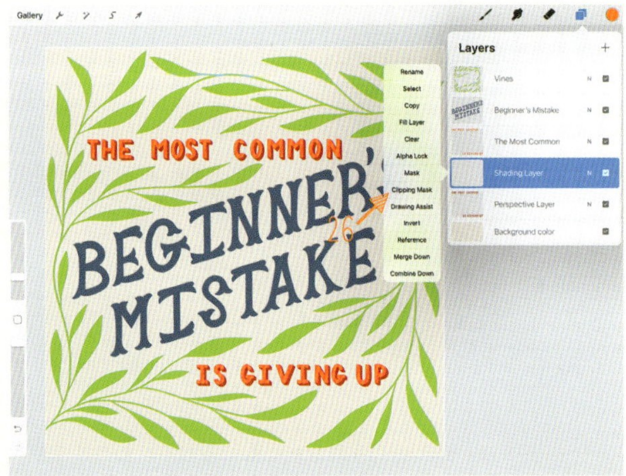

Tip: Clipping Masks are great to use when you want to add shading to a layer but you don't want to draw directly on that layer. This helps you preserve your original layer and keep the flexibility to change the color of the shading later.

STEP 27: Decide which side you want your shadows to be on (I have shaded all the undersides of the letters so it looks like light is coming from the top). Then brush each shadow on the letters, but don't worry if you get some of the shadow color on the wrong parts of the letters because we'll erase those extra bits in the next step.

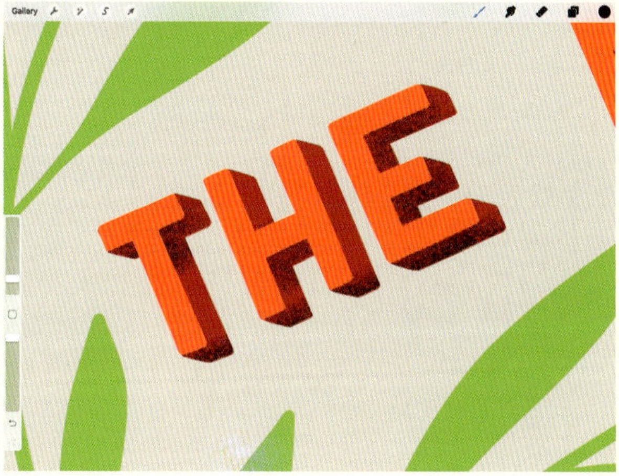

STEP 28: Use the eraser with the **Monoline** brush to clean up the shadow. The goal is to have crisp lines where the light would be shining on the shape. It helps to picture a light in the corner of your composition and then imagine where the shadows would be when the light is in that position.

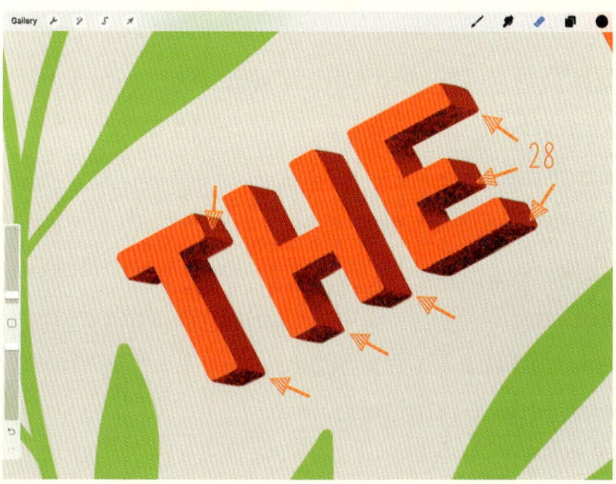

Next, I'm going to repeat the same process with the blue letters in my phrase, but rather than adding shadow I want to add angled lines on top of a perspective layer. To do this we have to create a new perspective layer, then use the **Selection** tool to copy and paste a portion of the vintage lines texture onto another new layer.

STEP 29: Create a perspective layer using steps 19 through 23, then create a new layer and select the **Vintage Ink Lines** brush.

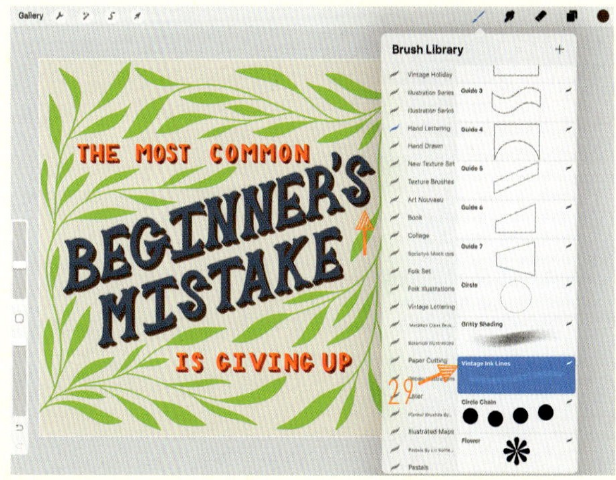

STEP 30: Reduce the opacity of the new **Perspective Layer**. Create a new layer and name it "Vintage Lines." Drag it between the Perspective Layer and the original text, and then swipe the brush across the canvas.

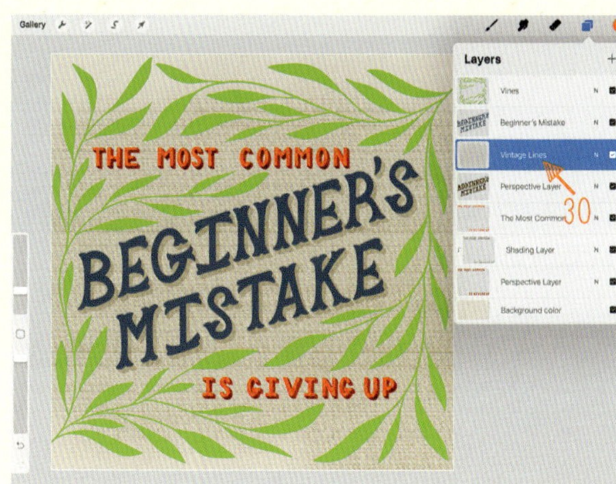

STEP 31: Tap the **Move** tool, and drag the little green dot at the top of the canvas to rotate the shape (turn off **Magnetics** to stop the magnetic snapping). Try to get the angle of the lines to match the angle of the new Perspective Layer. This doesn't have to be perfect but getting it close helps the perspective look more accurate.

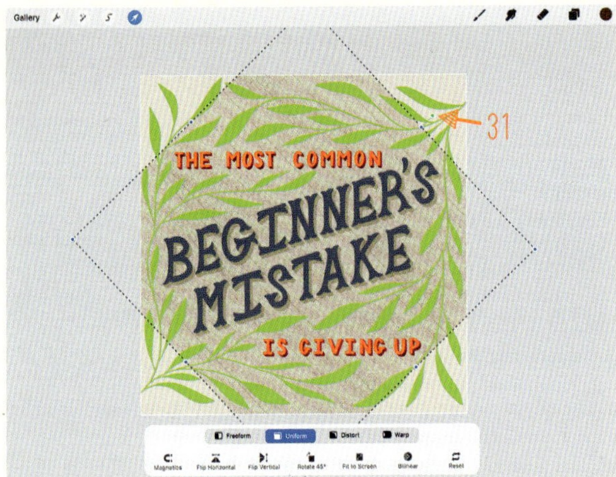

STEP 32: Tap twice on the **Perspective Layer**, and then tap **Select** in the flyout menu. This selects everything you have drawn on that layer.

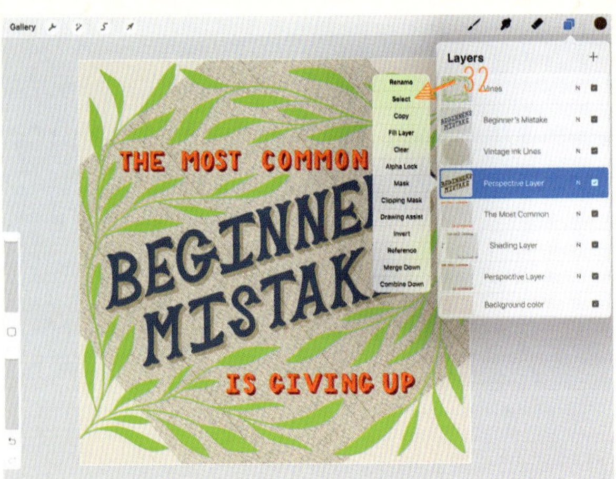

STEP 33: Now tap on the **Vintage Ink Lines** layer in the Layers panel, tap anywhere on the canvas once to close the Layers panel, swipe three fingers down the canvas and when the menu pops up, tap **Copy & Paste.** Essentially, we've selected an area and then copied that area from another layer.

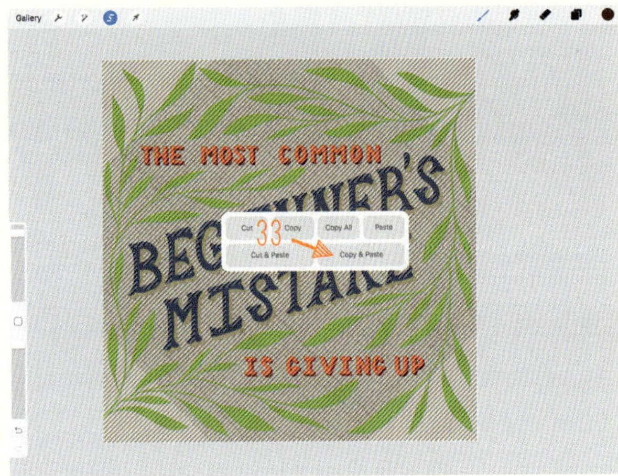

STEP 34: Make your original **Vintage Ink Lines** layer invisible, and you should be left with a cutout of the vintage ink lines that is only on the Perspective Layer area. Duplicate the layer a few times if you want the lines to be darker, always being sure to duplicate the original (the bottom layer). When you duplicate a layer in Procreate, it becomes slightly blurred, so duplicating only the bottom layer can prevent duplicates from appearing increasingly blurry. Once

you are happy with the darkness of the lines, merge all the duplicates together.

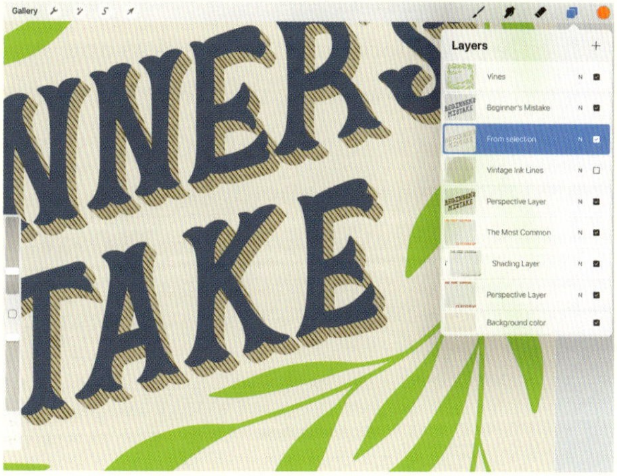

STEP 35: I want to add a little more visual interest to the words in the center to give them even more emphasis. Create a new layer above all the letter layers, and draw some decorative elements using whatever brush you'd like. I used the **Liquid Pen**, but feel free to experiment with different brushes. You can use lines, dots, leaves, florals, or any shapes you like to decorate your letters!

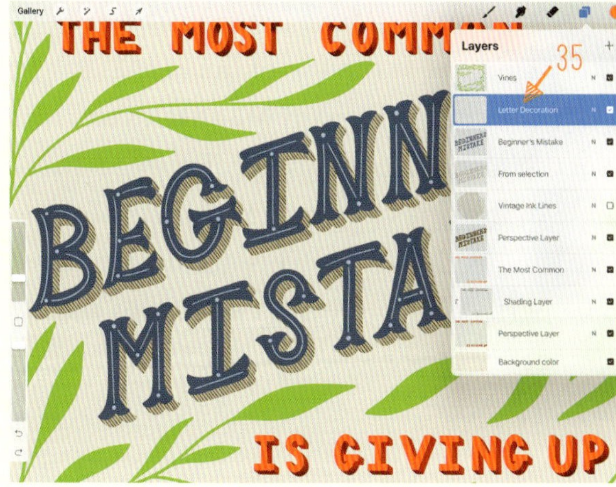

With just these few steps there are countless ways to add depth to your lettering. You can adjust the angle and width of a perspective layer, put a shadow behind the letters, or add layers of decoration. I always try a few options each time I create a new composition, because I never know what I'll discover just by playing around with shadows and perspective!

I created a few examples that you can experiment with on your composition (opposite), or you can create a new canvas and try some different options there. Note that each color should be put on a separate layer. This gives you the freedom to adjust the color of each element separately.

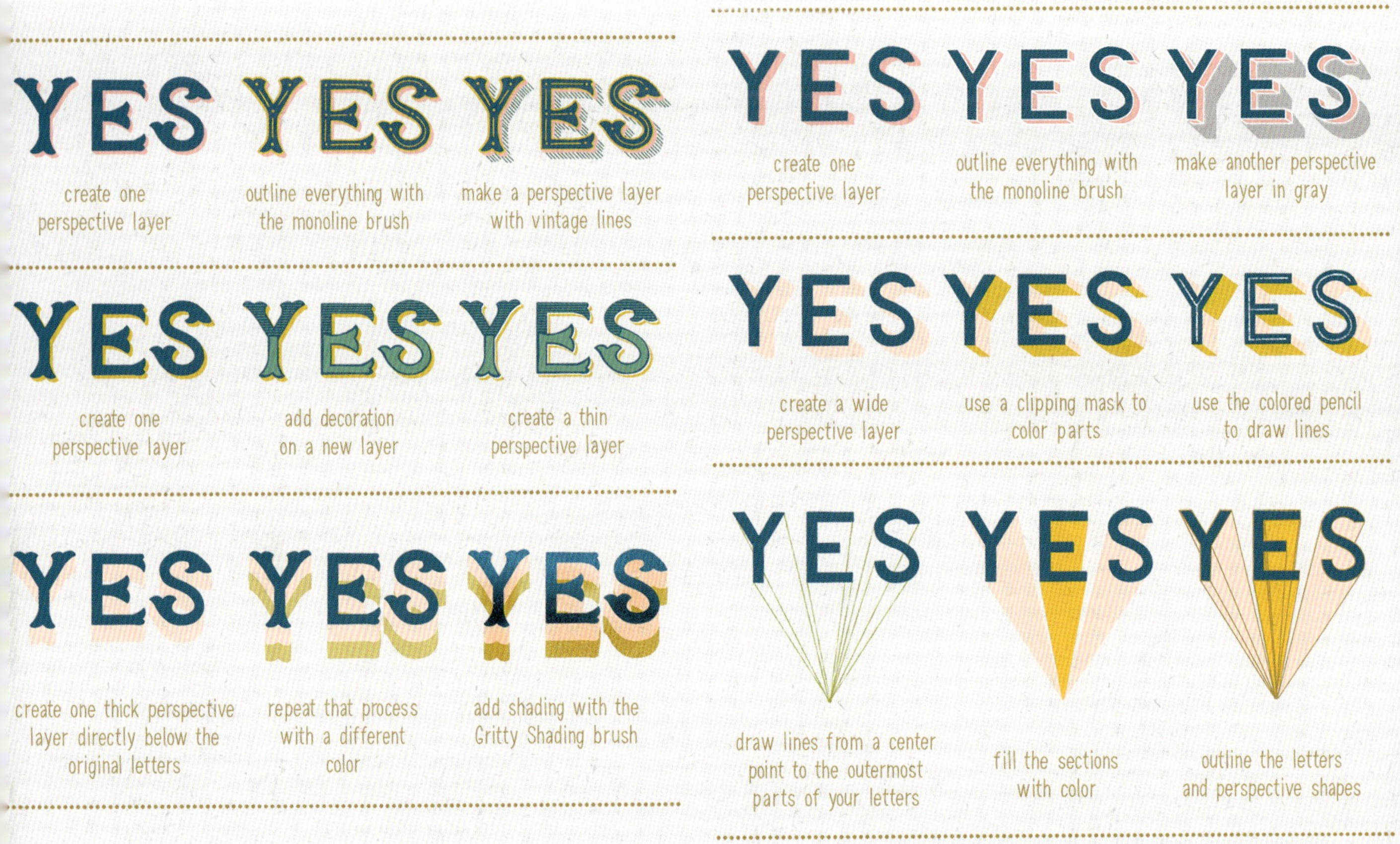

Tip: You could practice creating more complex perspective layers by recreating some letters from the lettering inspiration resources in chapter 2.

Let's Decorate!

The decorative elements of your composition are like the dressing on a salad—they aren't required but without them things feel unfinished. Just like changing the dressing changes the taste of a salad, changing your decorative elements can completely transform the feel of your lettering composition. Therefore, it's important to stay flexible and experiment with lots of options before committing to one. It's even more important to keep your decorative elements on different layers so you have the ability to easily change its colors, textures, and opacity.

I'll be using leaves as my decorative elements, but there are an unlimited number of ways to decorate your lettering. In chapter 7 you'll find a huge list of decoration ideas, so feel free to pull from those as you complete the lettering projects in this book.

To add your decorations, use the following steps:

STEP 36: Let's start with the leaves. First I'll create some veins on the leaves using the **Liquid Pen** as an eraser.

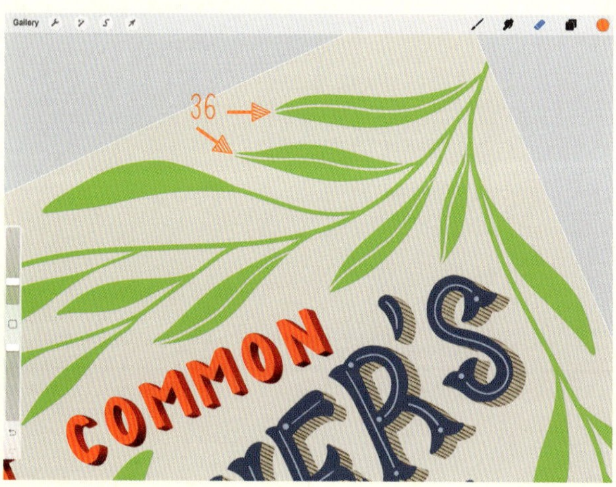

STEP 37: I think the lime green color gives the leaves too much emphasis, so I will use the **Alpha Lock/Fill** method to apply a more muted shade of green. I also want the leaves to have a little more depth, so I will to use the **Hand Drawn Dots** texture brush to erase over the whole layer of leaves. Before I do that, though, I will make a duplicate of the leaves layer because I'm not sure if I'll like the texture. The duplicate layer preserves the ability to go back to the original leaves later.

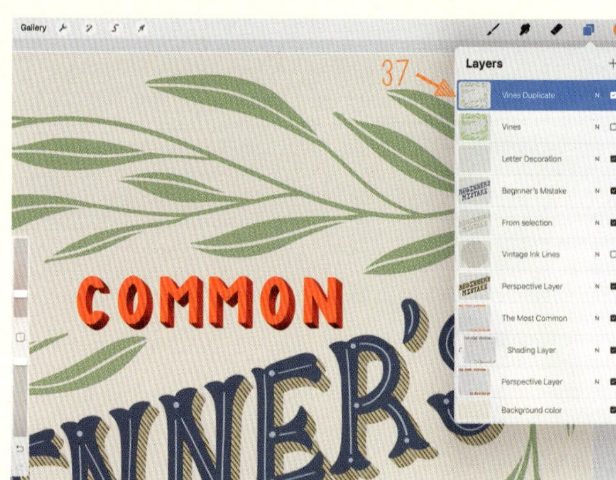

Tip: Make a duplicate of any layer on which you want to make permanent changes (like erasing a texture). You never know if you'll want to go back to the original version in an hour, or even a week later, so it's best to preserve your work to avoid having to recreate elements of your drawing. Just remember to never duplicate a duplicated layer, only duplicate original layers that you drew by hand!

STEP 38: Most of the colors are dark and dull, but having something bright and eye catching would help improve the contrast of the piece, so I will add some white berries (on a new layer, of course) using the **Liquid Pen.**

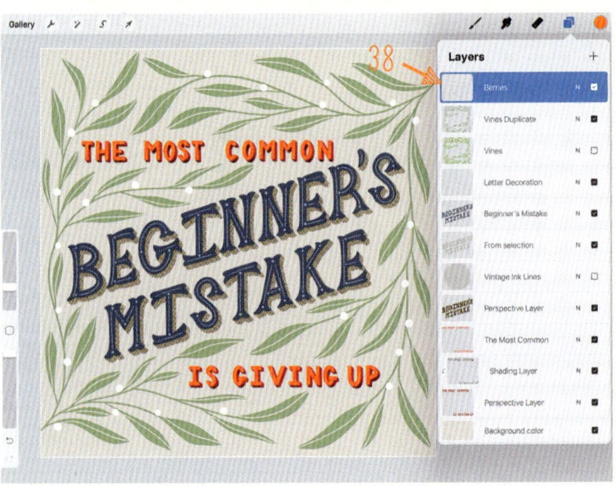

STEP 39: See how the blue is dark and concentrated in the center of the canvas? That looks somewhat unbalanced, so I will add little blue dots on the berries in order to spread the blue throughout the canvas. I gave the berries a little more movement by placing the dots in different positions within the white circles, rather than always putting them in the center of each berry.

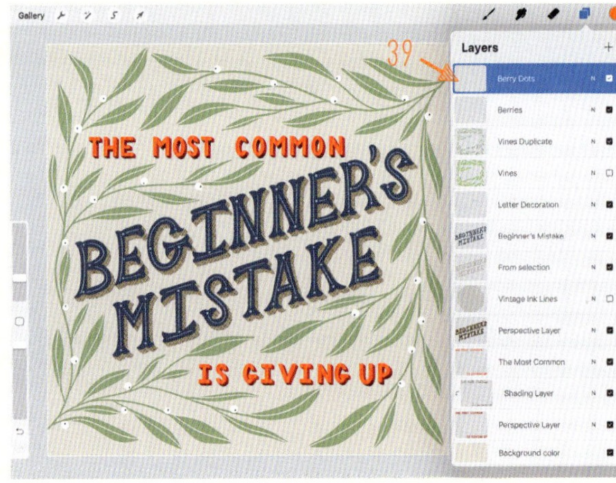

STEP 40: To add some texture. I will use the **Varied Paper Texture** brush with a dark brown color. I drag the texture layer up or down the layers panel to change the layers it overlaps and decide to put a dark texture layer on top of all the others. Then, I will set that layer to a **Blend** mode. (Notice how all the layers show an N [meaning "normal"] beside them except for this new texture layer, which says Lb. This indicates that I turned on a Blend mode called **Linear Burn.**)

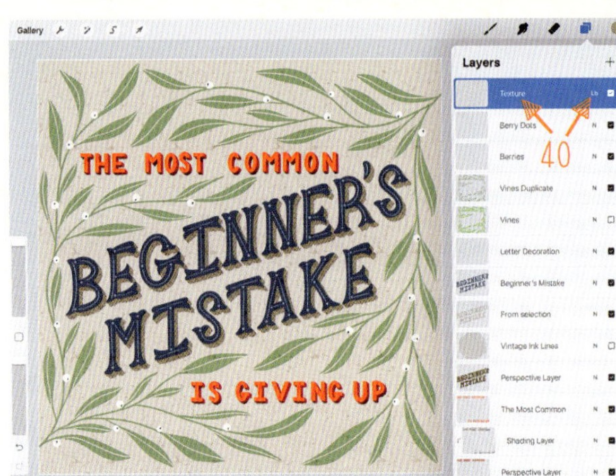

Blend Modes

Blend modes are exactly what they sound like: functions that blend things together. Imagine, for example, you have a piece of watercolor paper on your desk, and then you take some watercolor paint and brush it onto the paper. The two materials seem to blend together as the paint dries, and in the end they become one layer.

In digital art, drawings can look flat if we don't blend objects together intentionally, because unlike real paper, digital objects just sit on top of each other unless we tell them to do otherwise. That is why Blend modes are so wonderful. They make it possible to blend materials together so they look more natural.

Let's test out Blend modes with the following steps:

STEP 41: Tap the N symbol on the Texture layer. This opens up the Blend mode menu.

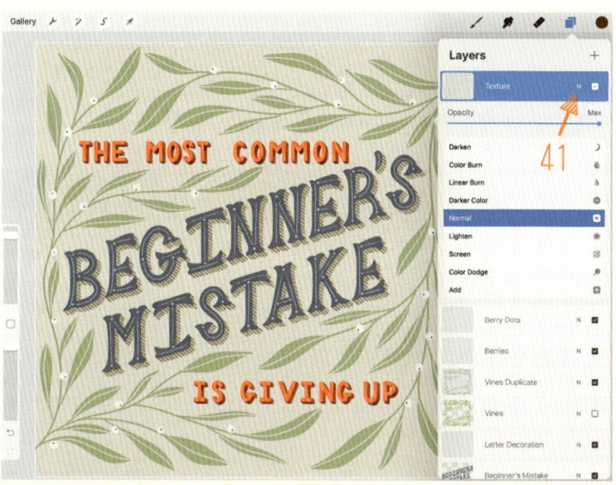

STEP 42: Tap on each of the options to see how the texture blends differently with the other objects that are under it.

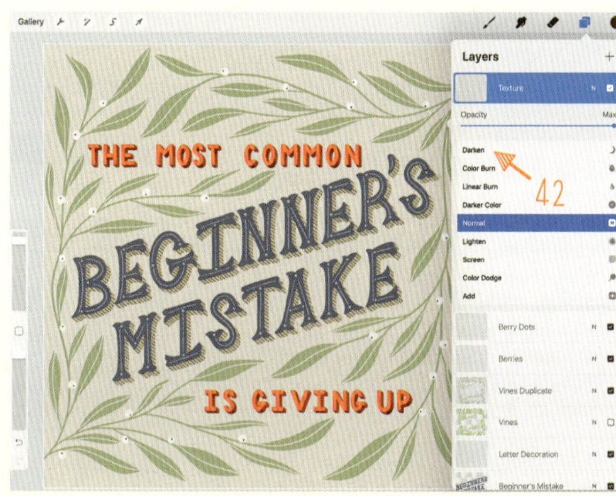

STEP 43: Scroll down the menu to see the full list of Blend modes. Try each option to see the various results. Each time I create a texture layer, I try out all of these options, because I never know what interesting blend I'll discover! Try the same process

with different texture colors to get a completely different result.

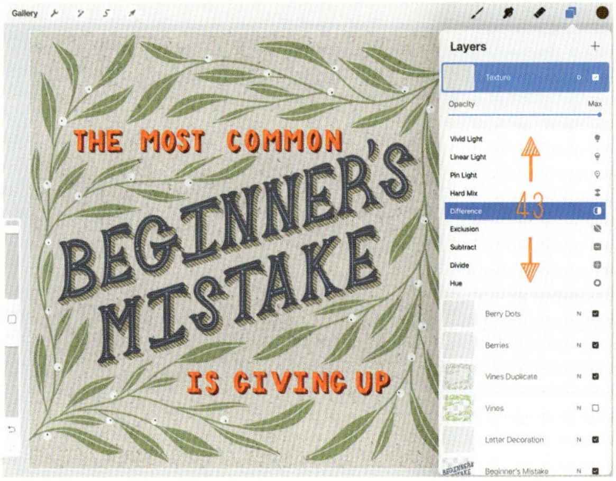

STEP 44: The final step I usually take with a project is trying out various color options. We've already covered how to color drop (if you want to change the color of individual letters) and use the **Alpha Lock/Fill** method (if you want to change the whole layer to a specific color). So let's look at one last way to change the color using the **Hue, Saturation, Brightness** tool.

Hue, Saturation, and Brightness

There are times when you just don't know what color to use. Let's say you've made a beautiful lettering composition but you aren't happy with the colors, and you aren't quite sure how to begin fixing them. This is where the **Hue, Saturation, Brightness** tool comes in. You can make big or small adjustments to a color on a layer in order to change its hue and intensity. Here is an explanation of what these three functions control:

- **Hue:** The color range (blues, reds, greens, yellows, etc.).
- **Saturation:** The concentration of color in a given shade (e.g., gray is desaturated whereas hot pink is very saturated).
- **Brightness:** How dark or light the color is.

For example, if I wanted to create a vintage-style composition, I would select a low saturation because vintage colors are usually dull and muted. If I wanted a 1990's feel, I would increase the brightness and choose bright colors like pink, yellow, and maybe even some highly saturated neons.

Here are the steps to apply these color functions:

STEP 45: Select the layer you want to change in the **Layers** panel.

STEP 46: Tap the **Adjustments** menu and then tap **Hue, Saturation, Brightness.** Next select **Layer** to apply the color adjustment to the entire layer (rather than making selective changes with your stylus).

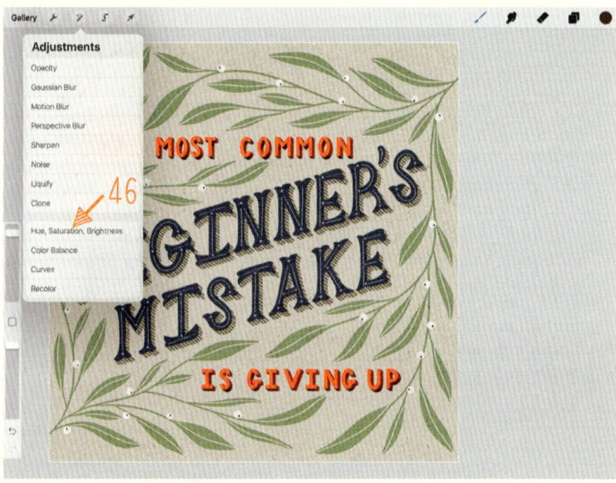

STEP 47: Adjust the sliders to your liking.

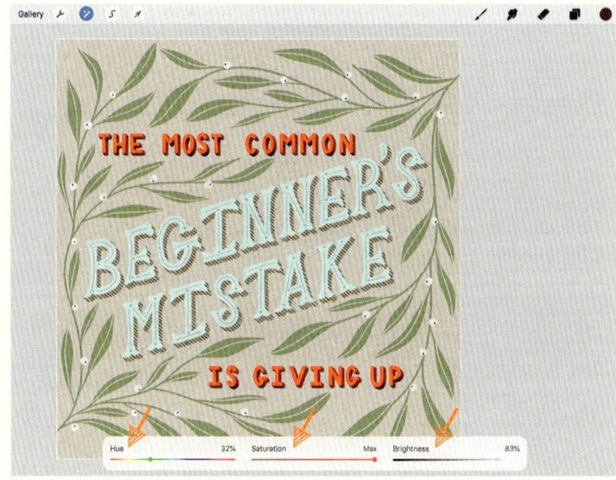

STEP 48: Create some Master Documents (like we did in chapter 3) and try a few different color versions using **Alpha Lock/ Fill** and/or **Hue, Saturation, Brightness** to adjust each color. You might also want to experiment with some different texture versions as well, trying different textures in both the background and foreground.

Here are a few various colored versions I created.

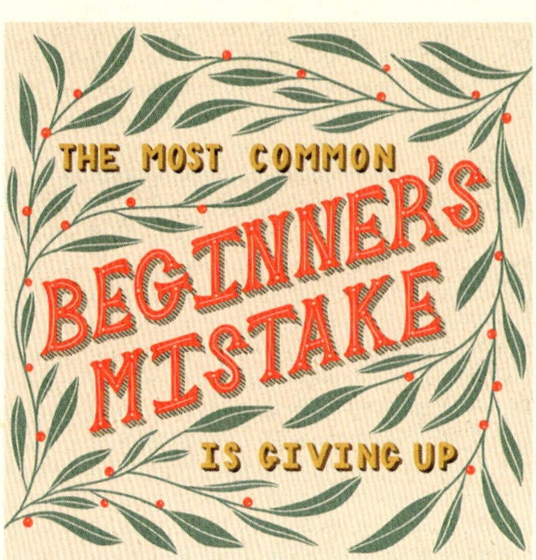

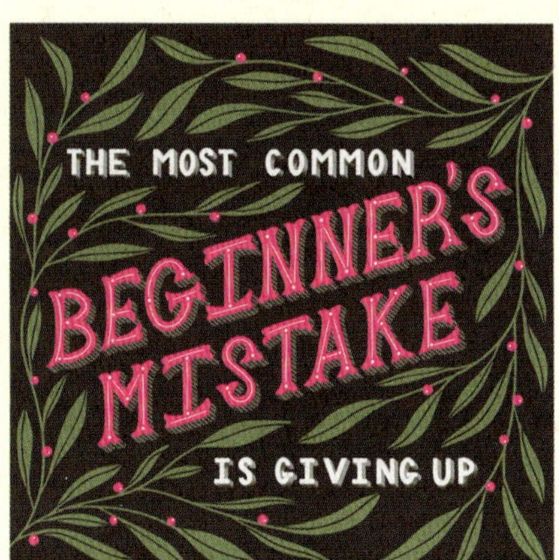

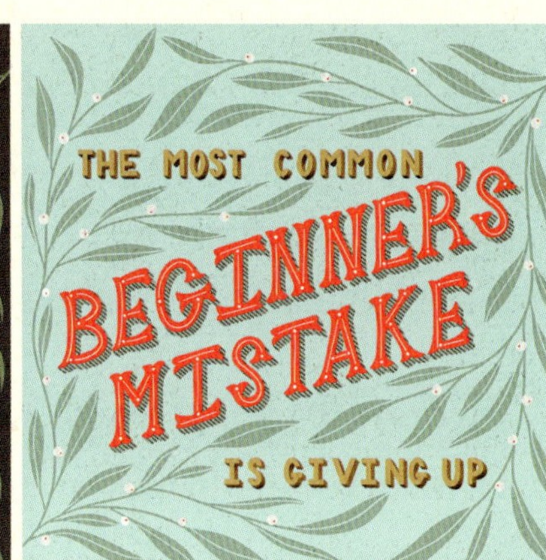

Critique and Adjust

Right after you have created a composition, you might feel very invested in the project and probably won't want to make any big changes (like redoing all the lettering, yikes!), so it's a good idea to step away from the project for a while in order to look at it with fresh eyes later on. We'll go deeper into the process of critiquing and improving your work in chapter 9.

When you're ready to make some changes, refer back to the **principles of design** we covered earlier in the chapter. Is your composition **balanced**? Doesn't it have good **contrast**? Did you use scale and color to create **emphasis** on the important parts of the phrase? Does the composition have a **harmonious** feel? If you answer "No" to any of these questions, start changing things! This is a great time to create a few Master Documents so you can feel free to play with options.

Keep Going!

You might want to try several versions of the same composition or try completely different compositions with different letter styles. Either way, just keep practicing! Each lettering piece you create will be better than the last, so keep trying new styles until you find your own. Let's look at a few ideas to get you started.

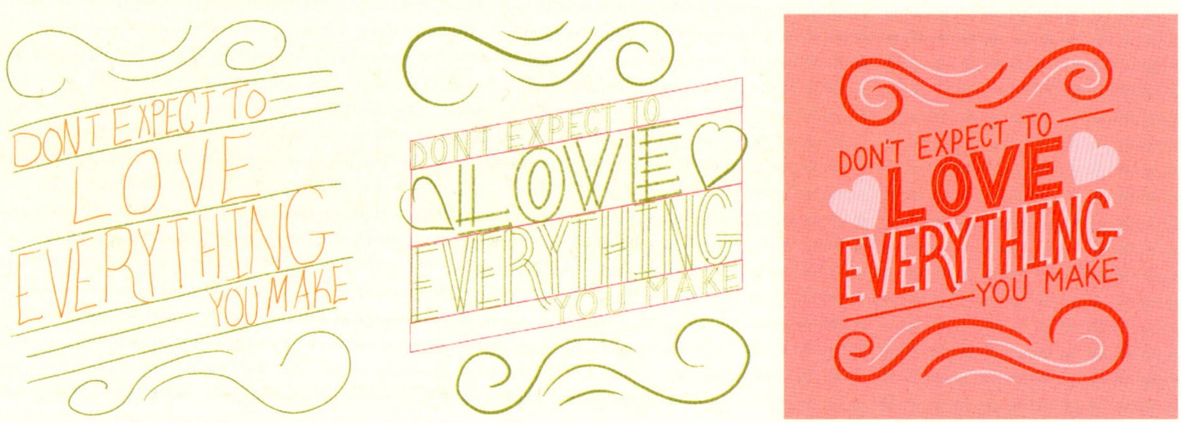

In this piece (above) I wanted to emphasize the words "**love**" and "**everything,**" so I made those words larger and more decorative than the other words. I also wanted to use a color that expressed the concept of love, so I used several shades of pink rather than choosing multiple colors. I added some flourishes on the top and bottom for two reasons: 1.) To fill up the canvas and 2.) To help balance the dark and light colors around the page. You will also notice I didn't add any serifs to these letters but I did make the small text with the **Monoline** brush so the letters have rounded edges. These rounded shapes contrast with the sharp edges on the other letters.

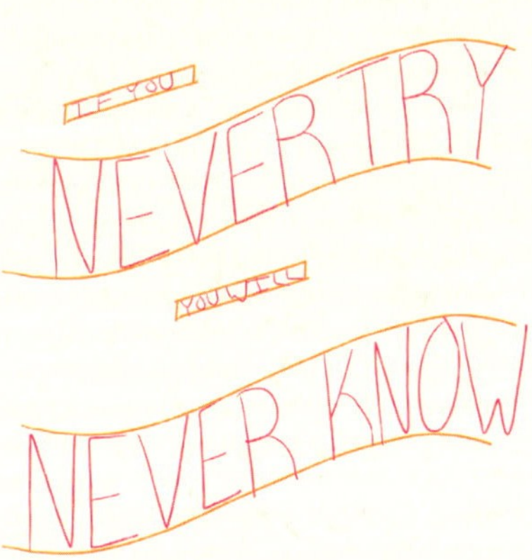

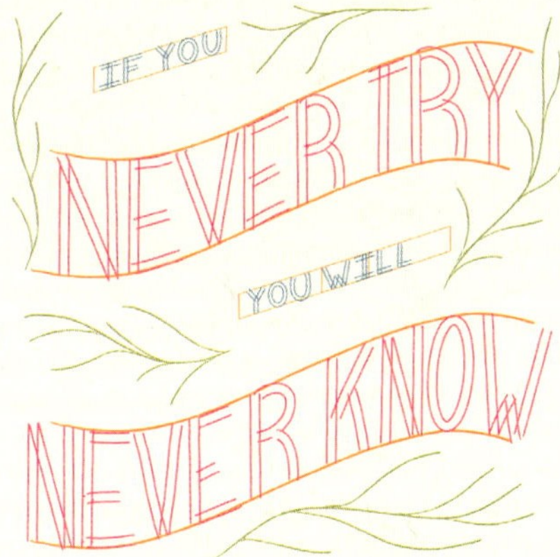

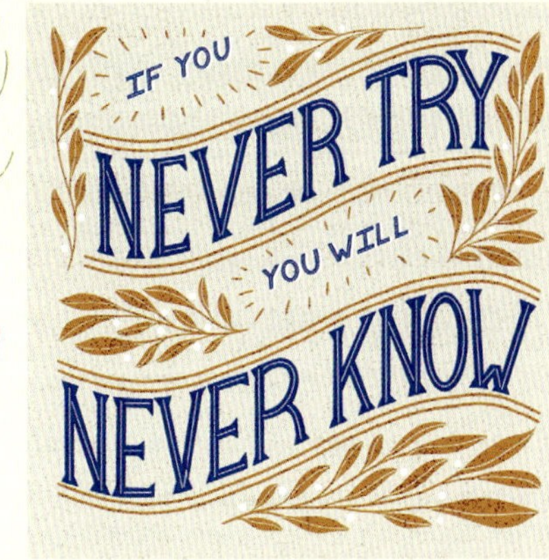

For the composition above I used simple sans serif lettering for the less important words, and bold serif lettering for the most important words. I added some lines around each set of letters to help add contrast to the two types of lettering. To add some subtle texture to the background, letters, and decorative elements, I used the **Barely There Grit** texture with a Blend mode.

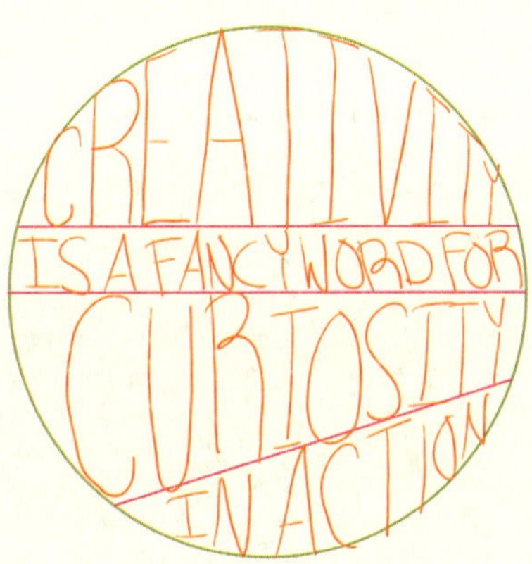

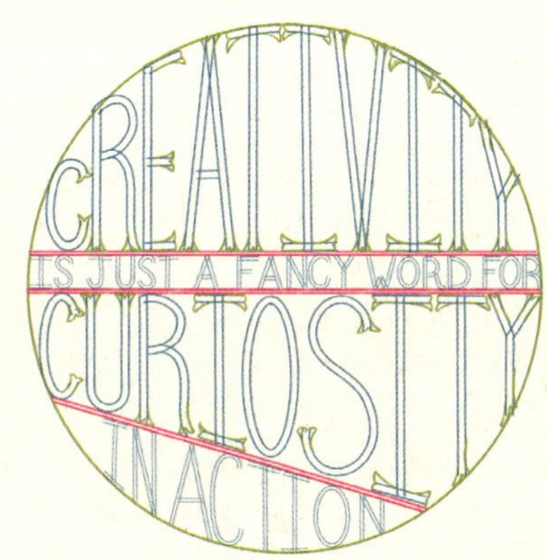

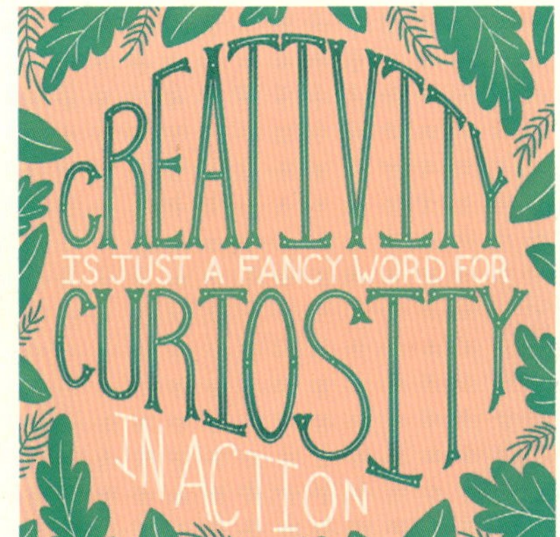

For this circular composition above, I wanted the words **"creativity"** and **"curiosity"** to be the most prominent part of the phrase, so I made them large and bright, while the other words are subtle and simple. I used the **Gritty Shading** brush on a Clipping Mask layer to add some vibrant highlights to both the letters and the leaves, which gives everything a shiny feel. I chose a tropical color palette, because the leaves I created had a tropical shape and feel to them.

For the next composition I found a set of beautiful lettering examples from the 1897 book *Specimens of Type, Borders, Ornaments, Brass Rules and Cuts, Etc.* by the American Type Founders Company. I used example No. 101C as inspiration for the orange letters and the flourishes in my composition. I used the **Symmetry** tool to make the flourishes symmetrical from left to right, and I used the **Colored Pencil** brush to give the flourishes some texture.

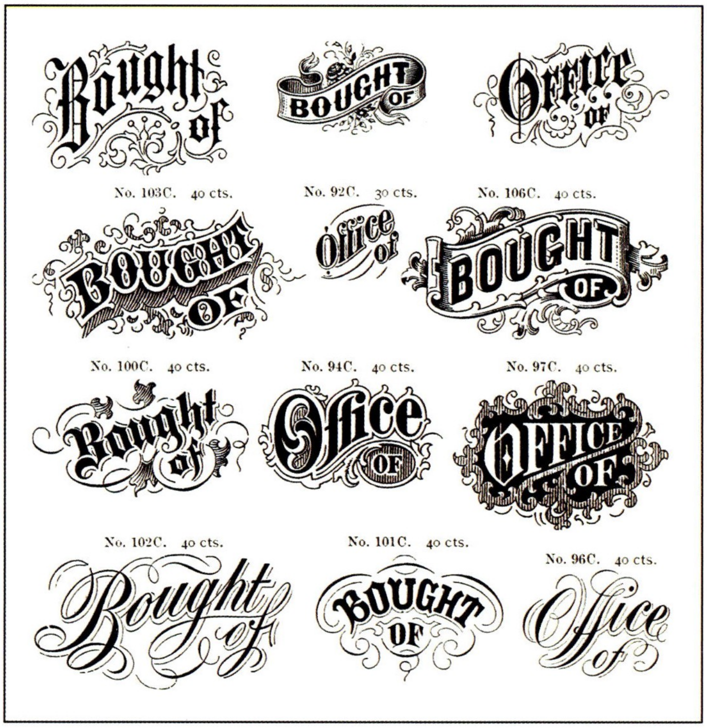

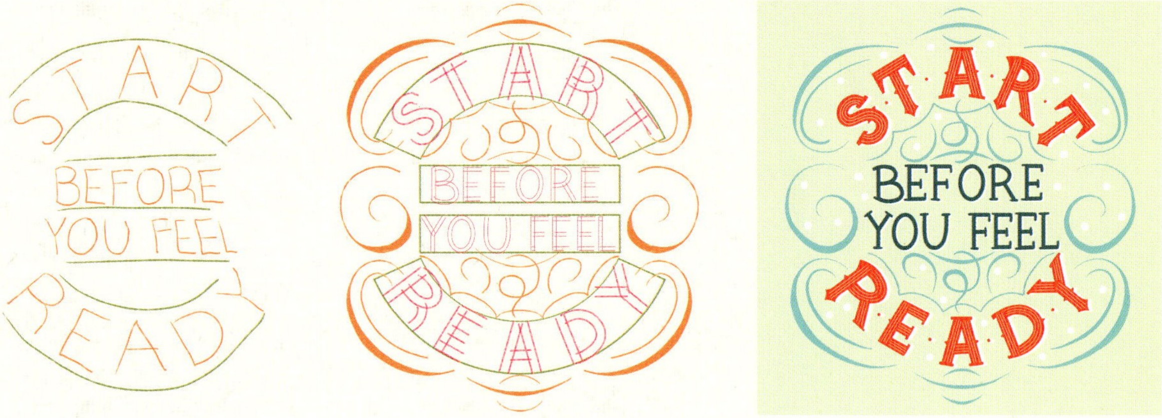

As you can see, just one little portion of a vintage lettering sample can inspire a whole composition, or even a whole series! If you're ever unsure about what kinds of serifs, decorations, or letter styles to use, just start scanning the **Downloads and Resources** page on my website (mentioned in chapter 1) and you'll quickly find some inspiration.

As you dig deeper into the resource images, you'll notice that we're still missing one big part of the lettering puzzle: script lettering. In the next chapter, we'll dive into script styles and techniques so you can start combining serif, sans serif, and script lettering to create varied compositions.

CHAPTER 6

Script Lettering

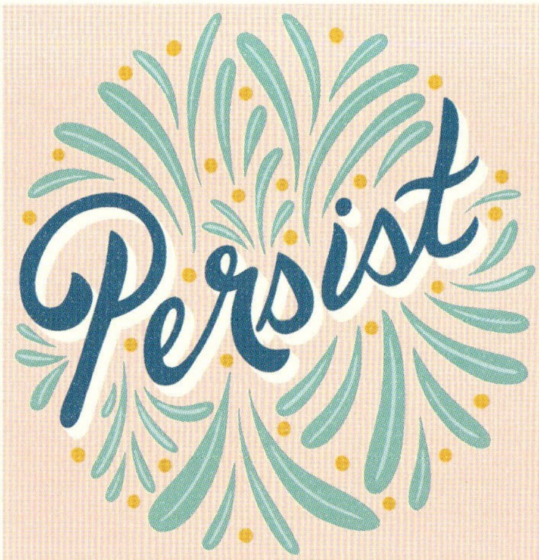

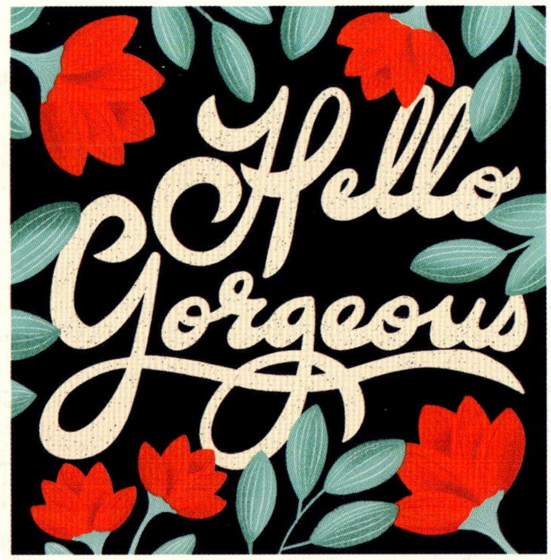

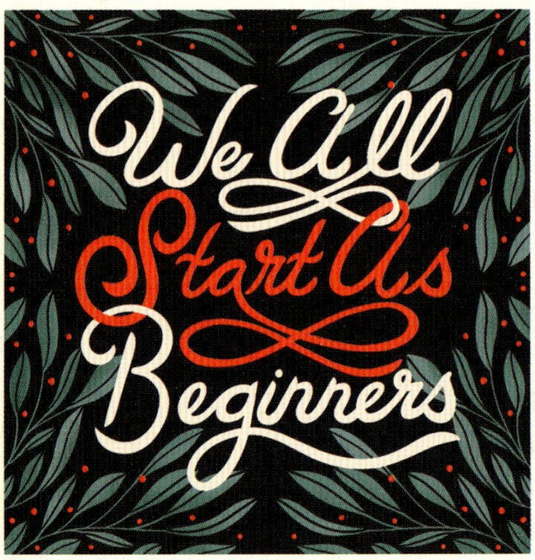

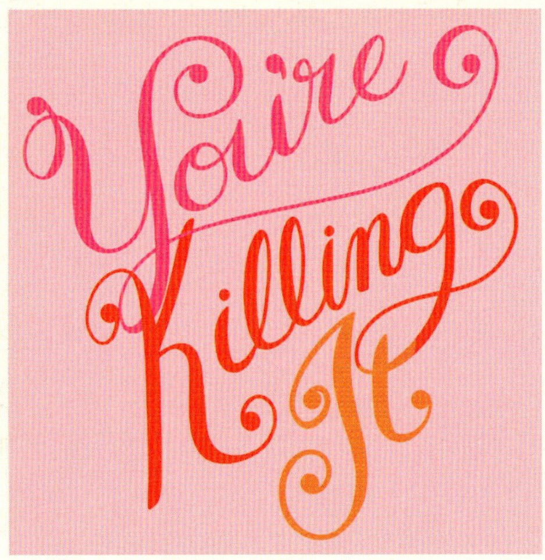

While it's hard not to love the fluid feel of script lettering, the challenge of making smooth and cohesive letters can cause beginners to develop a love/hate relationship with it. In this chapter, we'll cover everything you need to know to make the process of creating script lettering as easy and intuitive as possible, from spacing and connecting your letters to determining their shapes and style. Luckily, everything you've learned about lettering so far will come in handy as you enter the stylish and elegant world of script lettering.

To demonstrate the basics, we'll use a simple script called *monoline*. Monoline is great for beginners because it's just a single even line, so you never have to worry about adding weight to your letters. We'll cover how to add weight later in the chapter, but for now, let's focus on letter shapes, connections, and spacing.

Script Guides

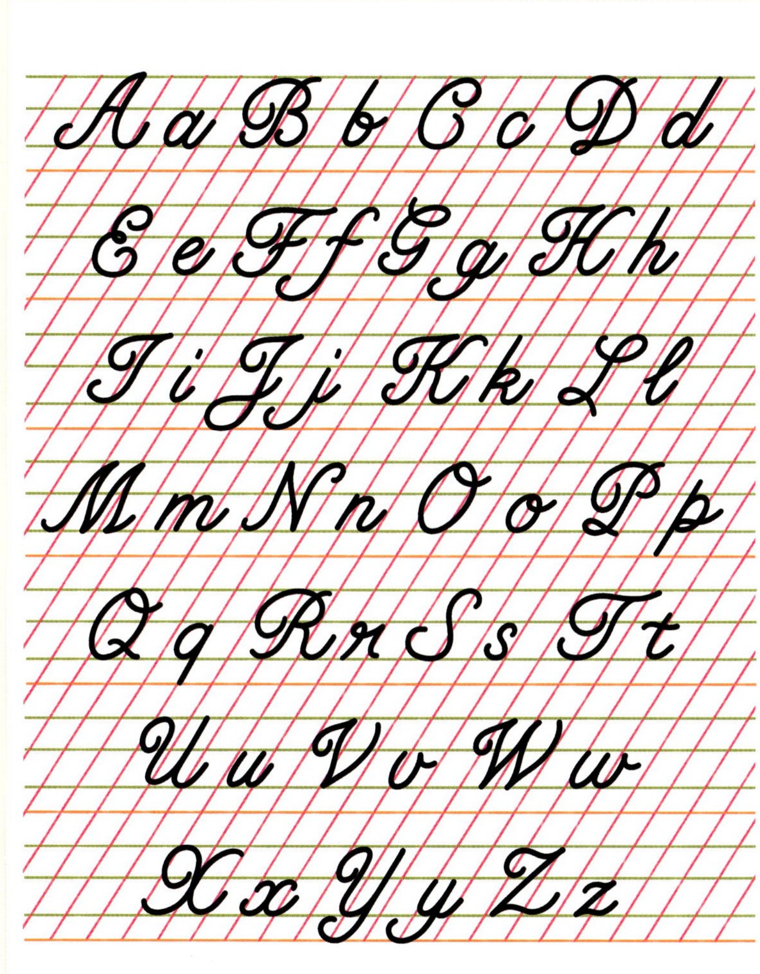

Script lettering uses the same guides that we covered in chapter 4, but we also use one additional guide to give the letters a slant. It's important to keep all the letters slanted at the same angle, because if a word contains letters on different angles, the script can appear incohesive or even illegible.

You can make the slant as extreme as you want, but usually, a slight angle is sufficient to create the effect of a graceful, flowing script. We'll cover how to put slant lines on your canvas later in the chapter, but for now, just keep them in mind as you use the practice sheets.

Note that this is just one type of monoline script. There are plenty more styles you'll discover as you dig into the vintage lettering images on the **Downloads and Resources** page on my website (described in chapter 1). Let's start with some practice.

You can download the *Uppercase Monoline Practice Sheet* and *Lowercase Monoline Practice Sheet* from the **Downloads and Resources**. Open a practice sheet in Procreate, and use the **Monoline** brush in the **Hand Lettering** brush set to trace each letter, and then try to redraw the same letter in the blank space beside it. It may take a few tries to get it right, and keep in mind that your letter doesn't have to match mine exactly. The purpose is merely to get an idea of the slant and curves in the letter style.

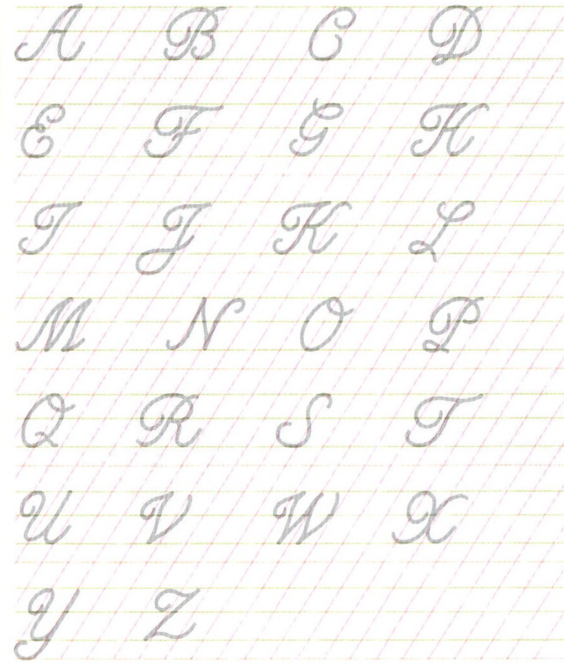

Uppercase Monoline Practice Sheet

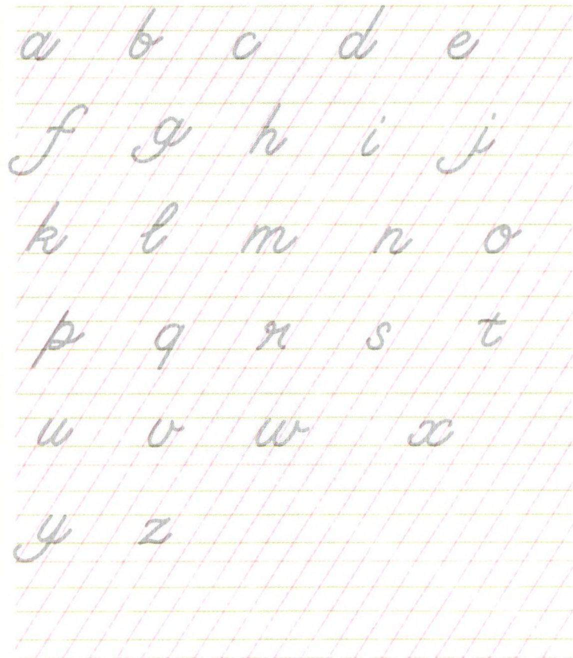

Lowercase Monoline Practice Sheet

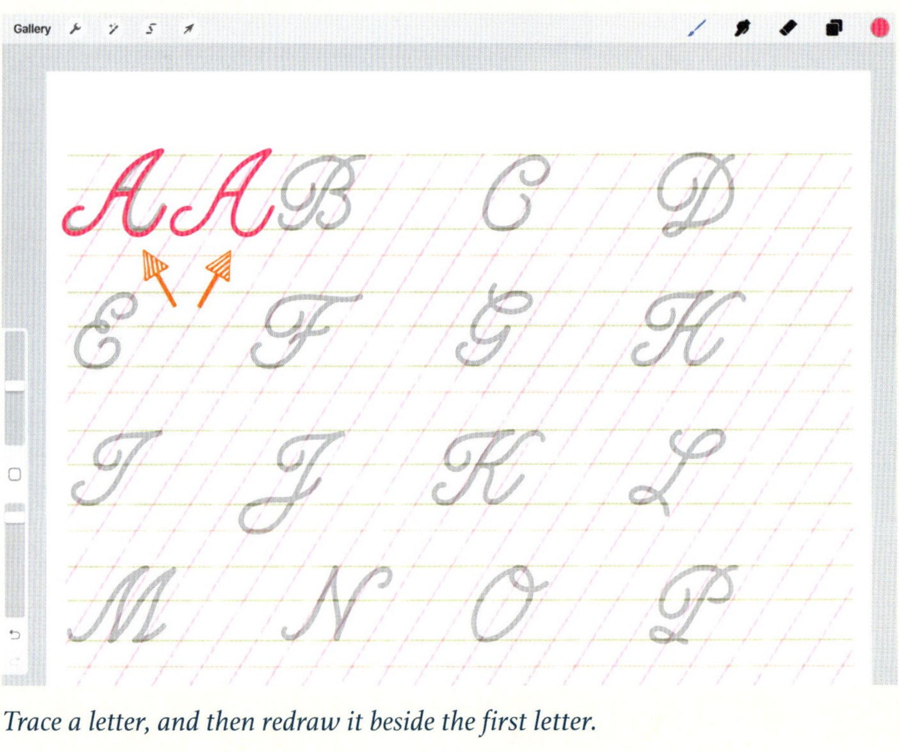

Trace a letter, and then redraw it beside the first letter.

Now that you've had some practice with tracing and copying letters, let's try writing some words. Download the *Blank Practice Sheet*, and open it in Procreate.

Once you open the practice sheet, follow these steps:

Blank Practice Sheet

STEP 1: Create a new layer, and then use the **Sketching Pencil** to sketch your text. This is a rough sketch so don't worry about making it perfect; just get the basic shapes down on the page. You don't have to create a whole word in one single stroke, so feel free to sketch each letter individually.

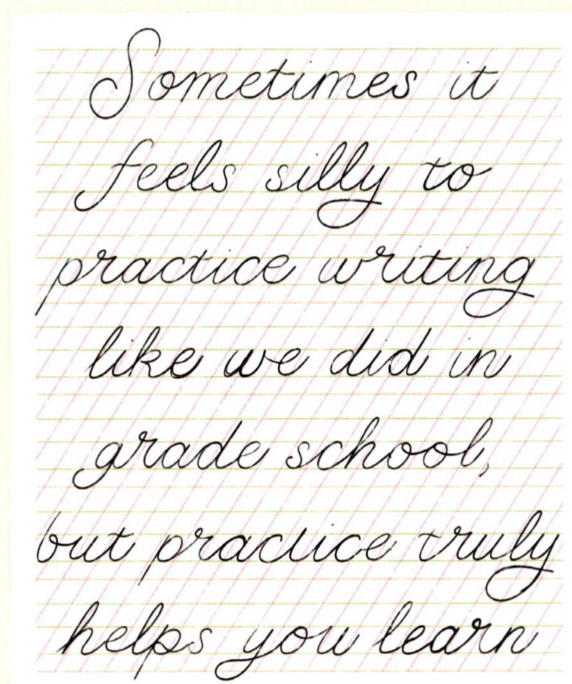

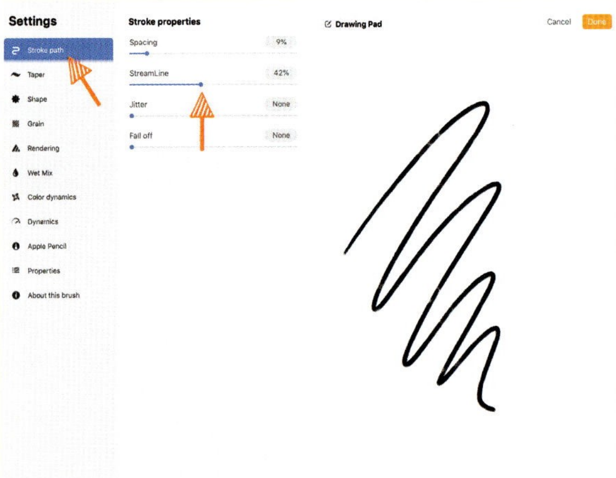

Reducing the Streamline makes the brush feel more lifelike.

Tip: If your Sketching Pencil (or any other brush in Procreate) feels "sticky" or like it's making your lines too smooth, reduce the **StreamLine** setting. To do this, tap twice on the brush to open the brush preferences. Tap on **Stroke path** to open the **Stroke properties**. Here you will find the StreamLine slider. Adjusting this down makes the brush more realistic, whereas adjusting it up will smooth out shaky lines. Sometimes StreamLine is helpful, but other times it makes it hard to sketch freely, so feel free to adjust it as needed.

STEP 2: Reduce the opacity of the Sketch layer in the Layers panel, and then use the **Monoline** brush to trace all of your letters on a new layer.

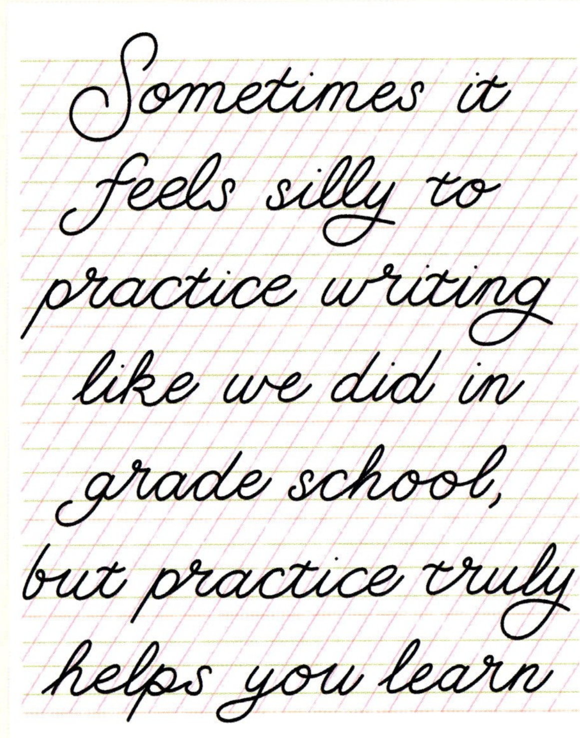

Don't worry if your letters look messy or unrefined. In fact, in the next section, we'll use your errors on these practice words to analyze your weaknesses, which will help you know what aspects you need to work on to improve your script.

Parent Shapes

Script letters are made from a few parent shapes that repeat throughout the script style. Take a look at this chart showing how this alphabet is made almost entirely from five parent shapes.

Of course, every script style is different, so the parent shapes will not always adhere exactly to this chart. The important takeaway is that scripts are comprised of a set of similar shapes that repeat throughout the alphabet. Therefore, while you may think you need to learn 26 letters to learn script, you actually only need to learn five shapes! The tricky part is keeping those shapes consistent throughout your lettering. Throughout this chapter we'll cover tips for maintaining the consistency of your parent shapes.

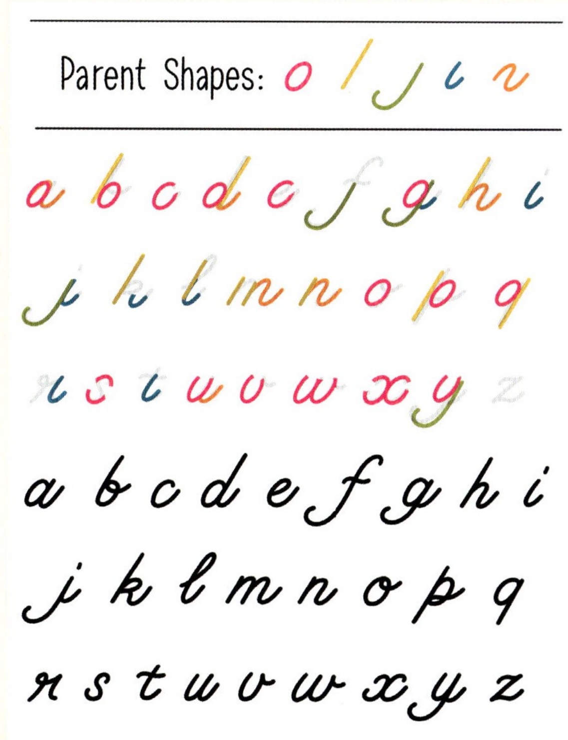

Script alphabets are almost entirely made up of just five parent shapes.

You can see in the chart that some letters use only part of a parent shape, for example the s and e, which use only parts of the **O** shape. As you can imagine, if the script contains conflicting parent shapes, the word will look odd. Consider this example. The script on the left looks even and cohesive. The script on the right is legible, but it looks a bit strange. Why?

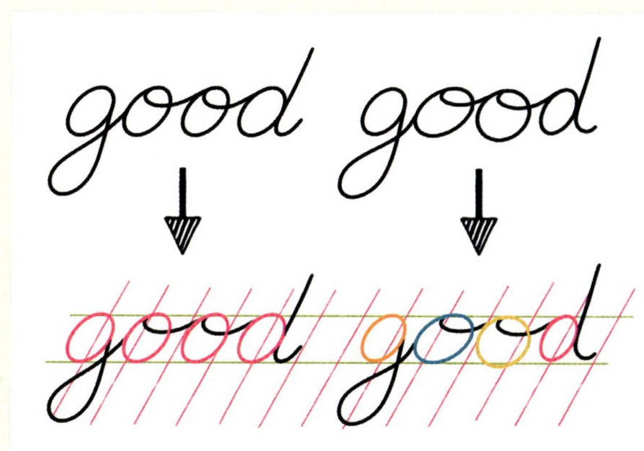

Examples of cohesive (left) and incohesive (right) scripts

The parent shapes in the example on the left are all the same shape and size. The parent shapes on the right are each different, which makes the letters look like they don't belong together. Once you decide on parent shapes, those same shapes need to be reproduced in all the corresponding letters. If a word contains conflicting parent shapes (like an **O** and an **E** that are different widths), the script will feel unbalanced. While letters with varying parent shapes are still readable, the viewer will usually perceive that something is not quite right.

The way we combine the parent shapes is just as important as the parent shapes themselves! Be sure not to lose part of one parent shape when you connect it to another. In this example (right), you can see the word on the left contains a series of whole ovals, whereas the example on the right contains semi-ovals on the **g** and **d** shapes where one parent shape slices through another. When combining two parent shapes remember to preserve the original shapes by having them merely touch, not overlap, each other.

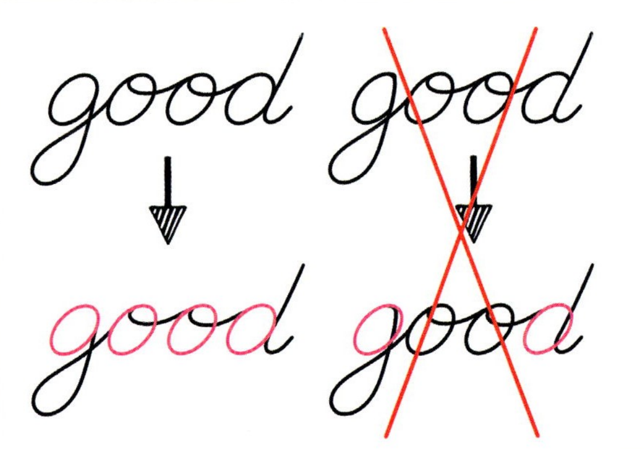

Examples of whole parent shapes (left) and partial parent shapes (right)

Now that you understand parent shapes, take a look at your practice words page. Do your words contain cohesive parent shapes? Do any of them contain letters with parent shapes that cut through another shape? Keeping your parent shapes consistent throughout your text is the first step to improving your script lettering.

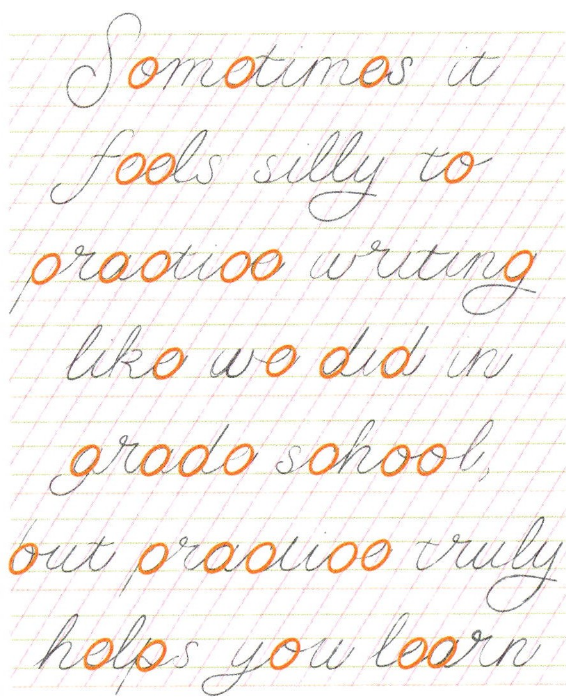

At this point it may be helpful to create a new layer on your practice sheet, and then sketch over your letters with a different color to fix any parent shapes that aren't the right shape or size. You could even draw a parent shape (like the **O**) once, then duplicate that layer many times and place it over all the **O** shapes on the page. This is a great way to check and compare parent shapes throughout a lettering composition.

Connections

The parent shapes are the foundation of your individual letters, but connections (the little lines that connect letters to each other) join them in a graceful and cohesive way, giving script lettering its unique beauty and cohesiveness. The angle, width, and height of the connections are crucial to creating this sense of cohesion. Connections, done well, should make your script look like it was drawn with one smooth pen stroke, which is why it is so important to avoid awkward connection points, which disrupt the natural flow of the script.

To avoid an artificial or clumsy feeling in your script, try to avoid the following three most common connection mistakes:

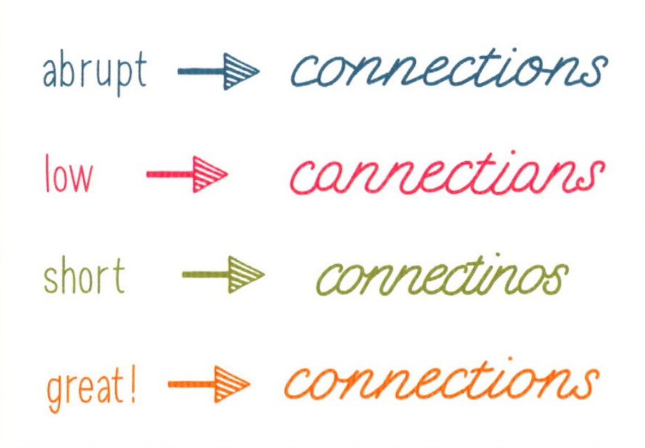

Examples of connection mistakes compared with proper connections

- **Abrupt connections:** These perpendicular connections point straight into the next letter like a fork stabbing into a piece of food, often making a T shape where the connection meets the next letter. More than any other type of mistake, abrupt connections disrupt the flow of your script by appearing to poke the next letter, rather than smoothly transitioning into it.
- **Low connections:** These connections are placed too low on the letter and often cause confusion (like turning the o into an a). If they extend lower than the letters themselves, thus going beyond the baseline, it causes your text to appear lumpy.
- **Short connections:** These connections are so short that they can make two letters appear as one. They don't leave enough breathing room between the letters.
- **Great connections:** The last example avoids all three mistakes. These connections have fluid lines, smooth transitions between the first and second letter, and plenty of spacing between each letter shape.

Take a look at your practice words and analyze your connections. Do they commit any of the common mistakes above? If so, create a new layer and redraw your connections with a different color. Then re-ink your script on a new layer.

Spacing

Spacing is one of the trickiest parts of script, but with a little sketching and adjusting, you'll be perfectly spacing your script in no time! You don't have to write your letters with perfect spacing on the first try, because in Procreate you can always adjust letter spacing by using the Freehand Selection tool to circle and move a letter. Don't worry if your natural handwriting doesn't have perfect spacing.

One way to check your script spacing is to draw a rectangular shape on a new layer, then duplicate that layer many times, and move the shape in between each letter. It should fit well in between each letter, but it doesn't have to be a perfect fit. Notice how in the second example the spaces range from too wide to too thin, and only a few spaces are alike.

Looking back at your practice words, does your spacing look even? If not, use the **Freehand Selection** tool to circle each letter that needs to be moved and shift it into the right place. Then, create a new layer above everything and re-ink your script keeping in mind any corrections you made for parent shapes, connections, and even spacing.

Don't feel discouraged if you had to make a lot of changes to your original sketch! Remember that no hand letterer is ever done learning to letter. Lettering is an ongoing practice of tiny improvements. As long as you're improving your skills you're on the right track!

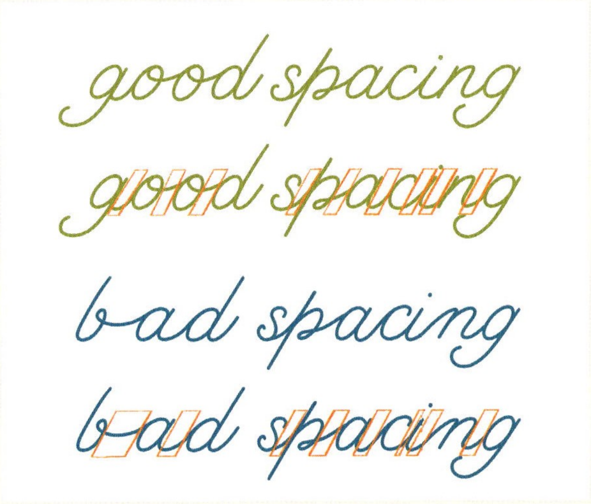

Examples of good and bad script spacing

Practice

Let's incorporate what you've learned so far into a finished composition. Choose a short phrase that you want to hand letter. You could start with some thumbnails or jump right into sketching the composition.

For the next project, I will letter the phrase, "Eat, Sleep, Create" using the following steps:

STEP 1: On a new 10″ × 10″ canvas, sketch the layout of your text.

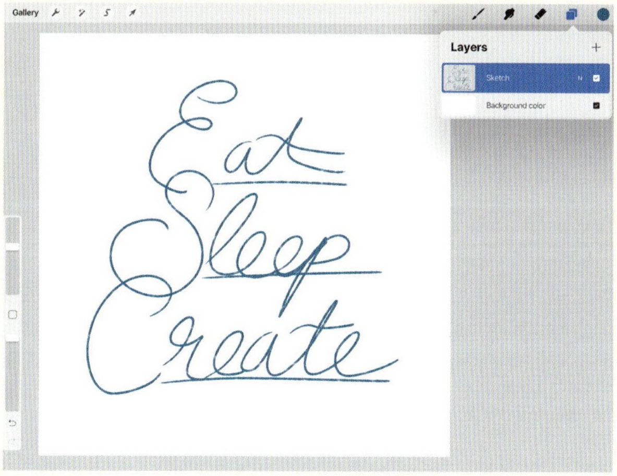

STEP 2: Add the lettering guides using the process you learned in chapter 5. I'm using guides for only the lowercase letters because I want my uppercase letters to be large and fluid; therefore the uppercase letters won't adhere well to guides.

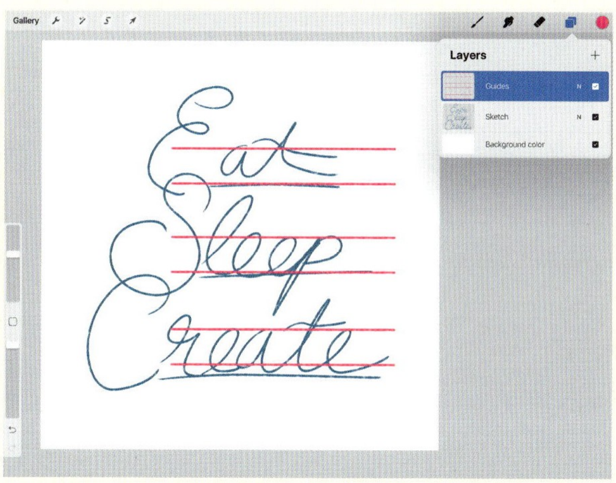

STEP 3: Tap the **Actions** menu to turn on the slant guides, which will help keep all your script on the same angle.

STEP 4: Tap **Canvas**.

STEP 5: Turn on the **Drawing Guide**.

STEP 6: Tap **Edit Drawing Guide**.

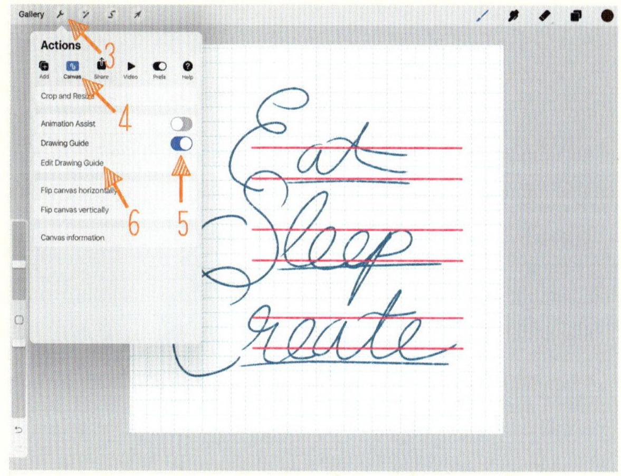

STEP 7: Select **Isometric** at the bottom of the screen as the guide type.

STEP 8: Use the little green dot to adjust the angle of your guides.

STEP 9: Adjust the **Grid Size** to your liking (I like my lowercase letters to be two or three rows in height on the grid because this helps me keep track of the letter widths.)

STEP 10: Tap **Done** to set the guide.

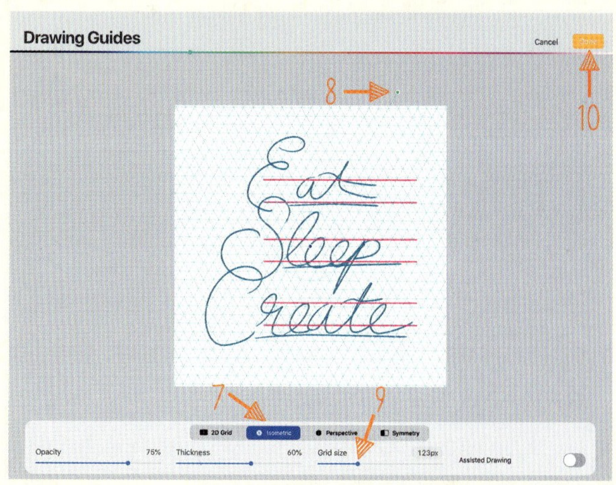

STEP 11: Refine your sketch. Take time to draw each letter individually, and think about parent shapes, spacing, connections, and angles as you sketch. You might even want to sketch the words once and then go over them again on a new layer to refine them. You could even draw one parent shape and duplicate it over all the other similar shapes (like we did on your practice words sheet), which will ensure that all parent shapes are consistent.

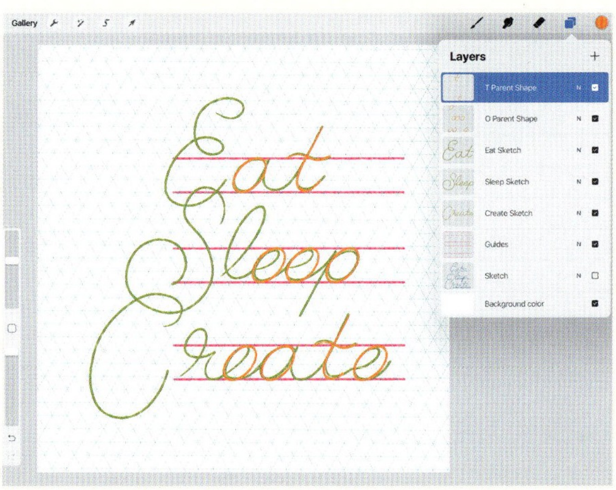

Tip: Put each word on a new layer when you create compositions with overlapping text. You will probably want to move words later on, and having them on separate layers makes shifting things around much easier.

STEP 12: It's time to ink your letters. Before you begin inking, test the brush size by drawing the smallest loop in your lettering. If the brush size seems too big for the smallest loop, then you will need a smaller brush.

STEP 13: Create a new layer, and use the **Monoline** brush to create smooth flowing lines. Remember that you don't have to draw each word in one single movement. It's better to focus on one letter at a time, and if you make a mistake, you can step back without losing a lot of work. Put each line of text on its own layer, so it's easy to move individual words around without adjusting the whole composition.

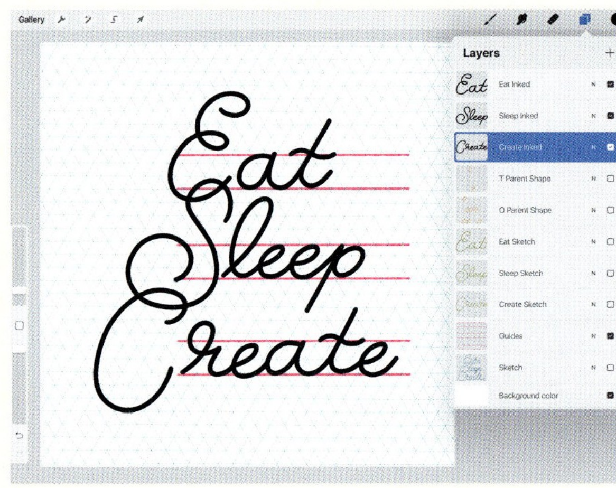

STEP 14: I want to remove the rounded ends from the lines. This is optional, so if you like the rounded ends, just leave them as they are! First, I will make all layers except the ink layers invisible, and I'll also turn off my grid by going to the **Actions** menu and turning off the **Drawing Guide**. Next, I'll use the **Monoline** brush to erase the rounded tips from the end of each letter.

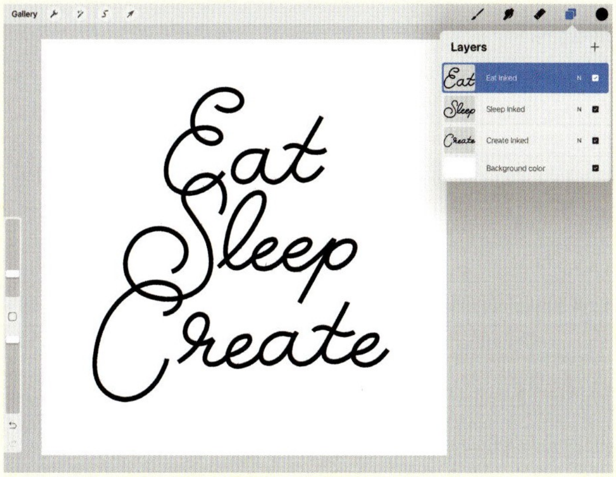

STEP 15: At this point, I like to create a Master Document of my inked text so I can start changing colors and add decorations freely without losing my original drawing. Next, I'll add a perspective layer by duplicating each line of text, selecting all three perspective layers (by tapping the first one and swiping right on the other two), and finally tapping the **Move** tool and moving the layers slightly down and to the left. It's important to select and move all three at the same time so the perspective angle is the same on all the words.

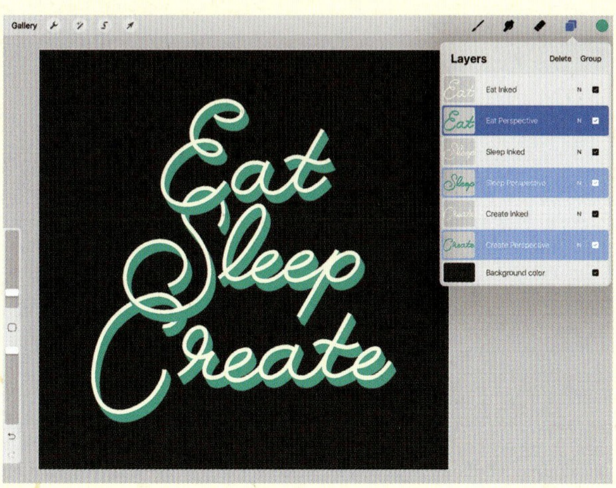

STEP 16: Now I'll play around with color options, setting each perspective layer to a different color using the **Alpha Lock/Fill** method.

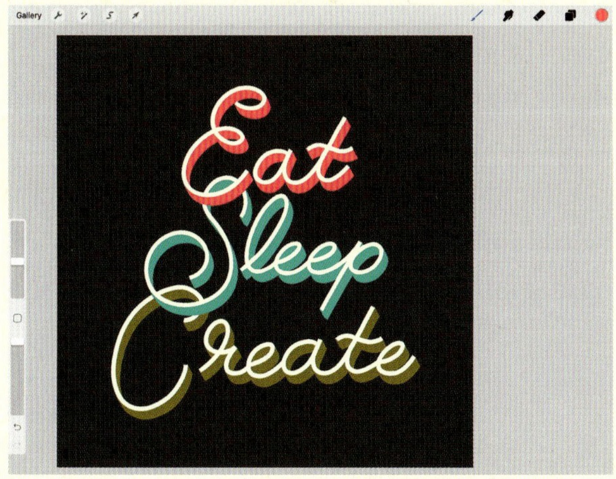

Although I like this option, I think the piece could use more variety, so I use a process that will allow me to color each letter individually. To do that, I'll use the **Alpha Lock** setting on the perspective layers.

Alpha Lock

Alpha Lock puts a layer in a state similar to a stencil, which means that only the portions of the layer that contain ink can be changed.

Follow these steps to use Alpha Lock:

STEP 17: Tap on the layer that you want to color, and then tap it again to see the flyout menu.

STEP 18: Tap **Alpha Lock** (or use the finger gesture shortcut of swiping two fingers to the right on the layer). After selecting Alpha Lock, you should see a checkerboard pattern appear on the layer icon in the Layers panel.

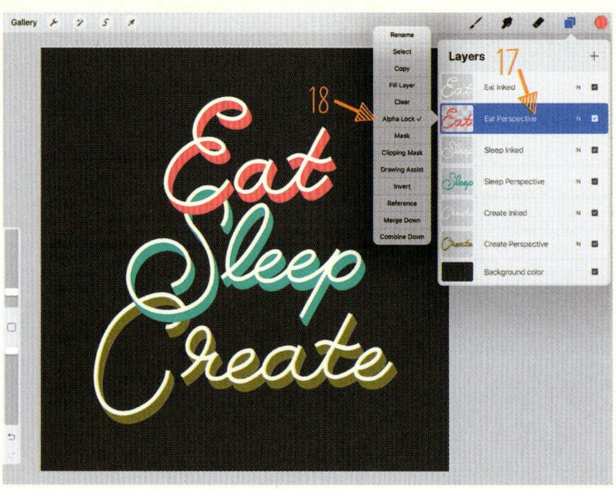

STEP 19: Choose a color, and start drawing on your letters. You'll see that the color appears on only the areas where your letters are already inked.

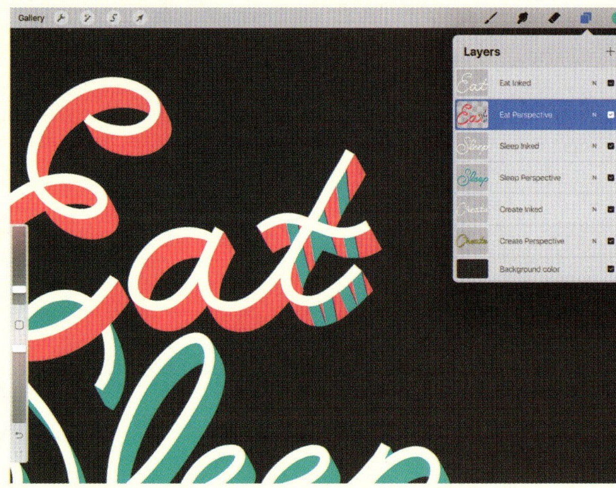

STEP 20: Turn Alpha Lock on for each perspective layer. Try making each letter a different color, alternating two, three, or four colors throughout the quote.

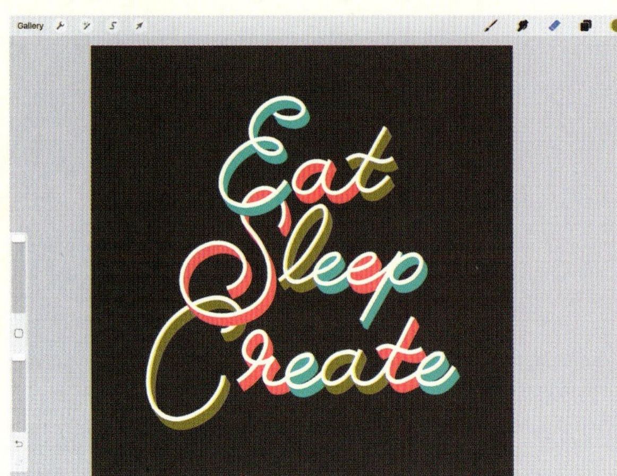

STEP 21: I want to add some visual interest to the background, so I'll add some dots with the **Liquid Pen** brush and use the **Barely There Grit** texture brush to add some black speckled texture.

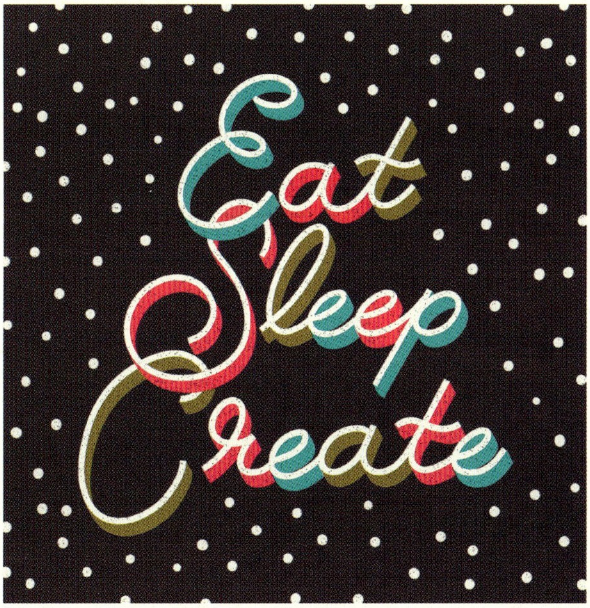

Even when I'm happy with the final result, I always try a few different color versions. You never know what you'll discover when you start experimenting with color!

Of course, this is just one way to finish this composition but the possibilities are endless. Take time to experiment with colors, decorations, and textures until you find something you like!

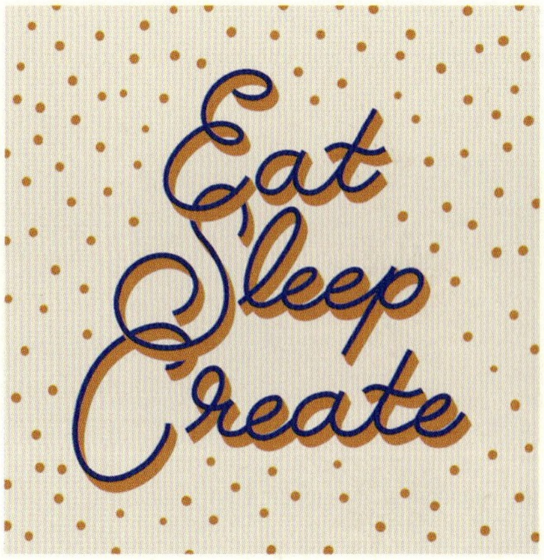

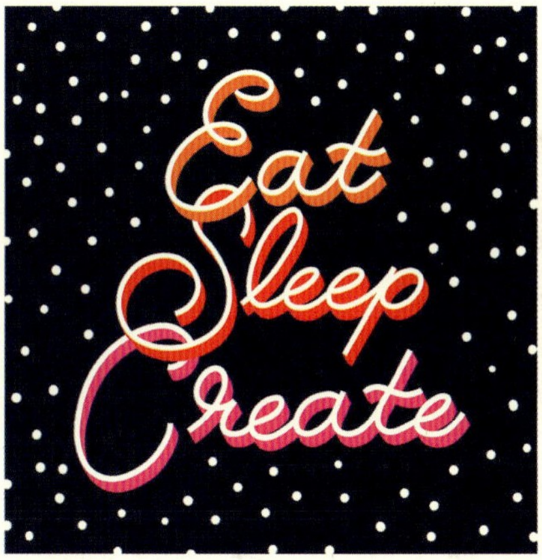

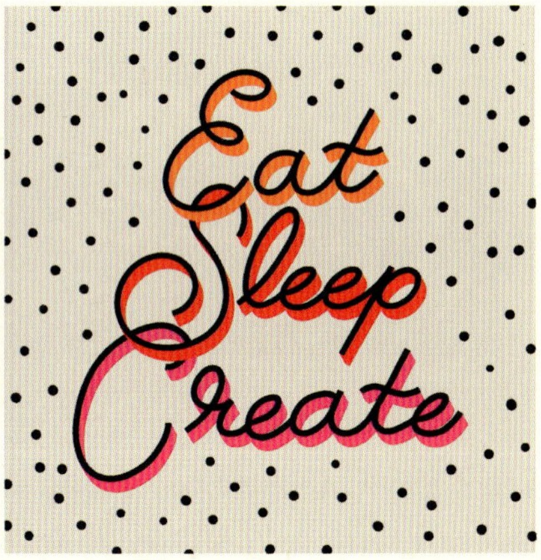

Adding Weight

Now that you've had some practice with monoline lettering, let's look at the final aspect of script lettering: weight. Adding weight means adding thickness to various parts of your letters. This technique helps to establish the style and boldness of a letter. Although most lettering styles add weight to the downstrokes of a letter, some styles break that rule, such as the fat-bottomed letter style (below).

For the majority of script styles we only thicken the downstrokes, which is the part of the letter that you create with a downward motion. Imagine you're using a paintbrush to paint your letters. When your brush goes in a downward motion you'll press down hard, which will create a thick stroke, and when your brush goes up the page you'll press lightly creating a thin stroke.

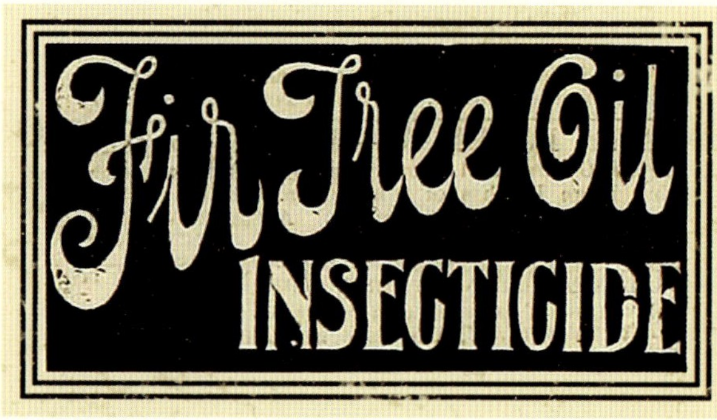

Example of fat-bottomed lettering found in an 1800's gardening magazine

Here are a few examples of how varying the weight can dramatically change the style of your lettering (below right). All of these examples started with the same base shape (the sketch in black), then I used the **Liquid Pen** brush to add weight in smooth curved strokes.

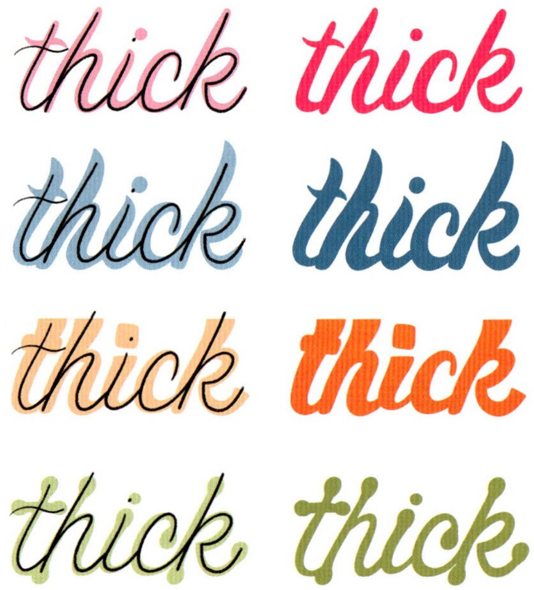

Examples of a few styles of letter thickening

> Tip: When adding weight to your script, make sure the weight is consistent throughout the words so the thickest part of each letter is the same weight on each letter.

Every type of script has a different style of weight, so you might want to scan through the vintage resources mentioned in chapter 1 to find a style you like. Here are just a few examples of script inspiration you'll find (opposite).

Another example is a beautiful Sign-Painter's style I found in a hardware magazine from the early 20th century (above). I wanted to create a similar script in my own compositions, so I made a practice sheet using the letters in the sign as my basis (right). You can see that I didn't copy the script precisely. Instead, I used the parent shapes as inspiration and then added some

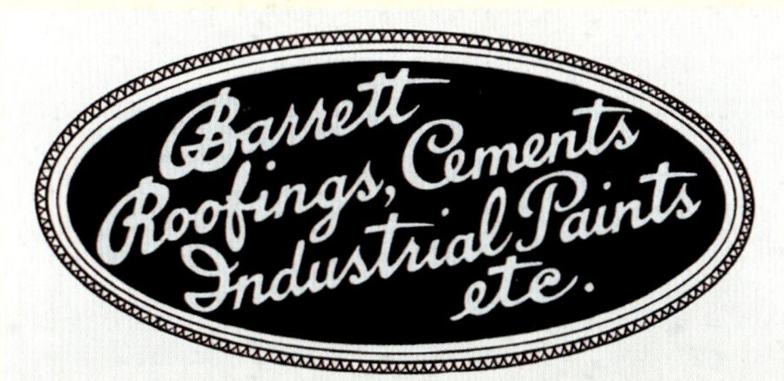

Sign-Painter's style script from an early 1900's hardware magazine.

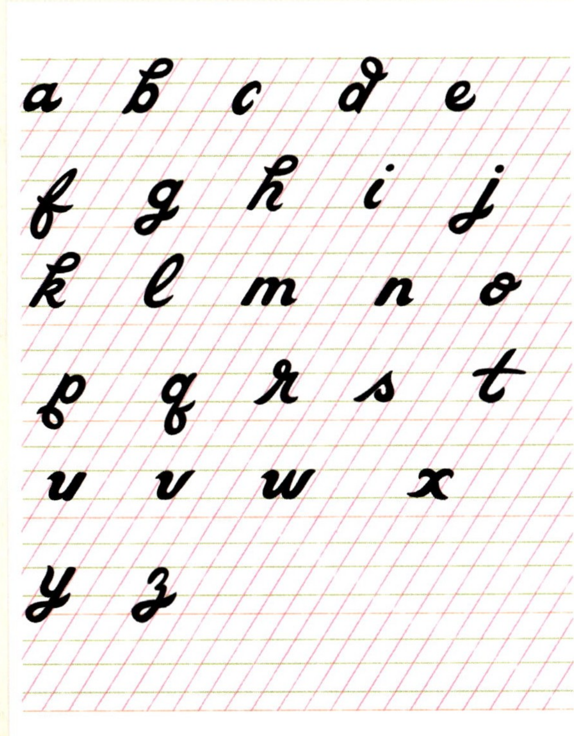

Sign-Painter's Style Practice Sheet.

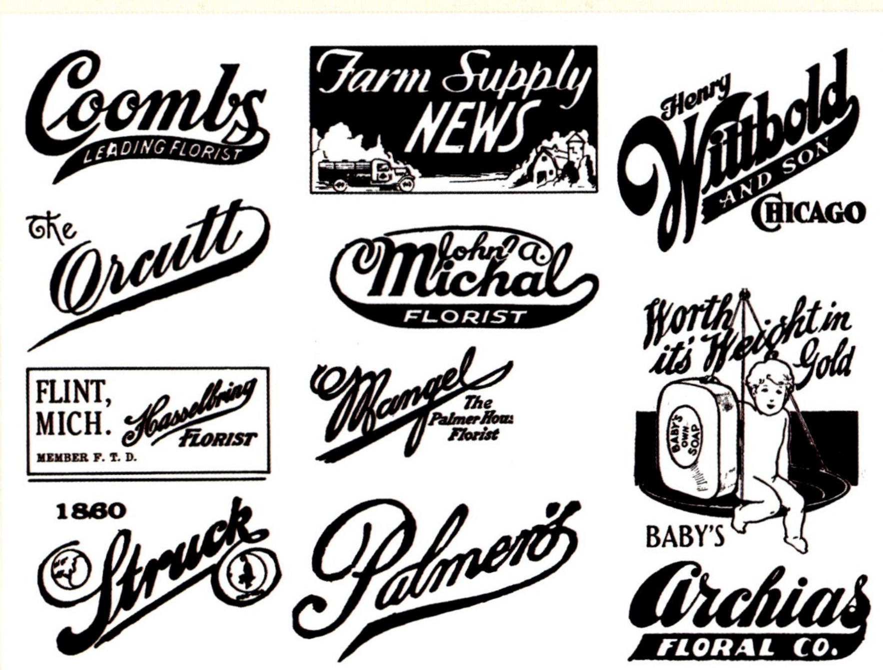

Script comes in many different weights and angles.

of my own features like the loops on the **b**, **d**, **h**, **k**, **o**, **p**, **q**, and **r** shapes.

This alphabet shows just one type of weight, but there are many others to discover and try. You can download this *Sign-Painter's Style Practice Sheet* or make your own using one of the letter styles you find on the **Downloads and Resources** web page mentioned in chapter 1. I like to use the **Liquid Pen** to incrementally build up the thickness over several strokes, focusing on one curve at a time. You'll notice that in the sign-painter script, and many other script styles, the insides of curves are flat while the outsides have a rounded shape (right).

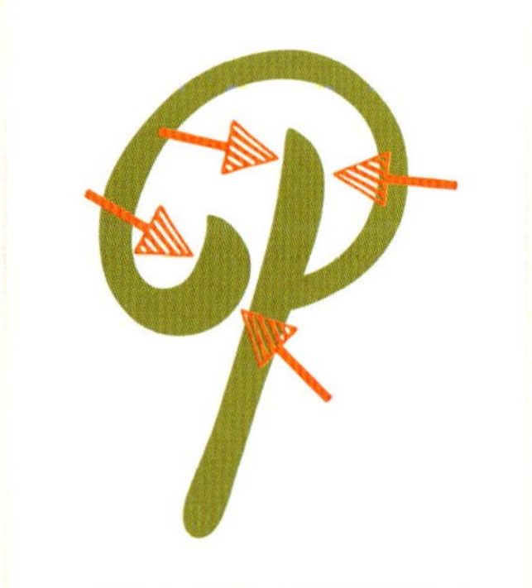

Notice where the curved and straight parts are on the Sign-Painter's script.

Create a Composition with Script

Let's create a finished composition using a script inspired by the sign-painter style shown above. I recommend using either a single word or a two- to three-word phrase. By starting small, you can focus your attention on refining your weighted script rather than worrying about fitting a large phrase onto the canvas.

Follow these steps as we letter the word "persist:"

STEP 1: As usual, start with some thumbnails to get ideas down in visual form. I will use the bottom right thumbnail, because I think the rounded shape will look nice with the rounded script.

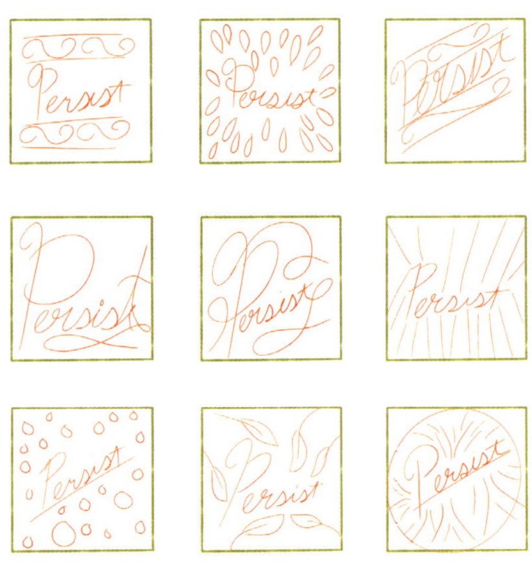

STEP 2: Do a rough sketch to get the placement of the letters and decorations down on the page. I leave extra space in between my letters, because I plan to add a lot of weight to each letter.

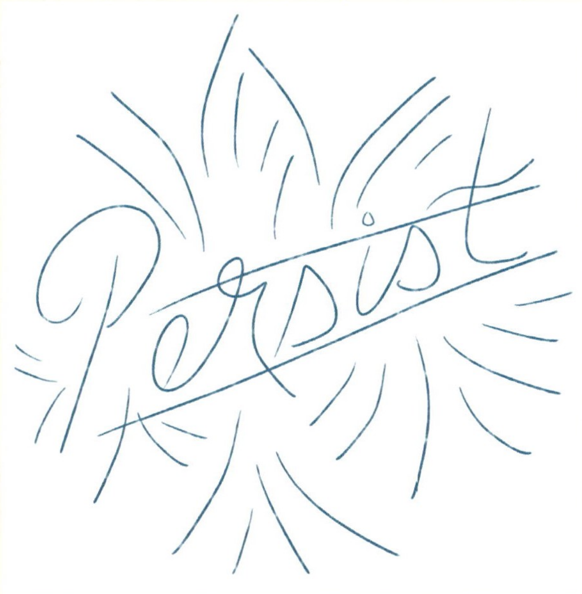

STEP 3: Add guides for your baseline, X-height, and cap height. Turn on the **Isometric** guide like we did for the previous project, and then do a more refined sketch of the text. At this point, you can also create a more refined sketch of the decoration on a separate layer.

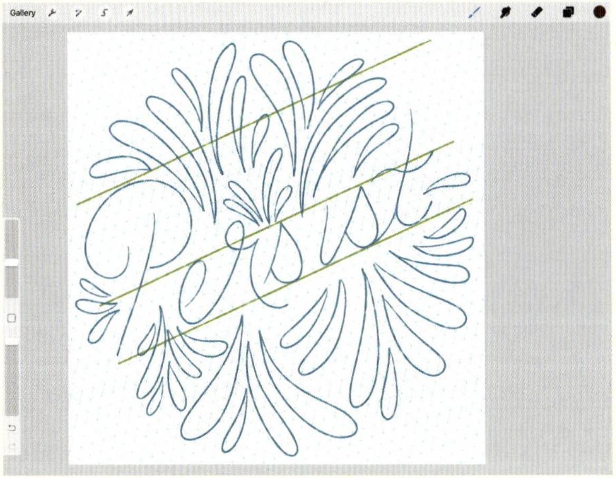

STEP 4: Before I ink the weight of my letters, I like to use the **Liquid Pen** brush to determine the thinnest parts of my script. This is essentially like doing a monoline script but with a different brush.

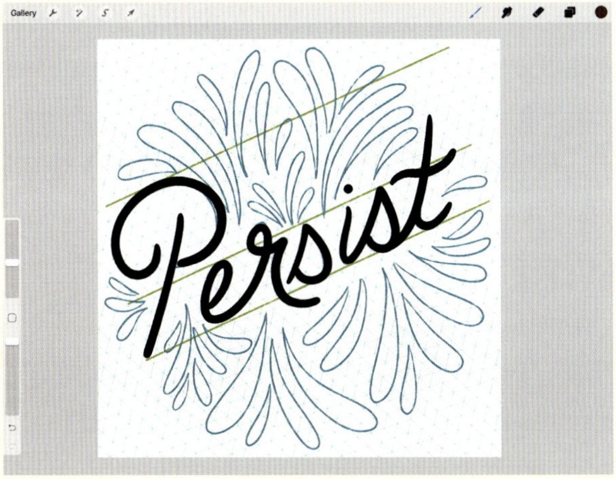

STEP 5: Now that the structure of the letters has been set, use smooth strokes to add weight to the downstrokes of the letters. I like to work on one curve at a time by zooming in closely and then brushing over that curve three or four times with a smooth stroke until the curve doesn't have any

uneven areas. Remember that it doesn't have to be perfect; it just has to be consistent. Once you decide on a thickness for your downstrokes, stick with that same thickness throughout the word.

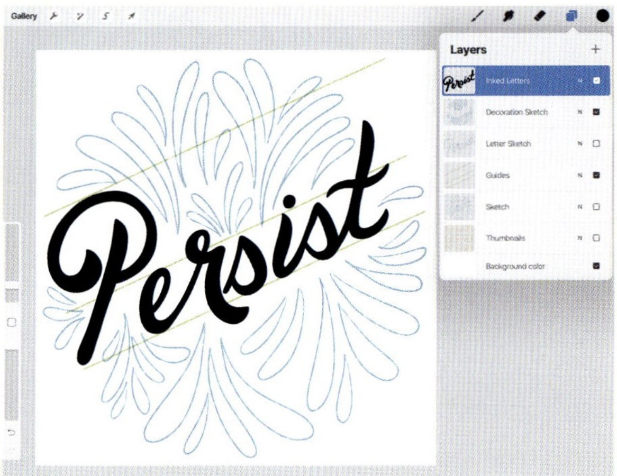

STEP 6: Follow the same process with the decorative elements.

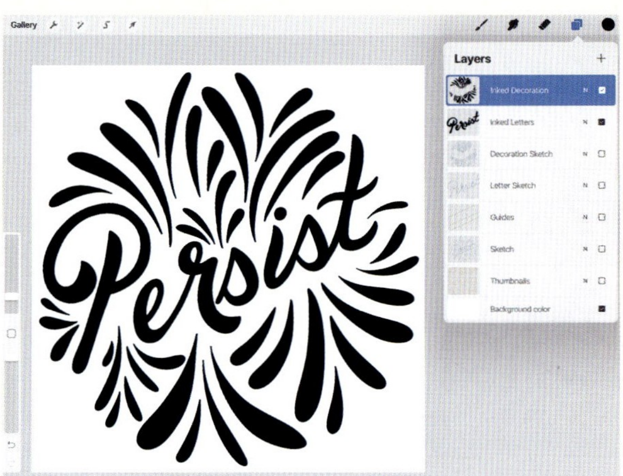

STEP 7: Experiment with colors, perspective, and textures like we did in all the previous projects until you land on a combination you like.

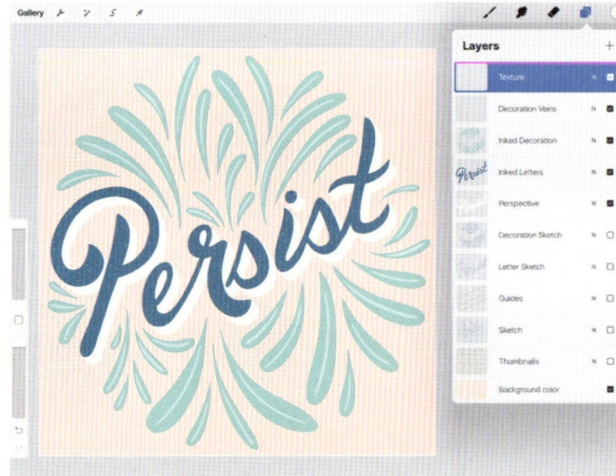

STEP 8: Now it's time to add in some sort of filler element. I will add some mustard-colored dots to fill some of the blank spaces and to create more color contrast to the overall design.

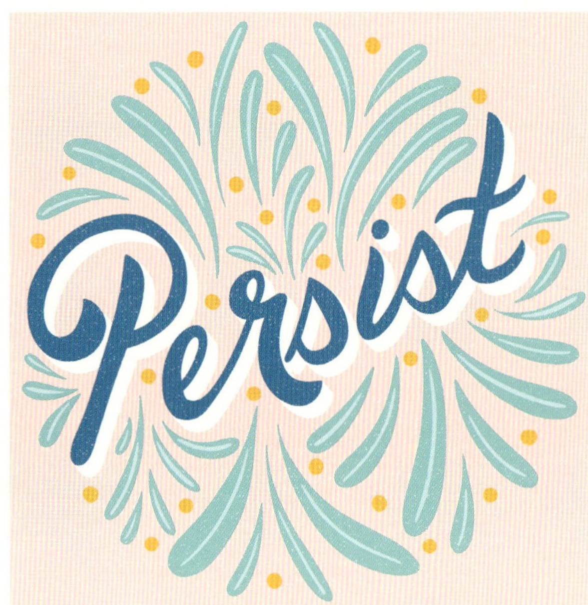

STEP 9: Finish by creating some Master Documents and then play around with various color versions.

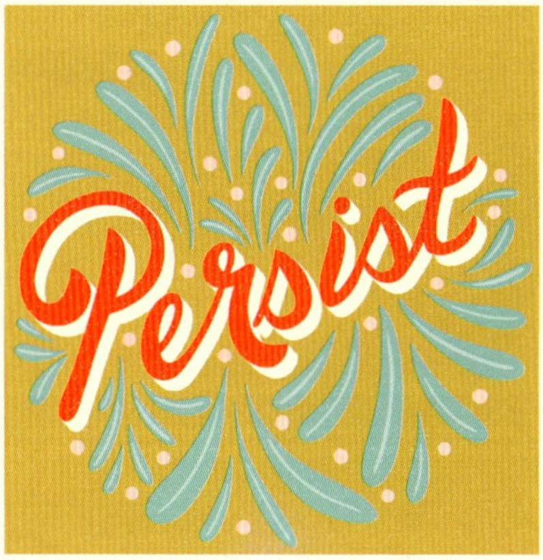

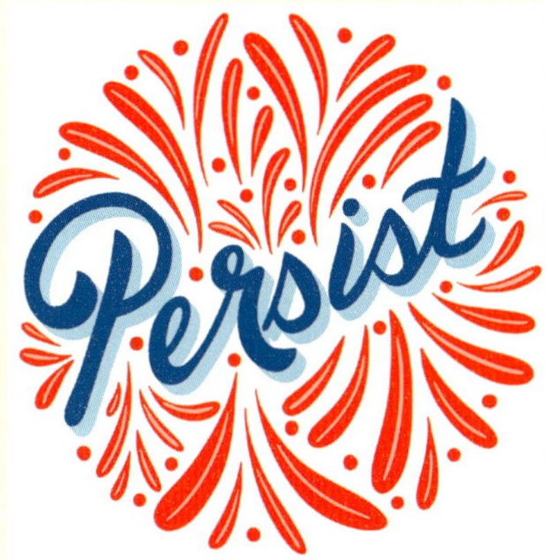

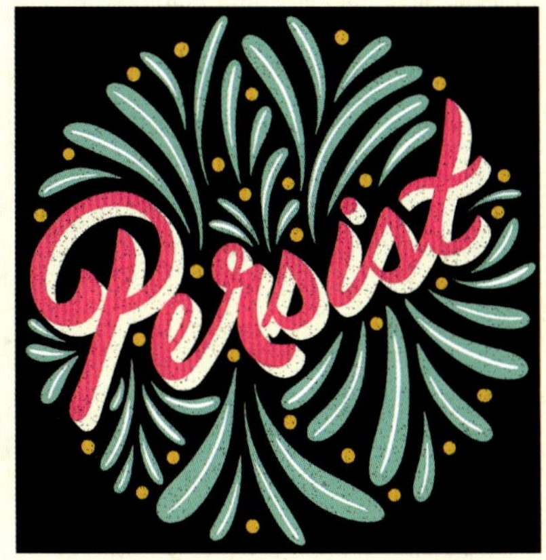

As you can see, once you start learning new script styles, there are an endless number of options for lettering compositions. For the next piece, I chose to have the lines of text very close to each other so I could add some flourishes that would weave in and out of the center line of text. To do this, I created the three lines of text, each on a separate layer, and then I erased part of the text where I wanted the two lines to overlap. You can see that I didn't include any decorative elements on my sketch. You don't always have to include these in your initial sketches, especially if you aren't sure what elements to use and if it's stopping you from beginning the project!

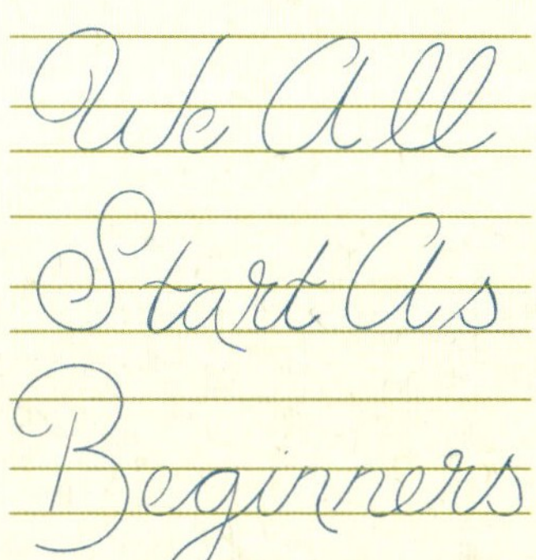

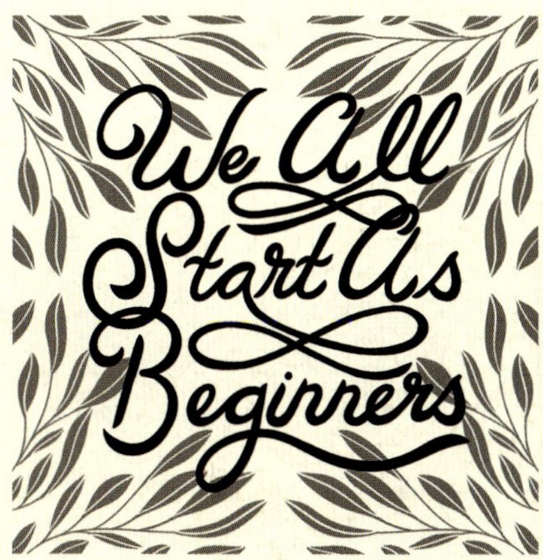

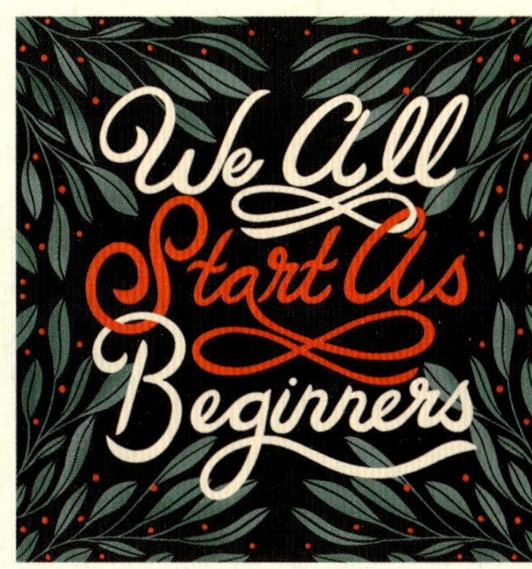

Not every piece needs to have decoration. Sometimes I prefer to let the lettering do all the talking, and will intentionally leave blank space around the words to draw more attention to them. For the "You're Killing It" script, I started with a thin **Liquid Pen** for my base lettering, then used a thicker **Liquid Pen** for the thickening. I then used the Circle brush to add circles on the ends of each letter. I put each circle on a new layer so I could easily adjust them to fit the letter perfectly. I also included a ligature in this composition. A ligature is a stroke that combines two or more letters and can serve more than one purpose in a composition. In this example, the loop of the g also serves as the cross of the t. Ligatures are a great way to bring a whimsical feel to your compositions and to create a cohesive look that ties the words together.

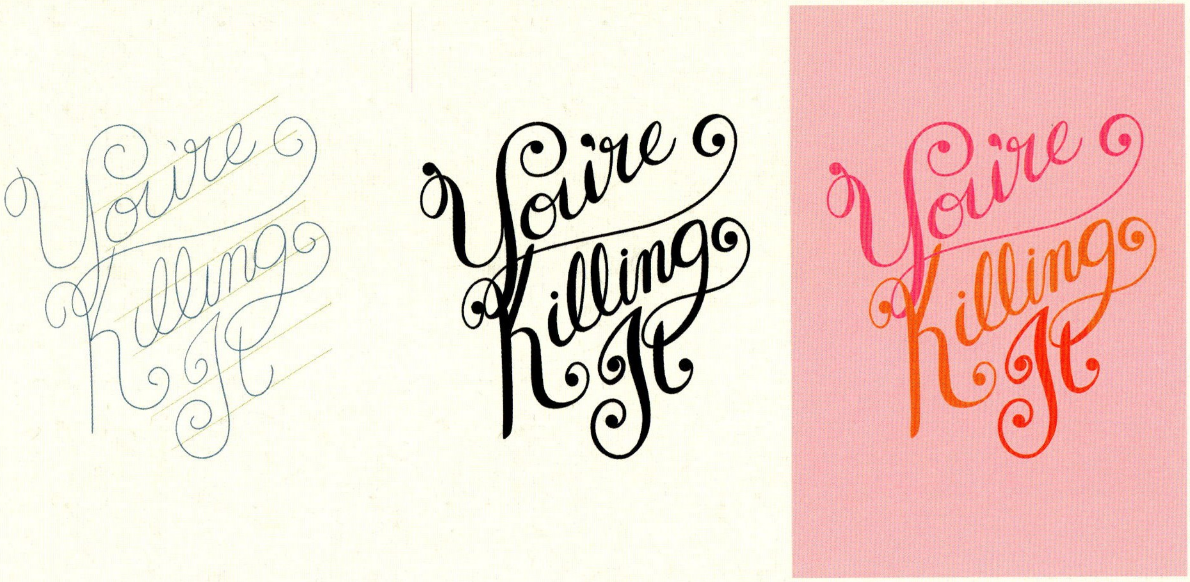

For the next composition I wanted to use a thick script that breaks one of the rules of adding weight. In this case, the weight is added to the bottom of the curve rather than the downstroke of the letter. For the decorative elements, I added some flowers and leaves layered with shading and lines. In the next chapter, we'll explore ways to create elements like these and look at lots of options for illustrated elements.

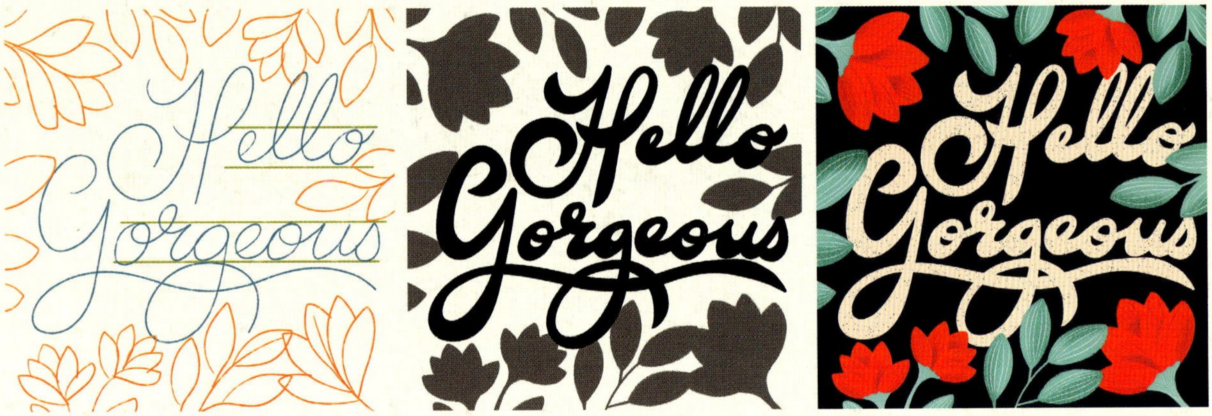

Now that you understand the basics of creating several different kinds of letterforms, let's start looking deeper into decorating your lettering compositions with illustrations, linework, and flourishes.

CHAPTER 7

Decorative Elements: Flourishes, Shapes, and Illustrations

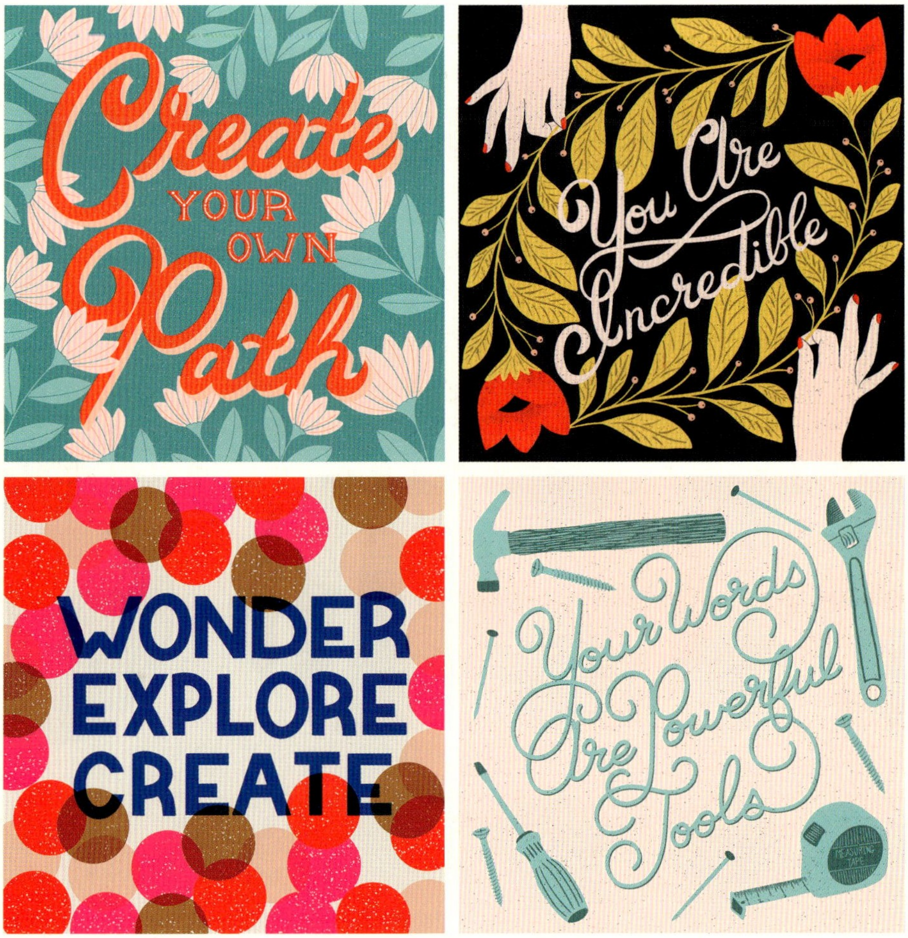

There are endless possibilities for decorating your hand lettering. You can create anything from abstract shapes to illustrations of your cat. In this chapter, I'll show you a few drawing techniques and I'll share some ideas for a wide range of decorative elements.

Let's start with the simplest type of decoration: abstract shapes. The great thing about abstract shapes is that you can't mess them up. The most important thing to keep in mind is that once you create a rule for your abstract shapes, you should follow that rule throughout the composition. If you start with big chunky teardrop shapes, you should repeat a similar shape somewhere else in the composition to create a balanced feeling.

Abstract Shapes

Any shape can be used to create many types of decorations. The shapes below were all made using the **Circle** brush in the **Hand Lettering** brush set. As you're trying out a new shape, consider as many options as you can think of to manipulate the shape, size, and texture. You could cut through a shape with an eraser, erase over it with a texture, duplicate it, cut it in half, or overlap it with other shapes. The possibilities are endless!

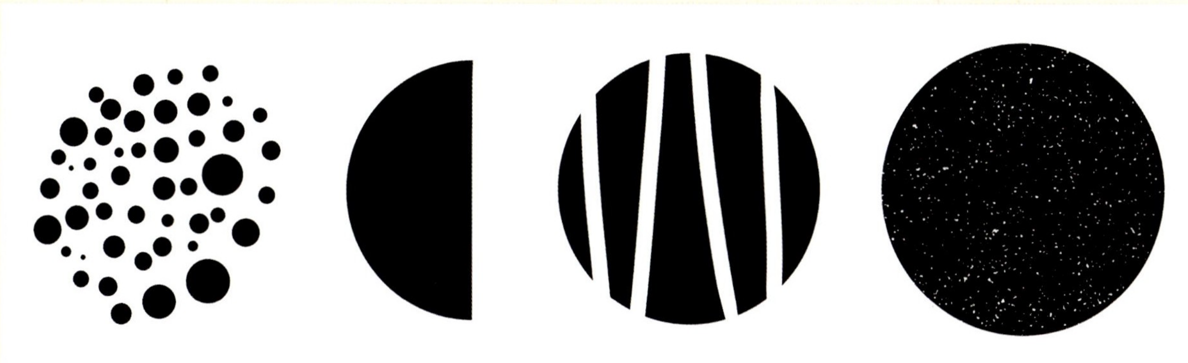

You can also play with the scale and texture on the abstract shapes, like these three pieces where I created the circles, set the circle layers to the **Blend** mode called **Multiply**, and then erased over the circles with the **Barely There Grit** texture brush. You can see that I experimented with the shape in various sizes and configurations before finding my favorite version, which is the one in the center.

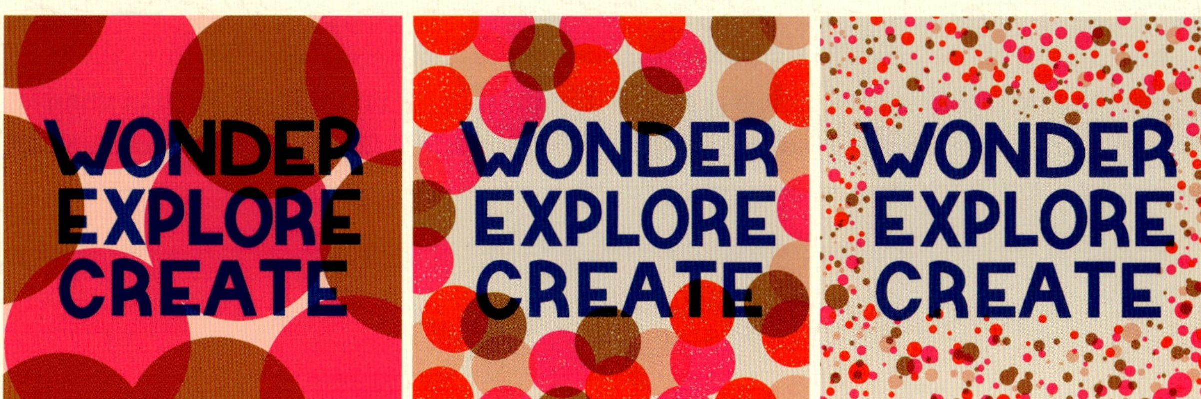

Three ways to use circles to decorate lettering

Make Your Own Stamp Brushes

We've already covered how to create abstract shapes (sketch them, then fill them in) but what if you want to repeat the same shape in other lettering projects? To do this, you would simply turn the shape into a stamp brush!

To create your own stamp brush, follow these steps:

STEP 1: Create a new document at 10″× 10″ at 300 DPI (all stamps must be made from square images and should be made on a large canvas to prevent blurriness). Use pure black ink with any brush to draw a shape. (Get a pure black by double tapping in the black area of the color wheel.) For my stamp, I drew a leaf shape and then used the **Liquid Pen** as an eraser to create the veins.

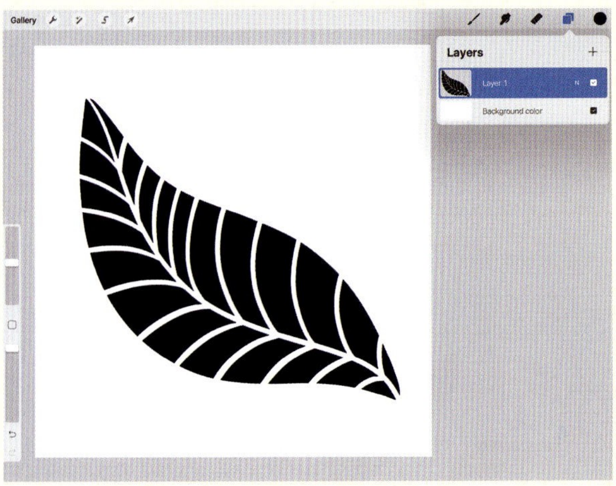

STEP 2: Save the image by tapping the **Actions** menu, tapping **Share**, and choosing **JPEG** as the file type. Then save it to your Photos library.

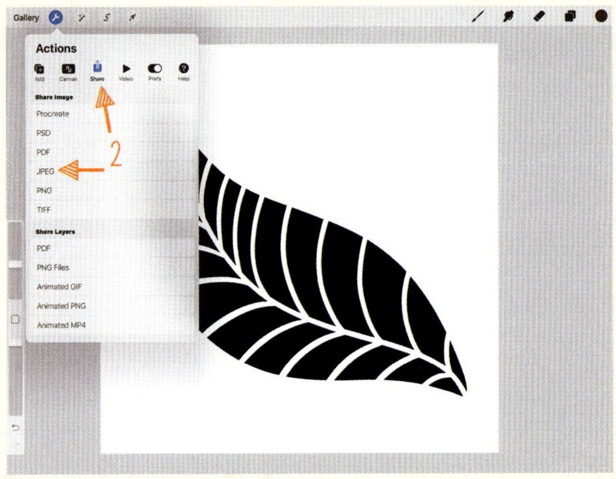

STEP 3: In the **Brush Library**, tap on the **Hand Lettering** brush set and then swipe left on the **Circle** brush and tap **Duplicate.** This creates a duplicate of the Circle brush, so you can input your own shape in place of the circle and rename the brush.

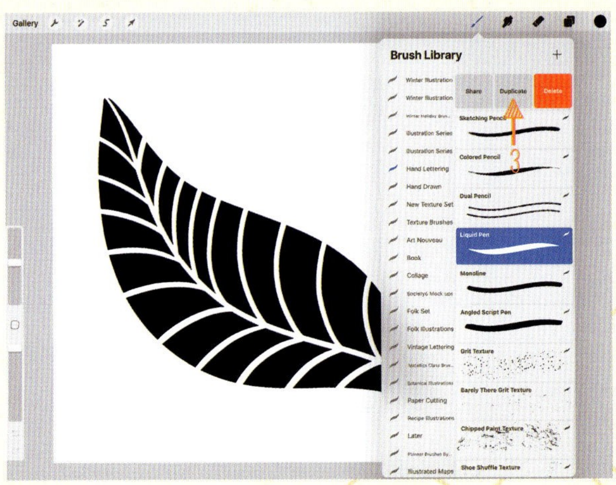

STEP 4: Tap on the new brush titled Circle 1 in the Brush menu to open the brush settings page, and then tap **Shape** on the left side of the screen. This will open up the Shape Source panel which is where you can input the shape you created. Above the shape, tap **Edit.**

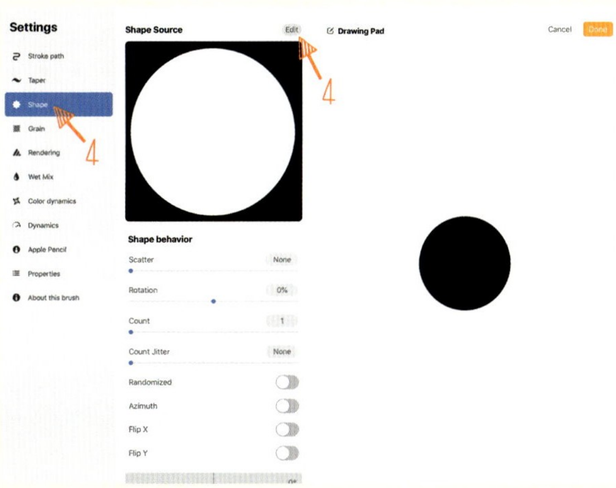

STEP 5: Import the stamp shape you created by tapping **Import**, then **Import a photo.** Once you tap on your photo, you should see it as the new shape source. Tap **Done** on the top right corner to set the shape.

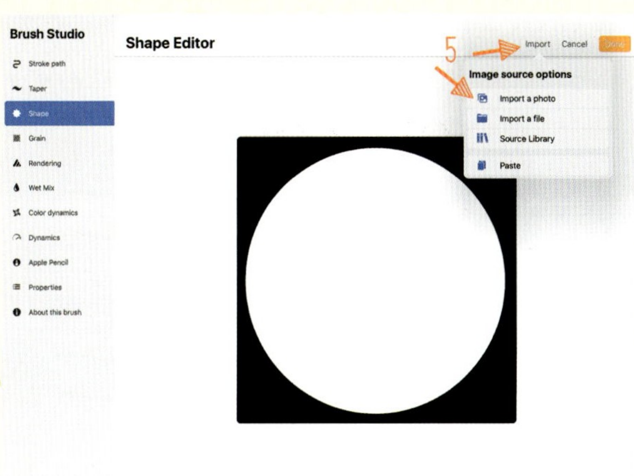

STEP 6: To rename the brush, tap **About this brush** on the left and tap the title to enter a new name. Tap **Done** on the top right corner of the screen to save your brush.

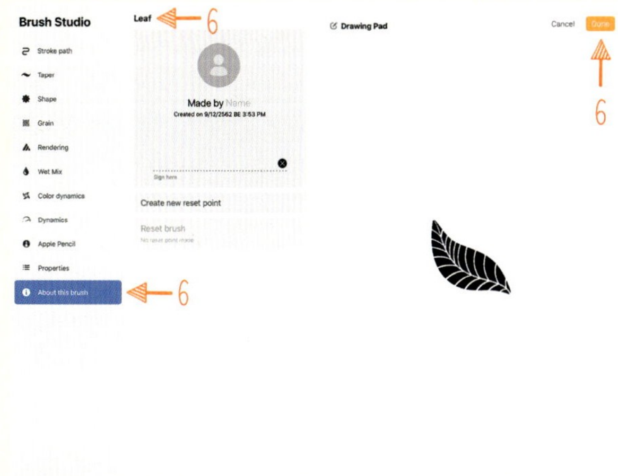

STEP 7: Test your stamp brush. Make your shape layer invisible and create a new layer. Tap with your finger to get the same size each time, or tap with your stylus to get a different size. I put each leaf on a new layer and then used the **Move** tool to flip, rotate, and position each leaf.

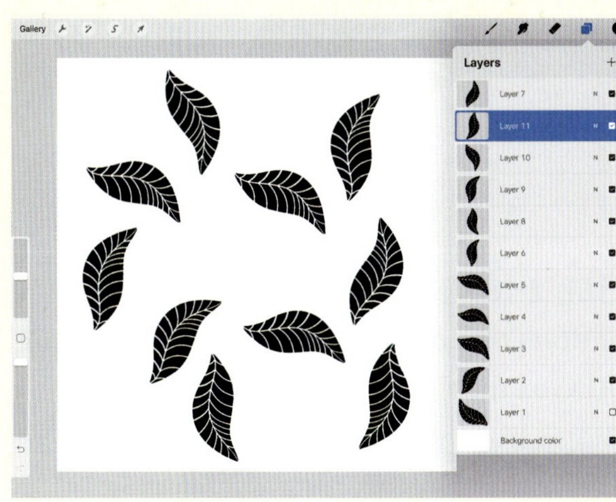

Natural shapes like leaves and flowers can be interesting when scattered throughout a lettering composition. They can even be arranged into a specific pattern, like a circular wreath!

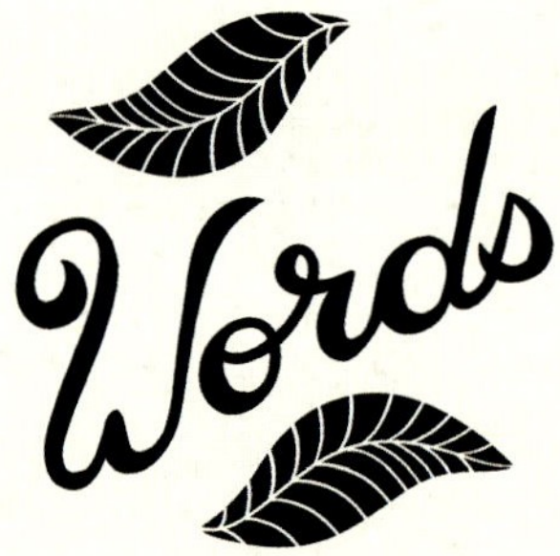

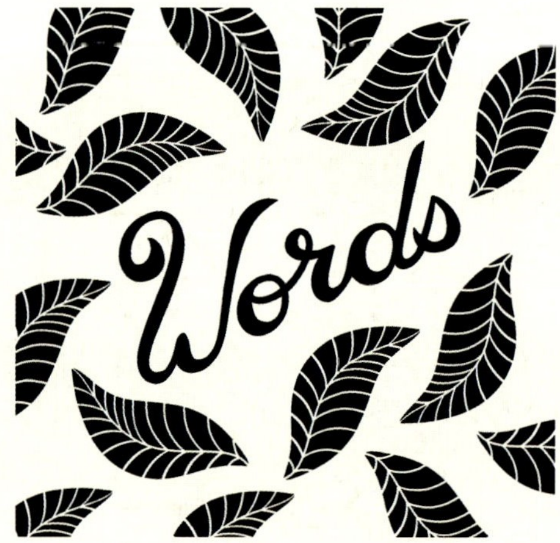

Shape Ideas

You can create decorative shapes by making brush stamps, or you can individually sketch some shapes and fill them with color. In this section, we'll look at some useful shape ideas that tend to work well in most any composition.

Straight lines and dots can be used to fill negative space and help draw attention to the words. Try them all in the same color, or use a different color for the dots. Use **Quickline** to get a perfectly straight line or draw freehand to get a handmade feel.

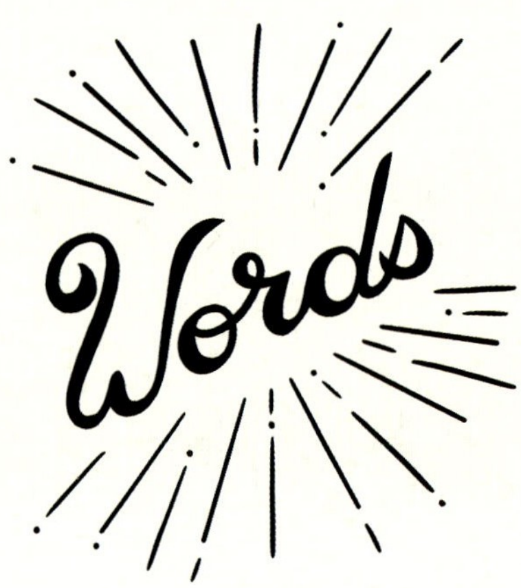

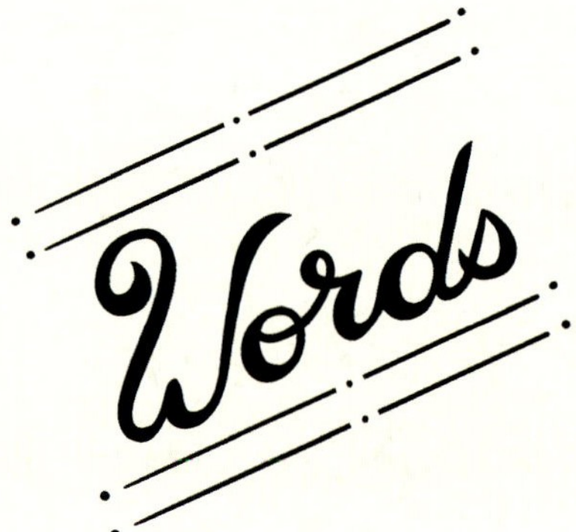

Teardrop shapes in a variety of configurations can frame a word or liven up blank spaces on the canvas. Combine them with dots or other shapes to create a more dynamic illustration.

Stars, dots, and sparkle shapes can add movement to the background of a lettering composition. You can either repeat the same shape throughout the composition or create a medley of various shapes.

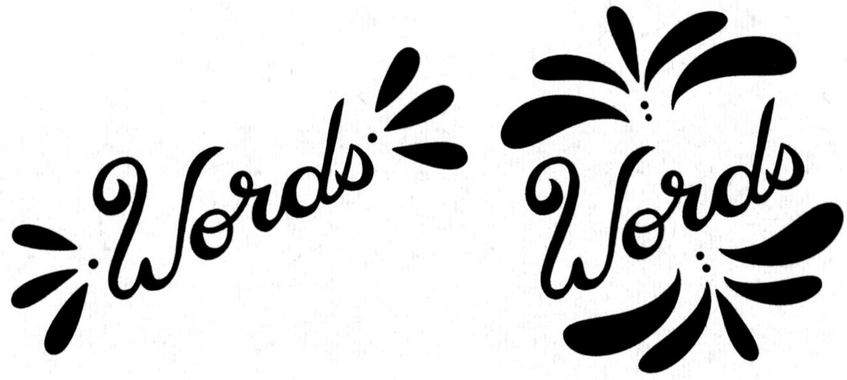

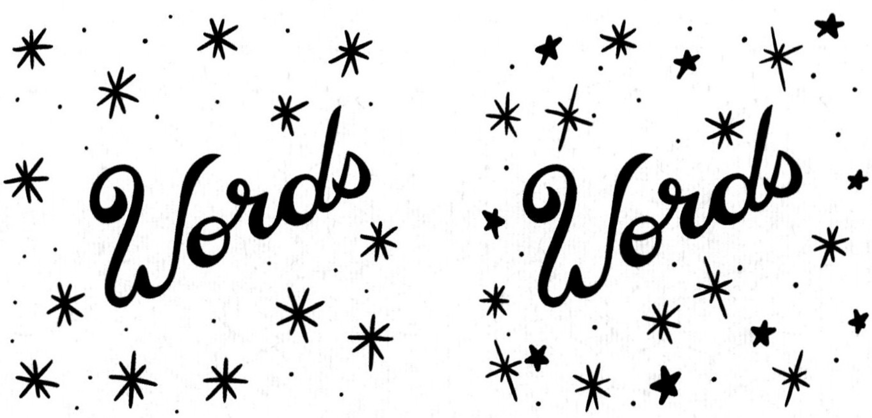

Flourishes

Flourishes are versatile curves, lines, or combinations of the two that can be used to fill your canvas with fluid linework. Flourishes can go in the opposite direction of a straight line (like the example on the opposite page, top) or they can continue the flow of a line (like the example on the opposite page, bottom).

Keep in mind is that the shape of the flourish should mirror the **O** shape in the script. If your **O** shape is circular like mine in the illustration below, then your flourishes should also be circular, whereas if your o shape is an oval, your flourishes should be ovals as well. Maintaining a uniformity between shapes keeps the composition cohesive and prevents the flourishes from drawing too much attention.

For these flourishes, I drew one side, then duplicated and flipped it horizontally so that the two sides would be perfectly symmetrical.

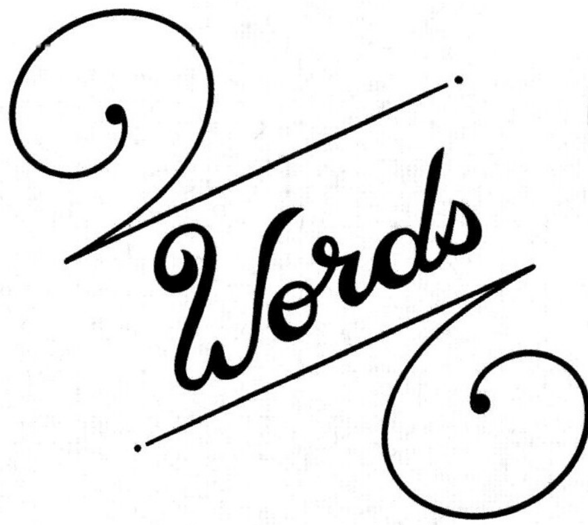

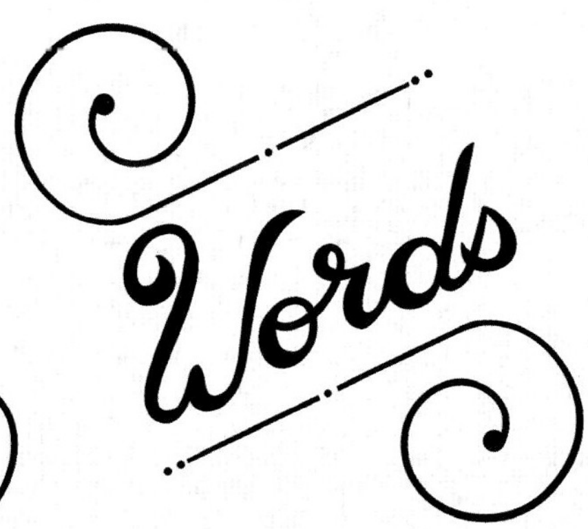

> Tip: When you draw flourishes, use smooth quick movements to make the curve. Try drawing your flourish three or four times until you get the exact curve you want.

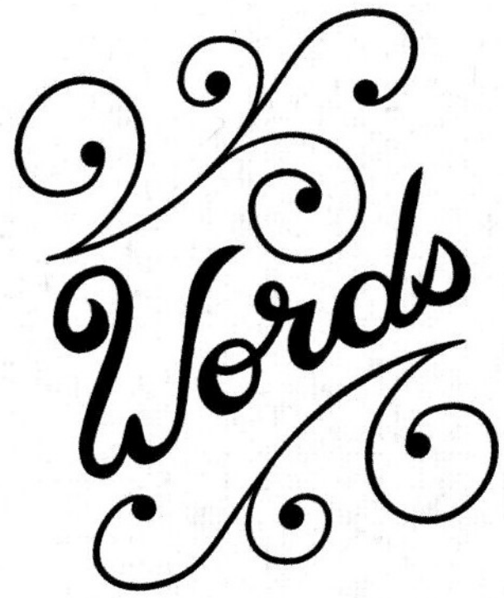

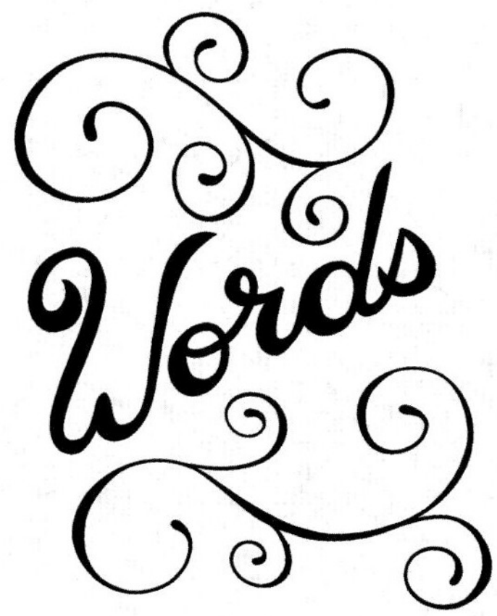

Flourishes can be made from a single curve or multiple curves put together. You can choose to thicken the downstrokes of the curves or make them a consistent width. You can also terminate the curve with a dot, oval, or any other shape that fits with the style of your composition.

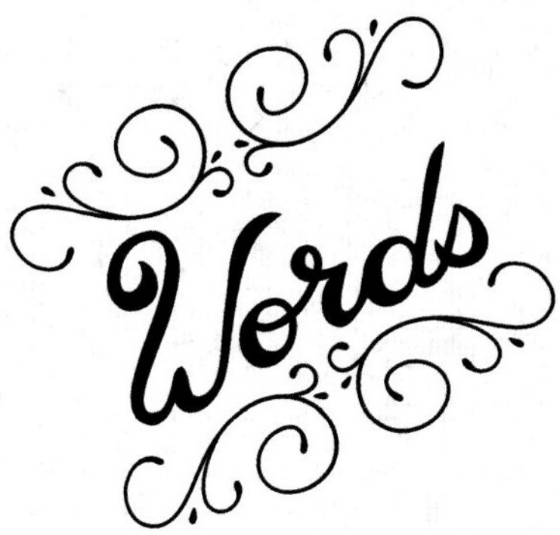

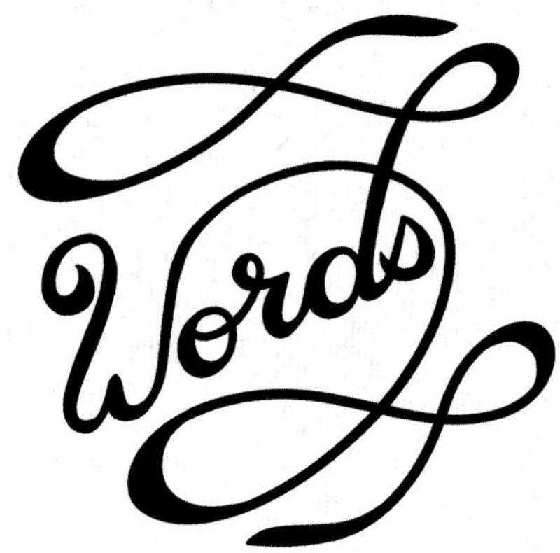

You can draw one flourish, then duplicate and flip it to create a mirrored effect like this example (bottom, left) or have the flourish extend directly out of the letters (like the example on the right).

In this example I combined monoline lettering with flourishes, making the flourishes come right out of the letters. With this method, flourishes can be a great way to fill your canvas without creating separate decorative elements.

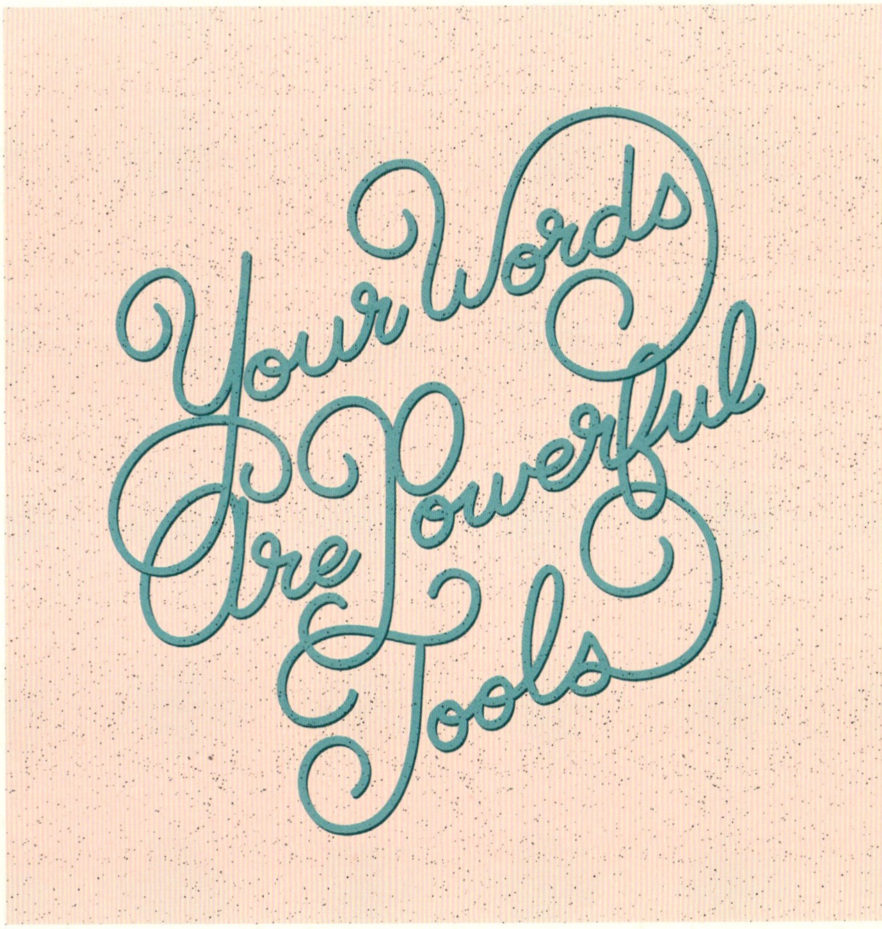

Of course, you can find many more flourish examples in the vintage lettering resources described in chapter 1, so delve into those to gain inspiration from the hand letterers throughout history!

Leaves

Leaves are one of my go-to shapes for filling lettering compositions. Leaves come in a variety of shapes and sizes and, like flourishes, are easy to wrap around words and can help fill negative space. We already looked at one style of leaf illustration in chapter 5, so let's look at a few other options for leaf shapes and finishing styles.

For the two compositions on the next page I used the same basic leaf drawing, but I finished them differently. For the piece on the left, I made each leaf a different tone and then used a **Clipping Mask** above the leaf layer to add highlights and shadows with the **Gritty Shading** brush. For the example on the right, I created veins by erasing on the leaf shapes and I added berries that match the color of the letters.

As you can imagine, any vine shape can be combined with any leaf shape to get a wide variety of styles. We will look at a few leaf shapes that you could try adding to your next lettering composition. I begin each leaf style by first sketching the base shape, then inking the shape, adding some veins, and finally, using a Clipping Mask over the leaves layer to add shadow and highlights using the **Gritty Shading** brush.

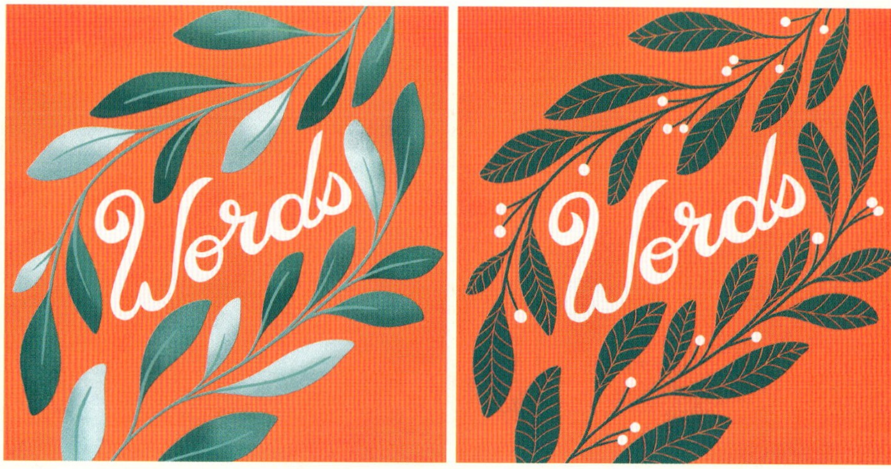

Two styles of leaf illustrations

Once you create a few of these leaves, you'll realize how easy it is to turn a picture of a leaf into an illustration. Any time you see a leaf you like, snap a picture of it so you have it in your inspiration library for later use!

The thin, long leaf shapes fit well into small spaces that need some extra visual interest.

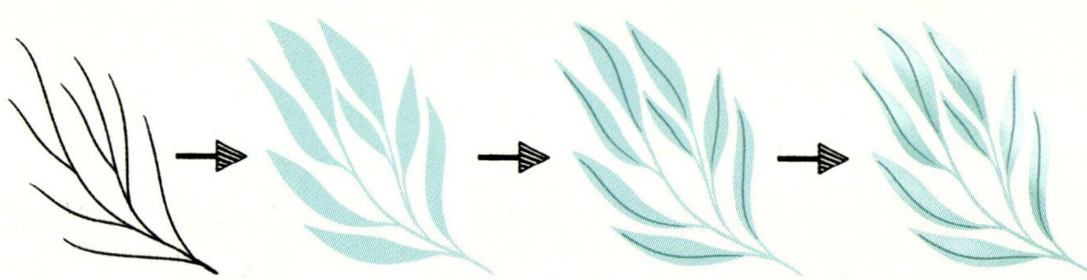

This heart shape leaf is great for adding chunky shapes to the background of a composition. Keep the shape irregular to add some variation and movement to the leaves.

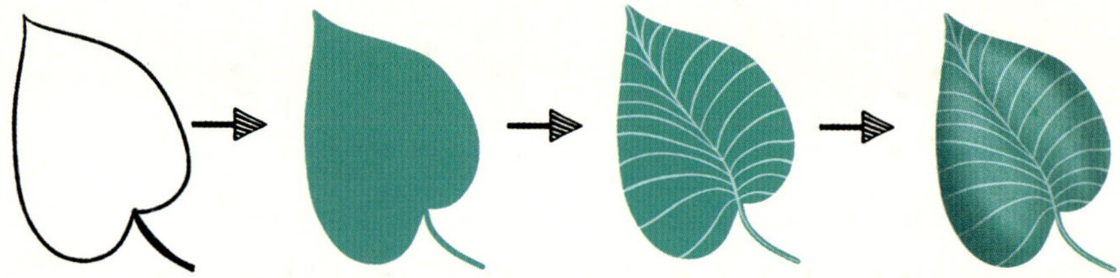

These fluid leaves are great for adding bold contrast (e.g., the vein color) to your composition.

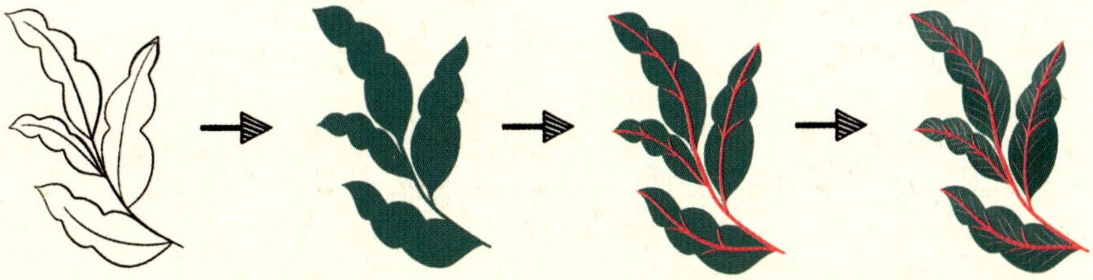

If you take a picture of a beautiful leaf and don't want to draw it by hand, you can place the image on your canvas (like we did with our color palette images in chapter 2), then trace the shape on a new layer and fill it with color, veins, and shading.

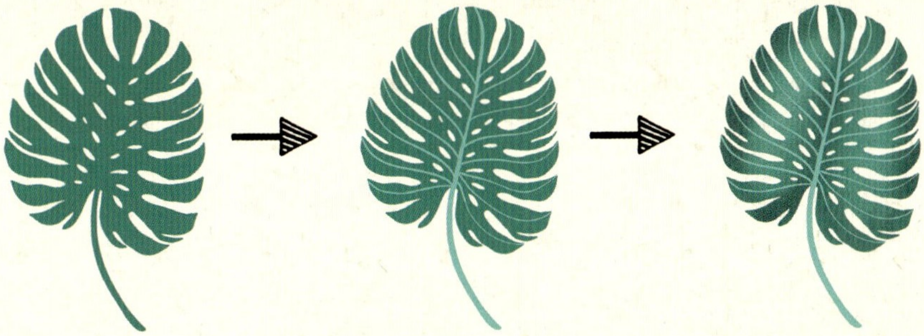

Flowers

Flowers are another classic element to add to your compositions. There are endless shapes and colors to choose from, making them an excellent way to spread complementary colors throughout your canvas. Let's look at a few common flower shapes that you can start integrating into your compositions.

For this flower I used the **Colored Pencil** brush to create some textured marks on the petals and leaves.

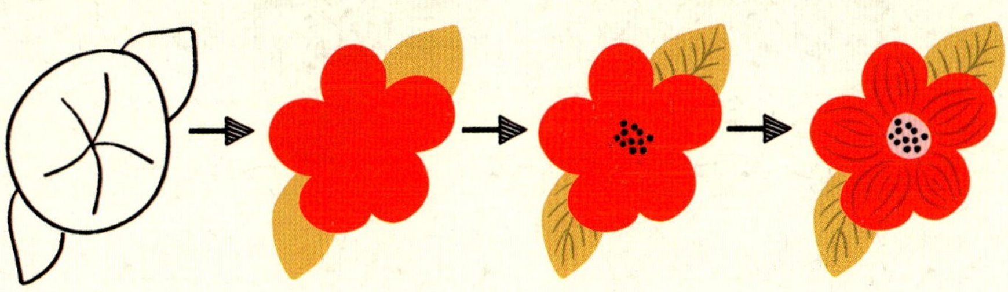

For this flower I kept each petal on a different layer so I could add shading to each one separately. To add the shading, I put each petal layer in **Alpha Lock**, then chose a color slightly lighter than the petal color and brushed it over the tips with the **Gritty Shading** brush.

This symmetrical folk-art-style flower was made by drawing just one half of the flower. I then duplicated that layer, flipped it horizontally, and moved it to the other side to create the whole flower. Color was added (on separate layers of course), and some extra petals and shading were layered on top.

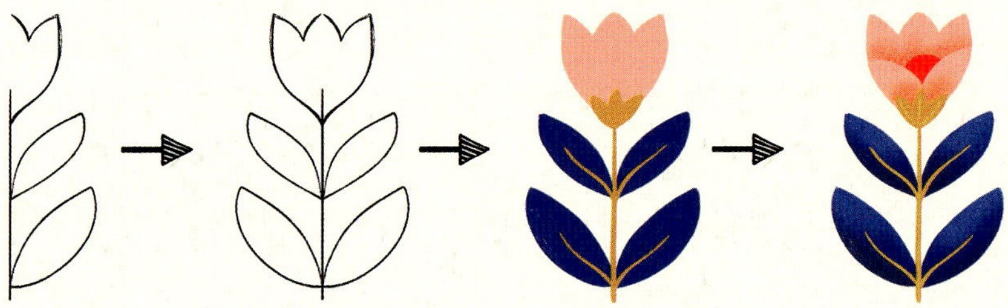

Just as there are many ways to create decorative elements for your compositions, there are also numerous ways to arrange them on the canvas. For example, in this composition, I wanted flowers to be both under and on top of the text, so I created two different layers with flower elements on each, and then placed one above and one below my text layer. I used reductive drawing (which will be covered later in this chapter) to create the flowers, and I used **Color Drop** to make the petals a different color than the leaves.

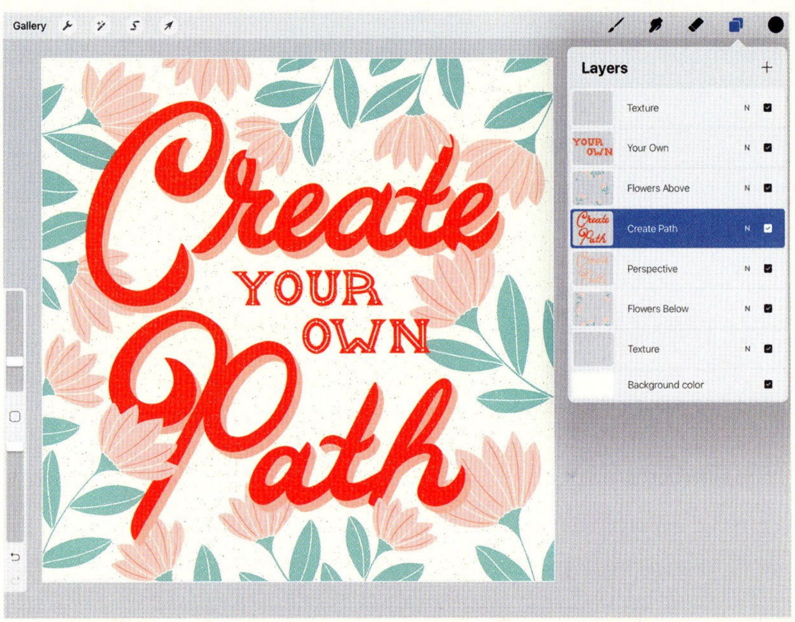

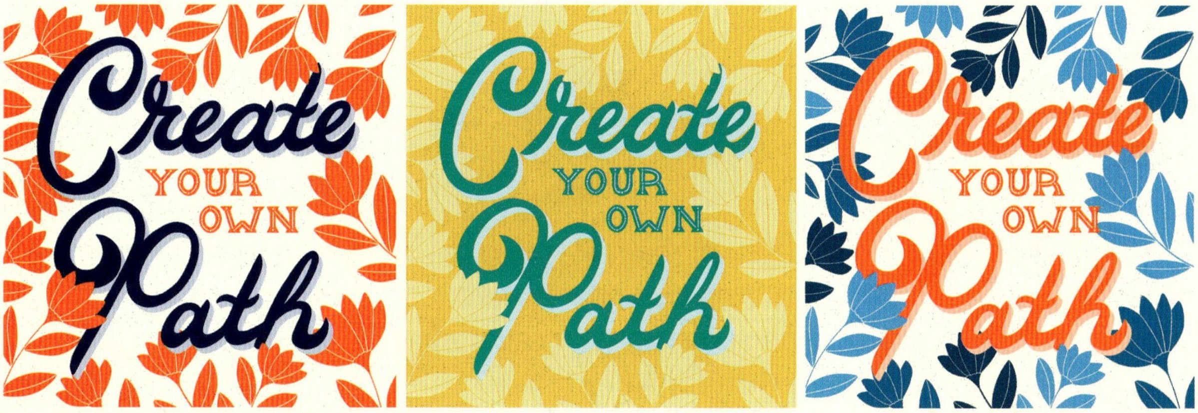

Next I tried various color versions of the same composition to see if there was a better combination of colors and textures.

I take photos of flowers anytime I see a new shape I want to recreate using the process above. You can add flower photos to your inspiration library so next time you need a unique flower shape for a composition, it will be there waiting for you!

Banners

Banners are a great way to highlight important text or break up a lettering composition that has a lot of words. Let's take a look at some popular banner styles.

For straight banners like this one, it's important for the angle of the words to be the same as the angle of the lettering guides. Therefore, I like to duplicate my lettering guide and then use the **Move** tool to pinch outward with two fingers to upsize the guide. Once the guide is in place, I use **Quickline** to add ends to the banner, and then I ink the banner shape on a new layer. Finally, some decorative elements like stitches or dots can be added.

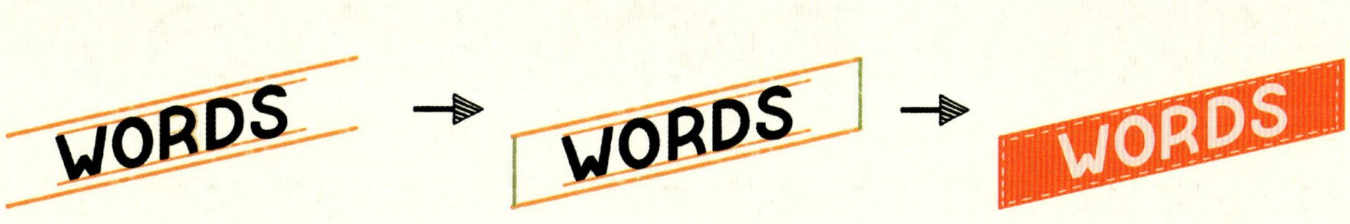

For curved banners, start by building your words as usual, and then make a curved line on a new layer. Duplicate the line, then move the duplicate above the word. Next, add some points to the ends of your banner, and use the **Freehand Selection** tool to move each letter individually so they match the curve of the baseline of the banner.

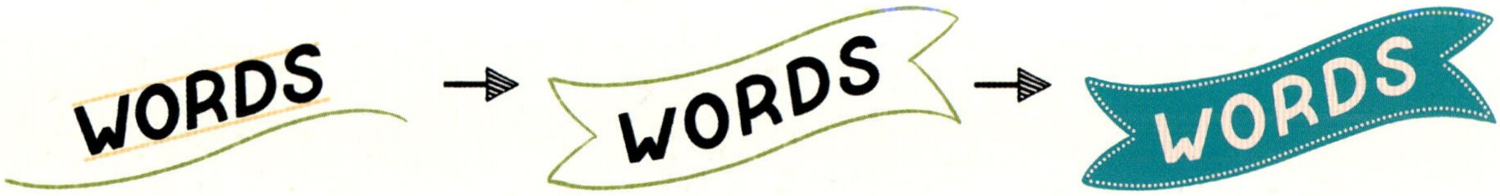

You can also overlap multiple layers of banners by duplicating the a banner set, and adding some connecting and ending elements.

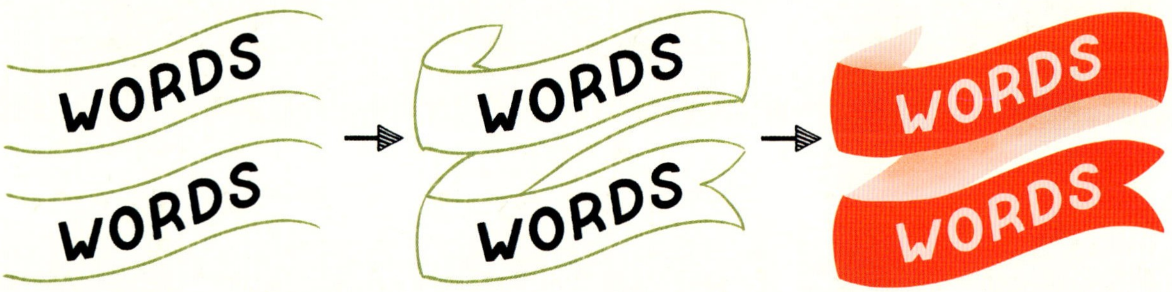

I made a set of six banner stamps (right) that you can use in any of your compositions. These can be found on the **Downloads and Resources** page mentioned in chapter 1. To use one, just open the **Hand Lettering** brush set, tap on one of the banner stamps, then tap once on your canvas.

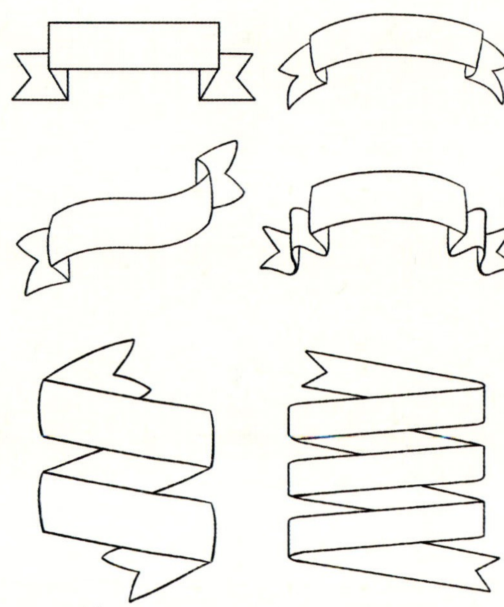

Find these banner stamps on the ***Downloads and Resources*** *page mentioned in chapter 1.*

Illustrations

You can turn any object into an illustration to pair with your lettering compositions. The illustrations can be as simple or as detailed as you like, as long as they're recognizable as the object you want to portray. Illustrated elements can help add context and interest to your compositions.

Consider this example (below) In the composition on the left, I used simple flourishes to decorate the lettering. On the right, I used some objects related to arts and crafts, which gives context to my lettering and communicates to the viewer that I'm referring to artwork or crafts.

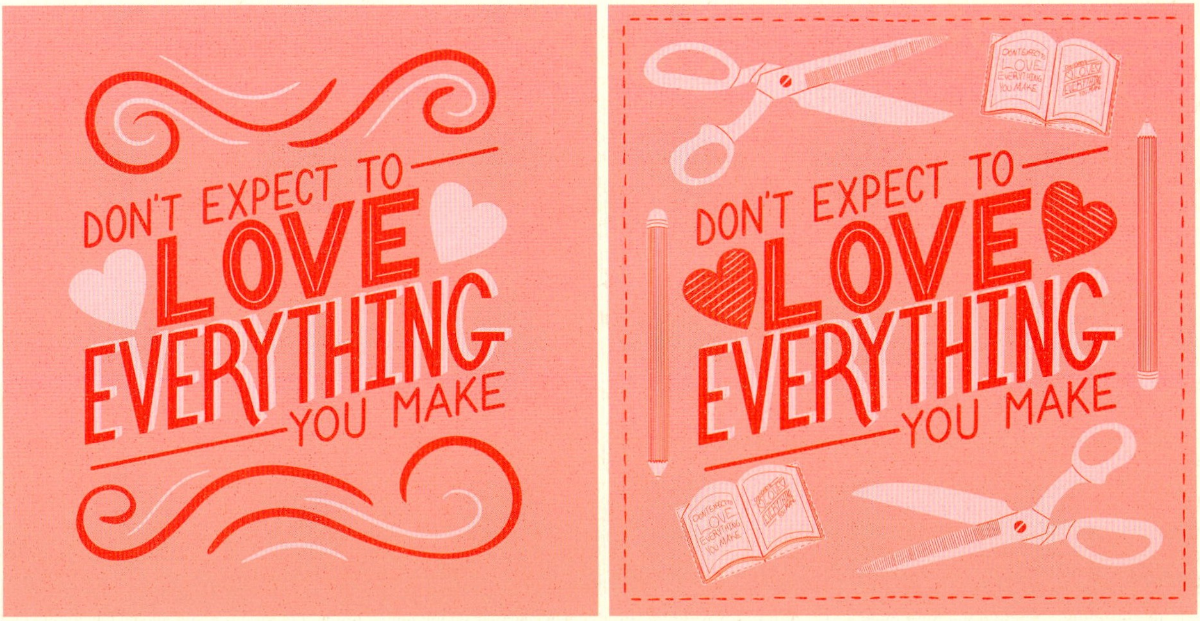

Illustrations can help put your lettering into context.

While both types of illustrations work equally well with the lettering composition, I might choose one or the other depending on my goals for the piece and how I intend to use it.

Let's look at a few simple ways to create illustrations of any object, so you can easily start incorporating illustrations into your lettering. We'll look at three popular drawing styles: line drawing, reductive drawing, and additive drawing.

Line drawing is the simplest way to draw an object. All you have to do is sketch or trace the object's outline, then fill it with color. I like to start with a rough sketch, create a new layer to ink my lines, and then add some color below the line layer. If you don't like drawing by hand, you can take a picture of the object, then place it on your canvas and make it semi-transparent in order to trace the shape. Just be sure to avoid copyrighted images or products when tracing or drawing images!

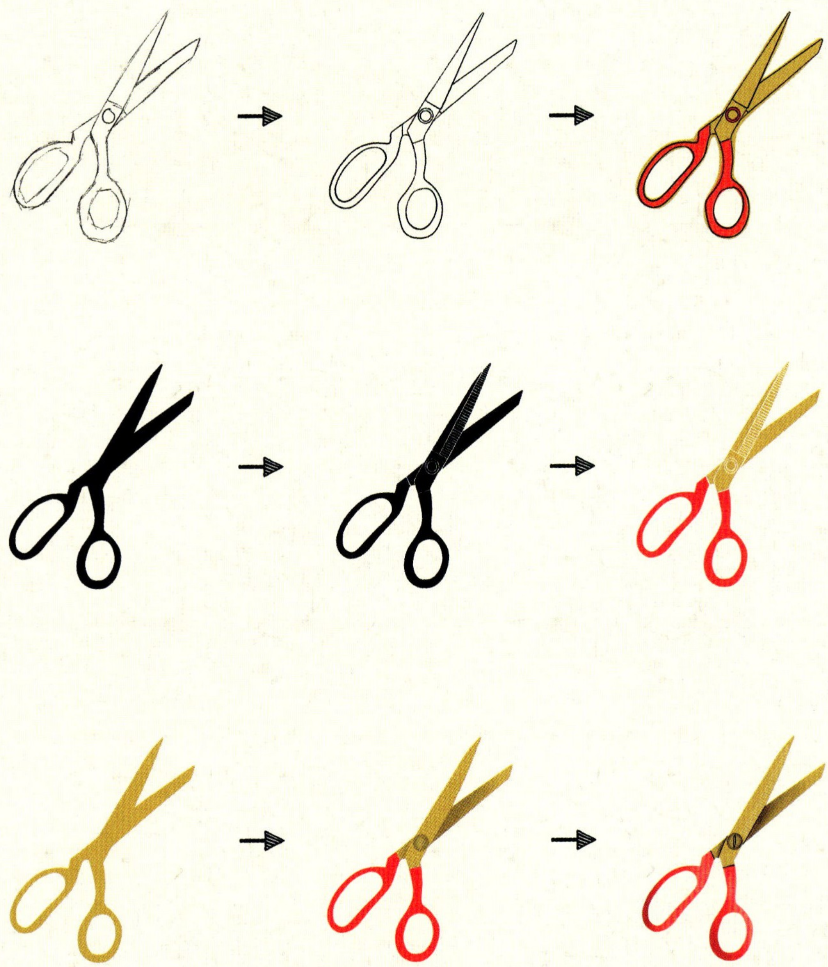

Reductive drawing is the process of removing material from a solid shape in order to reveal its form. You can easily control the amount of detail by choosing what to erase. The (optional) final step is to add color using **Color Drop** or the **Hue, Saturation, Brightness** tool.

Additive drawing is the process of adding layers (like we did with the flowers above) to create texture, highlights, and shadows. The first step is to create a solid silhouette of the shape. If I know I'll add shadows on one part of the object, I'll put the two pieces on separate layers (like the two sides of the scissors in this case). Next, I'll add some shading on a **Clipping Mask** layer using the **Gritty Shading** brush. Finally, I'll add in little details like the hash marks on the scissors, shadows on the screw, and highlights on the handles.

Try it out! Choose some objects that would add context or interest to your next lettering composition, and try illustrating them using all three methods described above. Testing out multiple ways of drawing the same object is a great way to quickly expand your skill-set and to start developing your personal style!

Next, try to integrate some illustrations into a finished composition. You could even re-use a lettering project you created previously and see what it would look like with some illustrated elements.

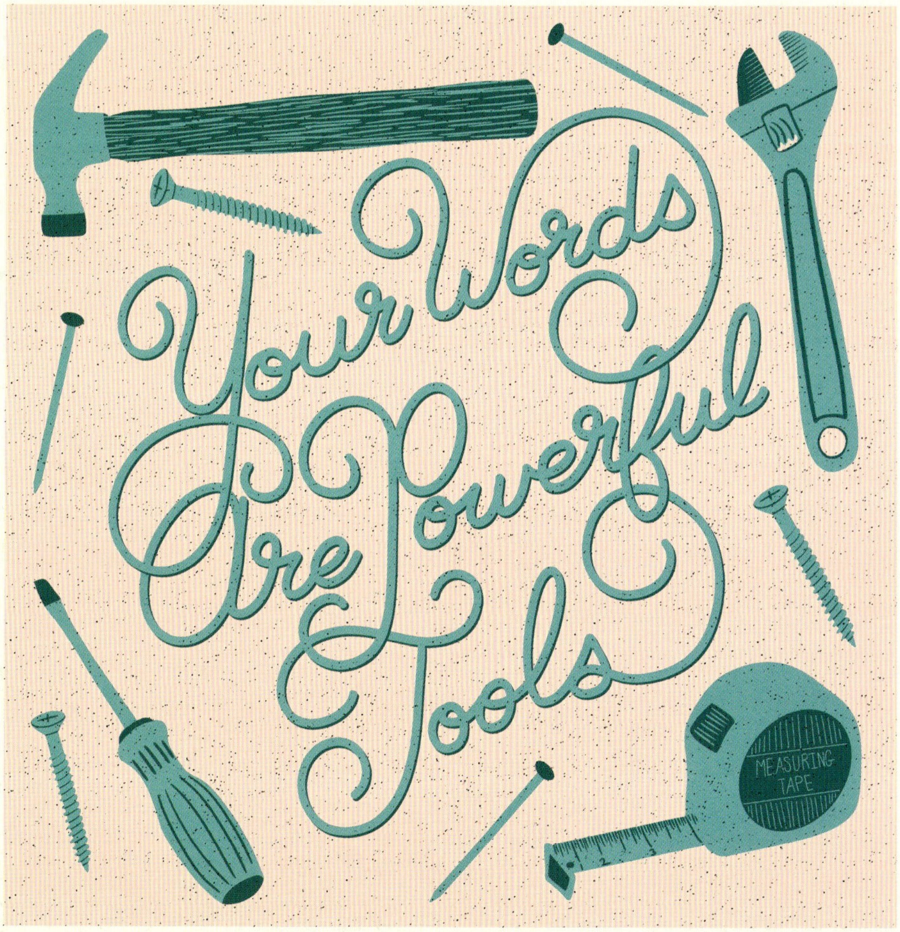

For example, I liked the monoline composition that I showed earlier in the chapter, but I felt like it was missing something, so I added some illustrations to create more visual interest on the canvas. While the quote isn't talking about literal tools, the play on words makes for a more fun and interesting composition.

So far, every composition we've created has begun with lettering and been followed by adding decorative elements around the lettering. However, there are times when you'll get a good idea for decorations before you even know what lettering to use. In that case, you can start by sketching and creating the illustrations, then add in the lettering that matches the theme and style of the decorations.

Of course, you will always think of more ways to decorate your work as you create new lettering pieces, so keep experimenting with new decorative elements each time you create a composition.

In the next chapter, we'll bring together all the skills you've learned so far to create complex and intricate lettering compositions that combine serif, sans serif, and script lettering with detailed decorative elements. If you feel like you need more practice on the foundational steps we've learned to this point, now is a great time to go back and practice the skills and processes covered in the previous chapters.

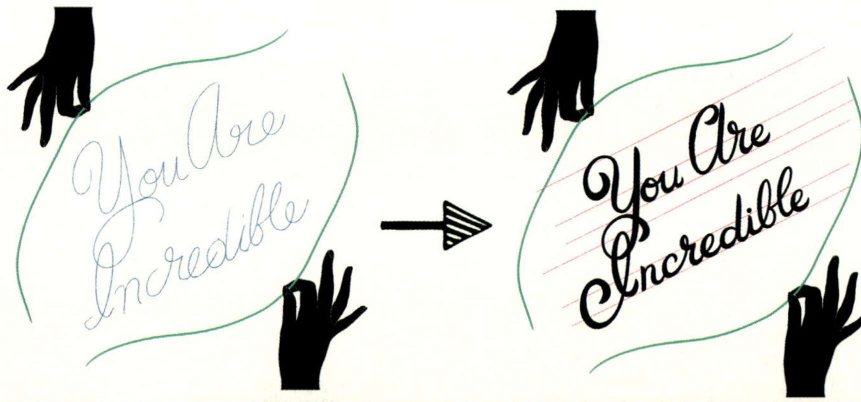

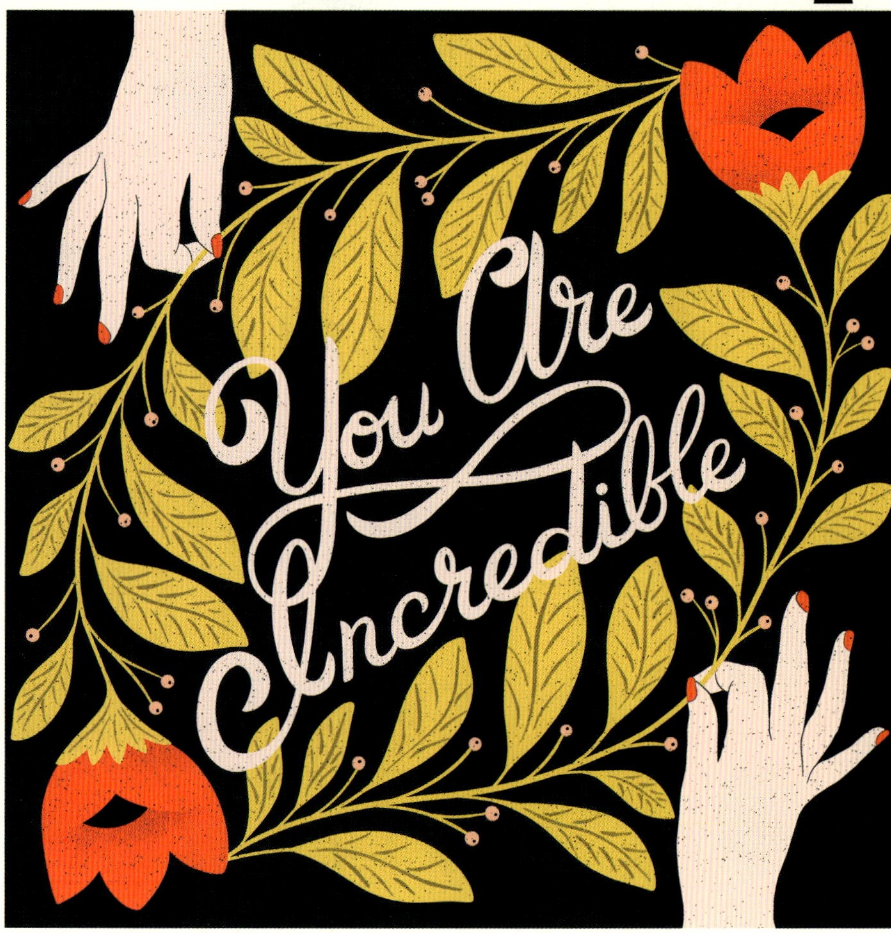

Sometimes you'll get an idea for decoration before you know what lettering to use!

CHAPTER 8

Combining Letterform Styles

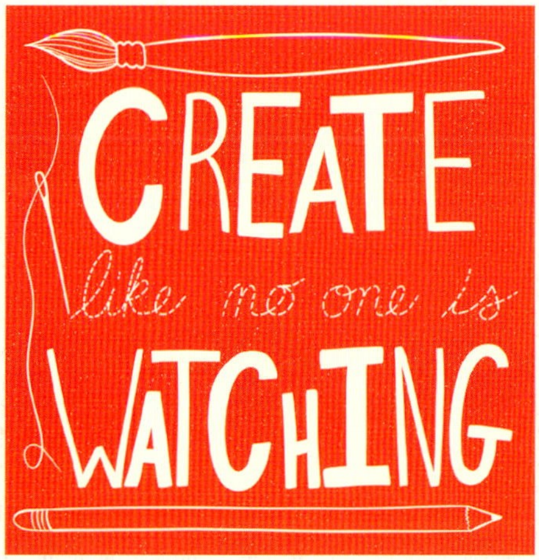

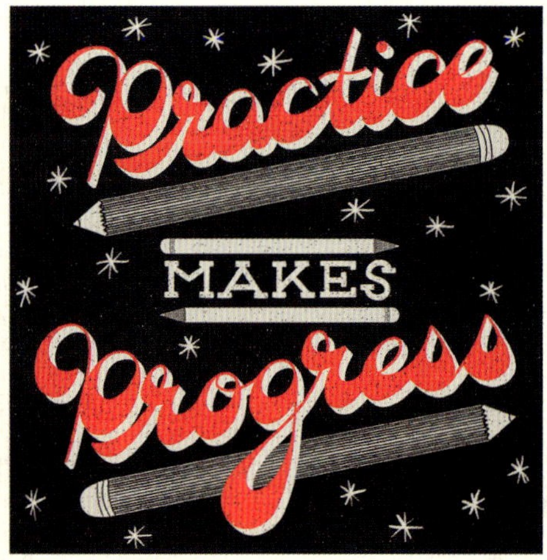

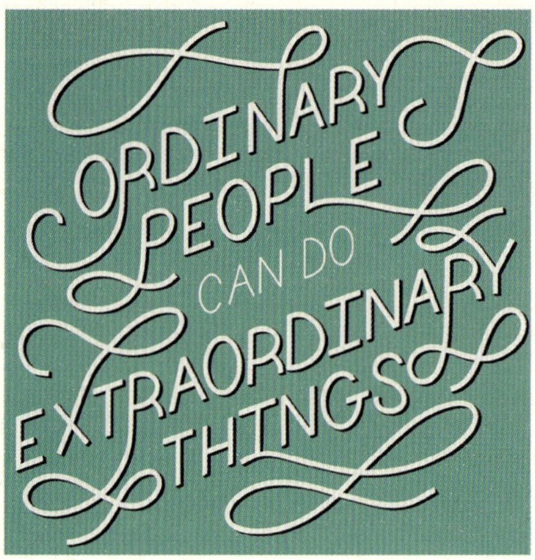

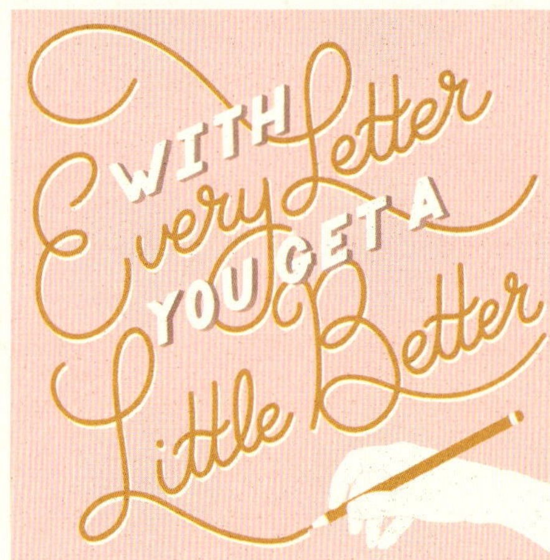

Now that we've covered the basics of building letterforms and decorating our compositions, let's take a look at how to combine letterform styles in a way that effectively communicates the message we want to convey.

In this chapter, we will cover the following principles, which will help you make decisions when combining letter styles:

- Consider the mood.
- Establish a hierarchy.
- Create contrast.
- Design intentional guides and slants.
- Pair opposites.
- Don't go overboard.
- Stay open to options.
- Stay organized.

Consider the Mood

Every letter style has a mood associated with it that helps communicate the message of the phrase. The mood can be a feeling, a genre, a time period, or a combination of all three!

For example, a calligraphy-style script might communicate sophistication and elegance, so it would be well suited for a wedding announcement or black tie-event. However, that same script on a child's birthday party invitation would be somewhat out of place.

When combining letter styles, consider the mood of the phrase first and then choose letter styles that don't conflict with that mood. At the same time, try to avoid using two styles that conflict with each other. For example, pairing a graffiti style with elegant calligraphy would result in a conflict of moods.

Graffiti is gritty and textural, and references a cultural and artistic style that can be seen as aggressive or edgy. Calligraphy is gentle and sophisticated, and alludes to a refined sensibility. Therefore, these two styles communicate very different messages and don't work well together.

Of course, there may be cases where you intentionally want to create a clash of moods, but for most compositions the goal is to find a single mood and stick with it throughout the piece. Once you choose a letter style with a clear mood, use other letter styles that share the same mood, are complementary to it, or are neutral enough that they don't conflict with the primary words.

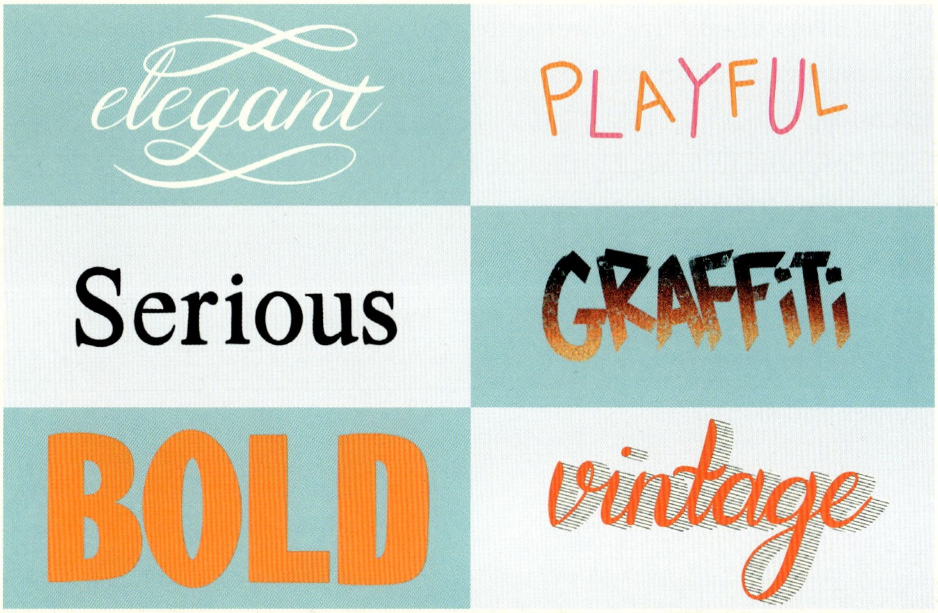

Establish a Hierarchy

Your job as a letterer is to clearly communicate to the viewer what part of the phrase is most important. Each time you start working on a phrase, you should first consider the importance of each word. You can number the words in order of importance or circle the most important words as a reminder to make those words stand out.

One way to begin thinking about a possible hierarchy for the words in a composition is to imagine that the only way to present the quote is by typing. Which words would you put in all caps or italics to tell the viewer those words are most important to the idea?

For our next project, I will use the phase below, and I need to determine which words to emphasize. Read the sentences below in which different words have been emphasized with all caps, and consider how the emphasis changes the meaning:

- With EVERY letter you GET a little better.
- WITH every letter you get a LITTLE better.
- With every LETTER you get a little BETTER.
- With EVERY LETTER you get a LITTLE BETTER.

You can see how a shift in hierarchy can change the meaning of a phrase. The first and second versions are a bit strange because they emphasize words that aren't truly important to the intended meaning of the phrase, which results in a confusing message. I think the last option makes the most sense for this phrase, so I will use bold, loopy lettering for the primary (or most important) words and plain sans serif lettering for the secondary words. With this piece, I want to communicate positivity, creativity, and progress. I think the playful script fits this mood, and it is bold enough to overpower the secondary words.

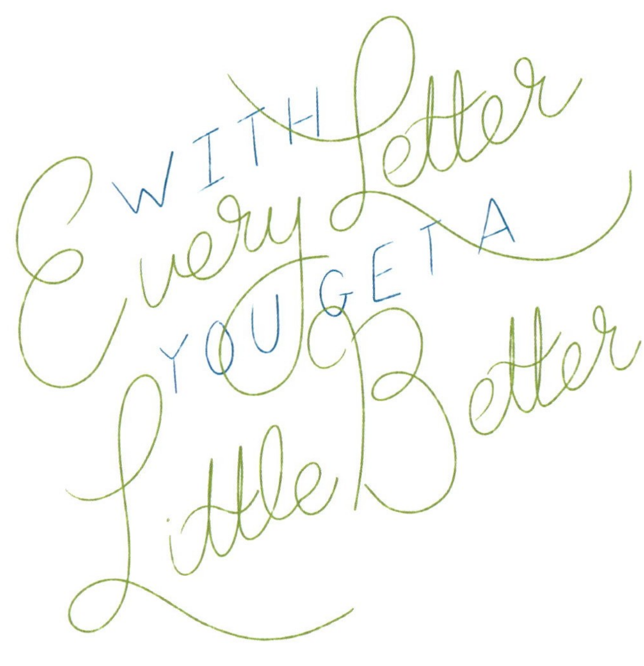

Create Contrast

Once you decide on the hierarchy for your phrase, you can consider the many ways to differentiate the letter styles in your composition using contrast. You can use size, thickness, color, serifs, and placement to identify which words are most important. For example, you might make the more important words twice as thick as the less important words or use a bold perspective layer on the more important words. These techniques help to avoid competition between letter styles and tell the viewer how to read the phrase using the emphasis you've placed on specific words.

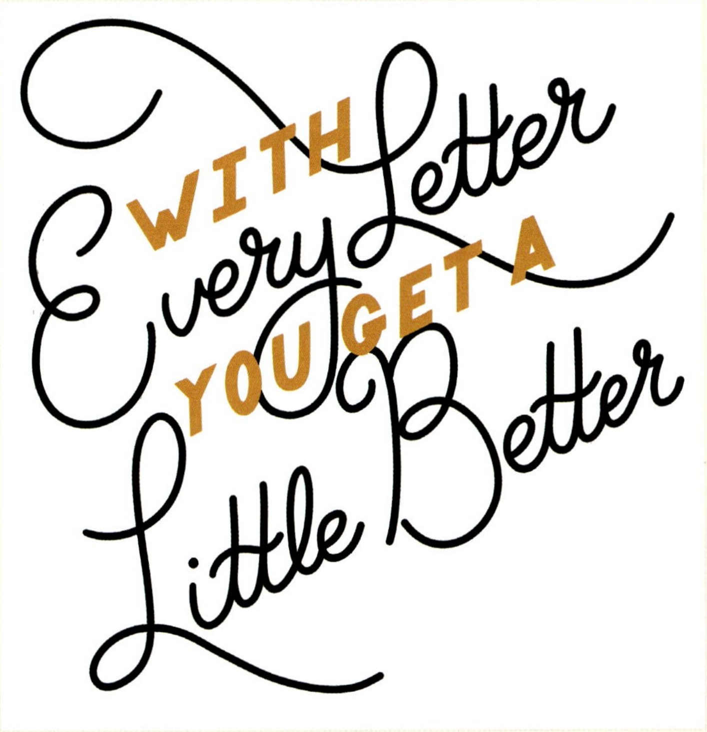

In this example, I made my sans serif lettering three times the thickness of my monoline lettering, and I gave the monoline letters lots of curls and loops to create clear contrast between the two letter styles.

Design Intentional Guides and Slants

As you create the guides and slant lines for your composition, it's important to think about consistency. For example, if you have one set of words at a 45-degree slant and the other at a 47-degree slant, they might look similar but they'll still create a feeling of discord within the composition. It's better to make the two slants either exactly the same or totally different so that the viewer can clearly see the intentionality of your letter slants. The same goes for the baseline.

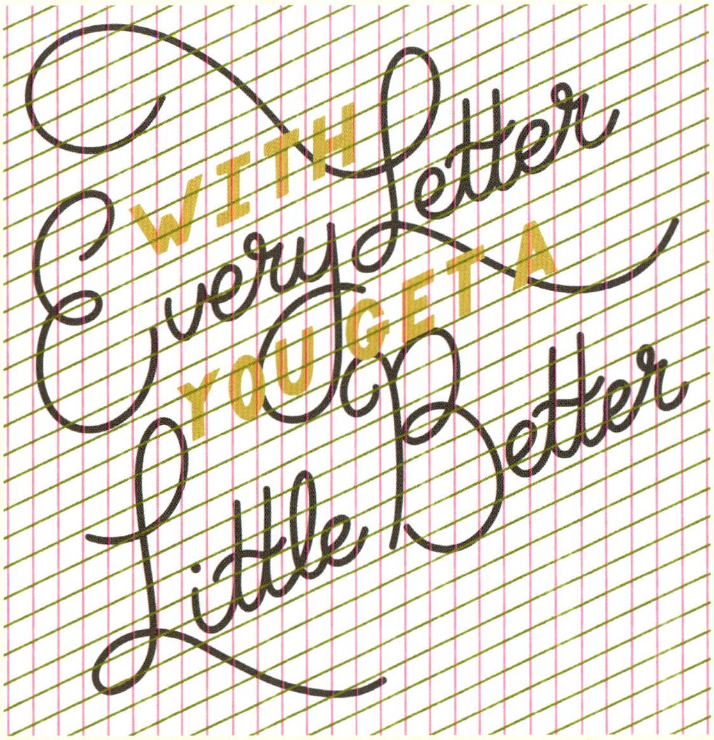

Notice how the baselines and slant lines match for the serif and sans serif letters.

You can see in this example (left), the baselines are all at the same angle for both the monoline and sans serif letters. The vertical slant is straight up and down on all the letters.

Pair Opposites

The easiest way to combine letter styles while creating contrast and a clear hierarchy is to choose two opposite styles, without mixing moods of course. For example, because I chose a thin, curvy monoline script, I combined it with a chunky, plain sans serif. If you're at a loss of what style to pair with a script, just keep it simple and use a plain sans serif.

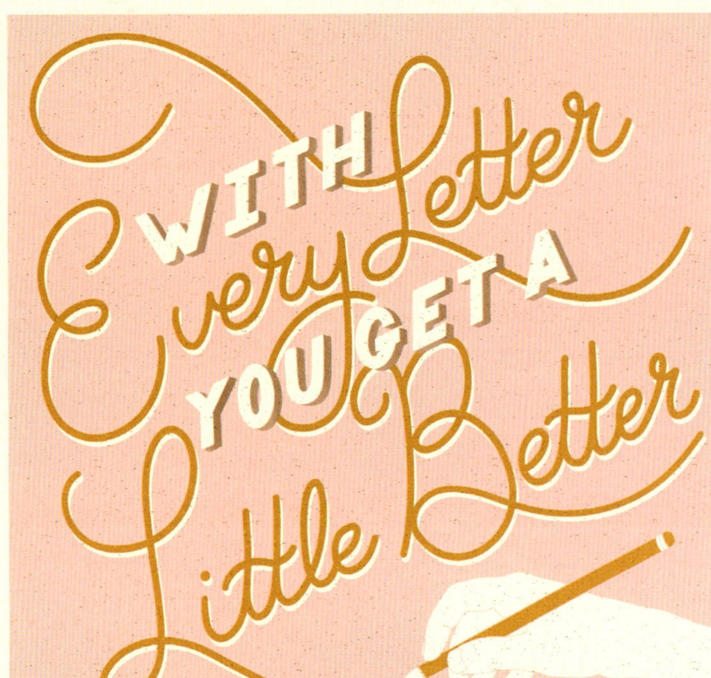

Despite not being exact opposites, serif and sans serif styles actually pair quite well together. Just be sure to use contrast to differentiate the two styles.

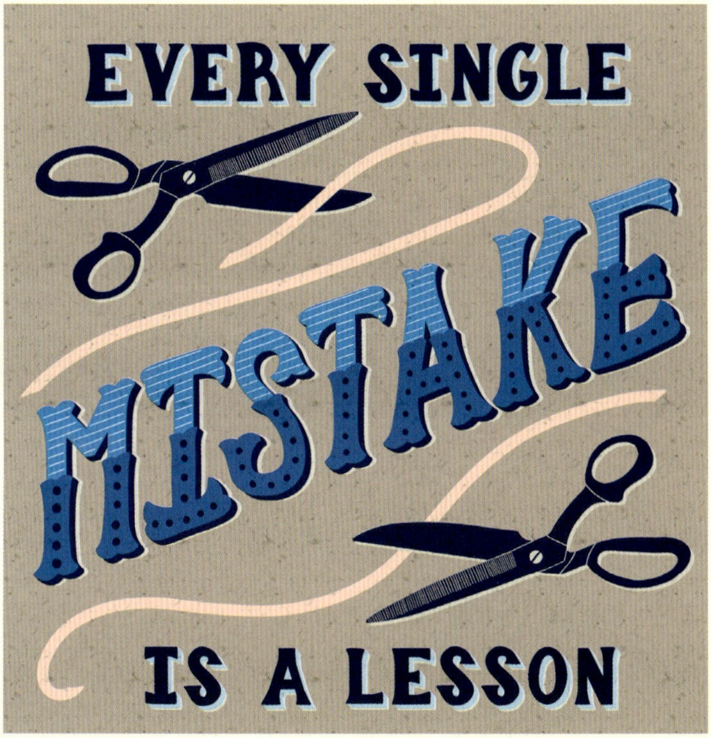

Don't Go Overboard

For beginners, combining two letter styles without creating any conflict can be challenging. When you feel comfortable with combining two styles, try adding a third! Keep in mind that using more than three letter styles is risky, even for expert letterers. Most designers recommend sticking to two styles most of the time. However, we know that rules in art are meant to be broken so try combining more if you get the urge!

Stay Open to Options

It's unlikely that your first idea for a composition will also be your best idea. I don't think I have ever finished a composition with the exact same plan I had in the beginning! As you're creating your composition, try to stay open to alternative ideas. Even if you're happy with how it looks, why not try the letters in a different size or width? Why not try adding another perspective layer or adjusting the colors? This process of adjusting and refining is something that every creative must do in order to find the best solution for a composition.

Stay Organized

As you start creating more complex compositions, and using a lot of layers to keep everything separate, your Layers panel may get a bit confusing. I like to group layers in order to easily shift and adjust layers that must stay together (like the perspective and shadows for a letter style).

To group layers, follow these steps:

STEP 1: On the Layers panel, select the layers you want to group by tapping on one, swiping right with one finger on the others, and then tapping **Group** at the top of the Layers panel.

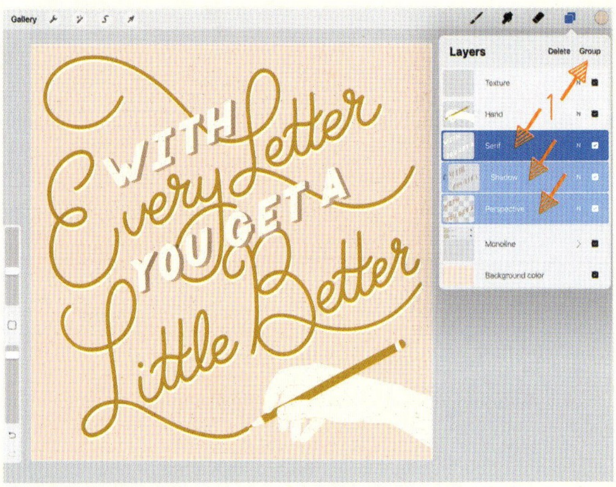

STEP 2: Tap twice on the words "New group," tap **Rename**, and then name your group.

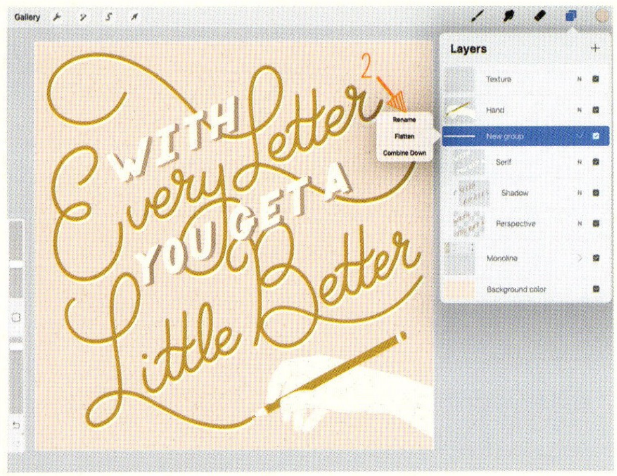

STEP 3: Use the arrow beside the group name to open or collapse the group.

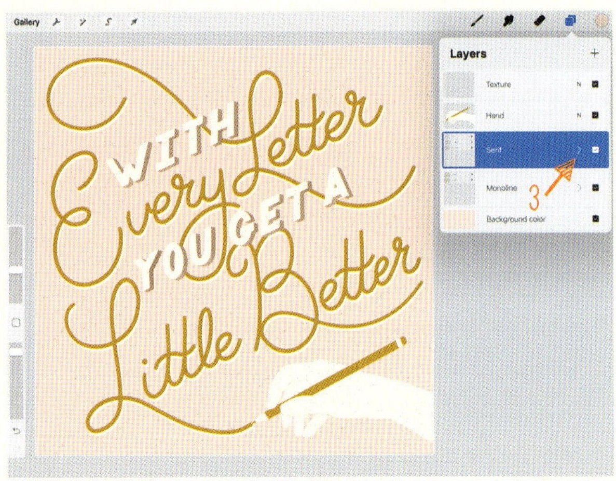

The Principles in Practice

Now that we've looked at the principles for combining letterforms, let's put them into practice. In the next composition (top right), I started with a chunky, curvy script, so I needed a contrasting script to complement it. The slab serif is the complete opposite of the angled, fat-bottomed script: It's thin, angular, and it sits on a straight baseline.

If you're ever at a loss for what lettering styles to pair, just try using a smaller, simpler version of the primary words. In this example (bottom right), I made the secondary words in the same style as the primary words, but I didn't give them any perspective or flourishes, which places the emphasis on the most important words.

In this composition (opposite, top), I wanted to clearly reflect the mood of the phrase in the mood of the letter styles. To do this, I combined a playful, offbeat sans serif with an illustrated script. The theme of the phrase is to let loose and create without fear or concern about doing it right. Therefore, a fun, rule-breaking letter style is the perfect vehicle to communicate that feeling.

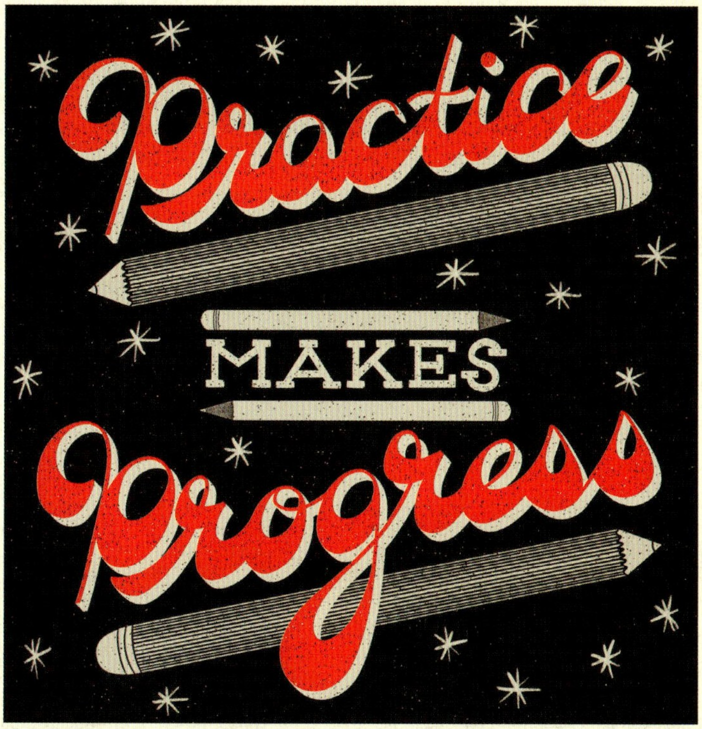

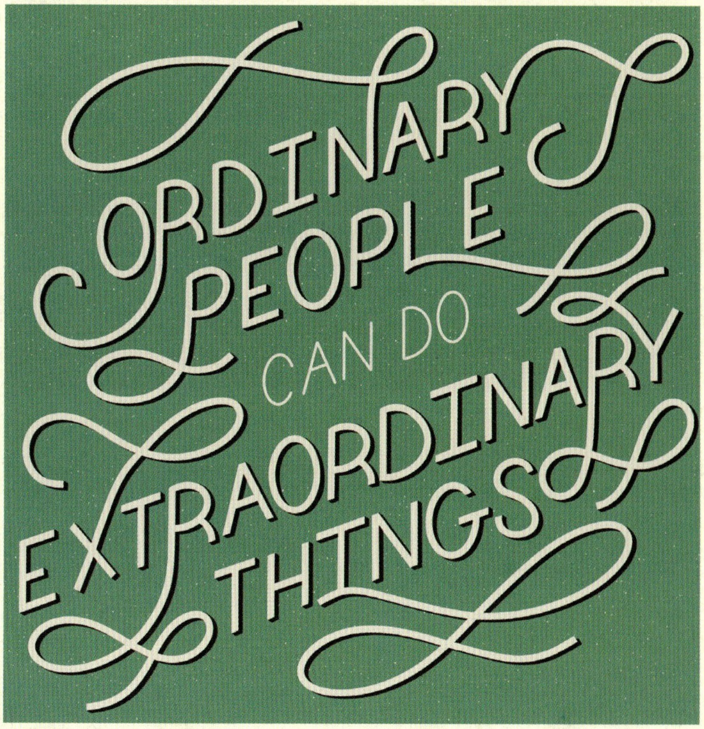

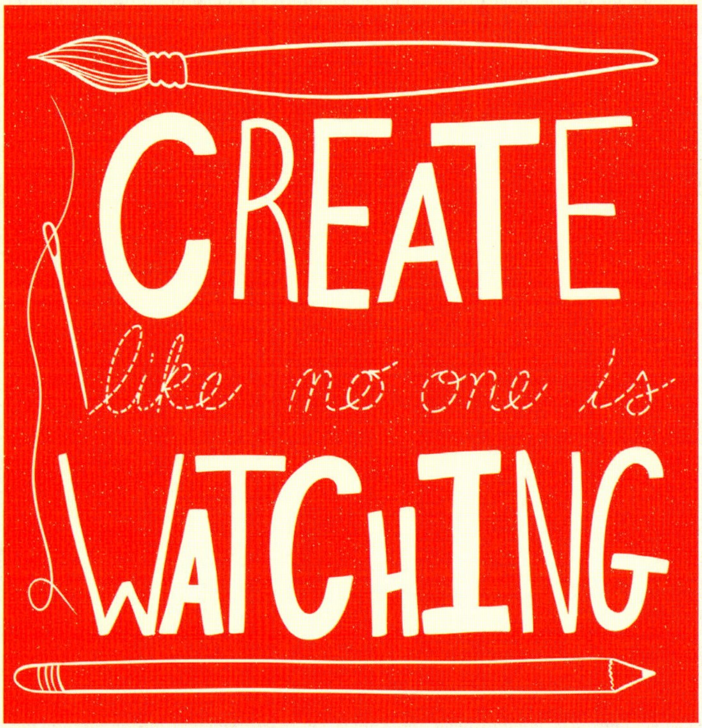

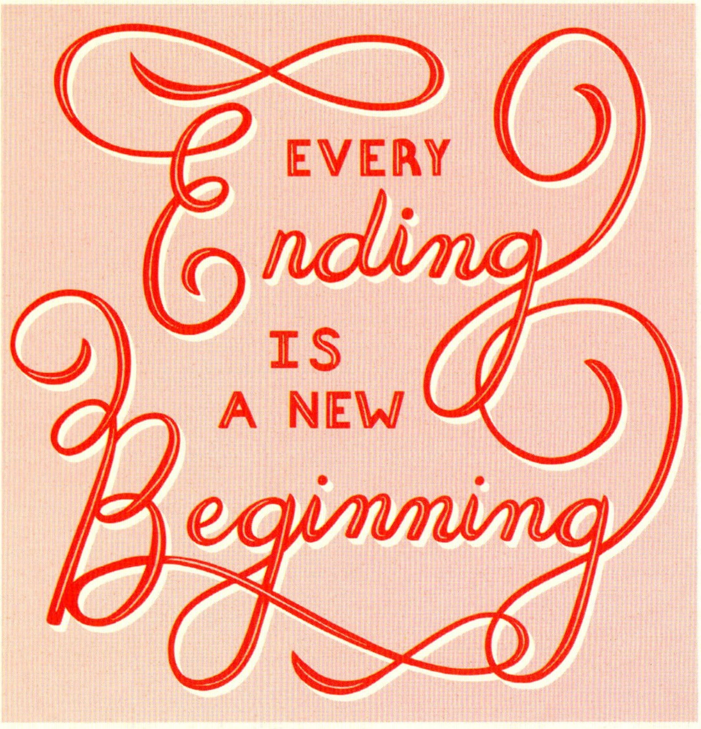

For the last composition, I wanted some bold, loopy lettering for the primary words and a simple sans serif for the secondary words. I wanted to unify the two types of lettering, so I added the same kind of line on the thickest parts of each letter. If you're having trouble getting two types of letterforms to work well together, add some kind of unifying element to both of them so the eye reads them as a set. You can see that I made a perspective layer only on the primary words, because I wanted those to stand out more than the secondary words.

Now that you've had a ton of practice creating letterforms and combining letter styles, it's time to start sharing your work with the world! In the next chapter, we'll look at ideas and methods for sharing your work online and in print.

CHAPTER 9

Sharing and Critiquing Your Work

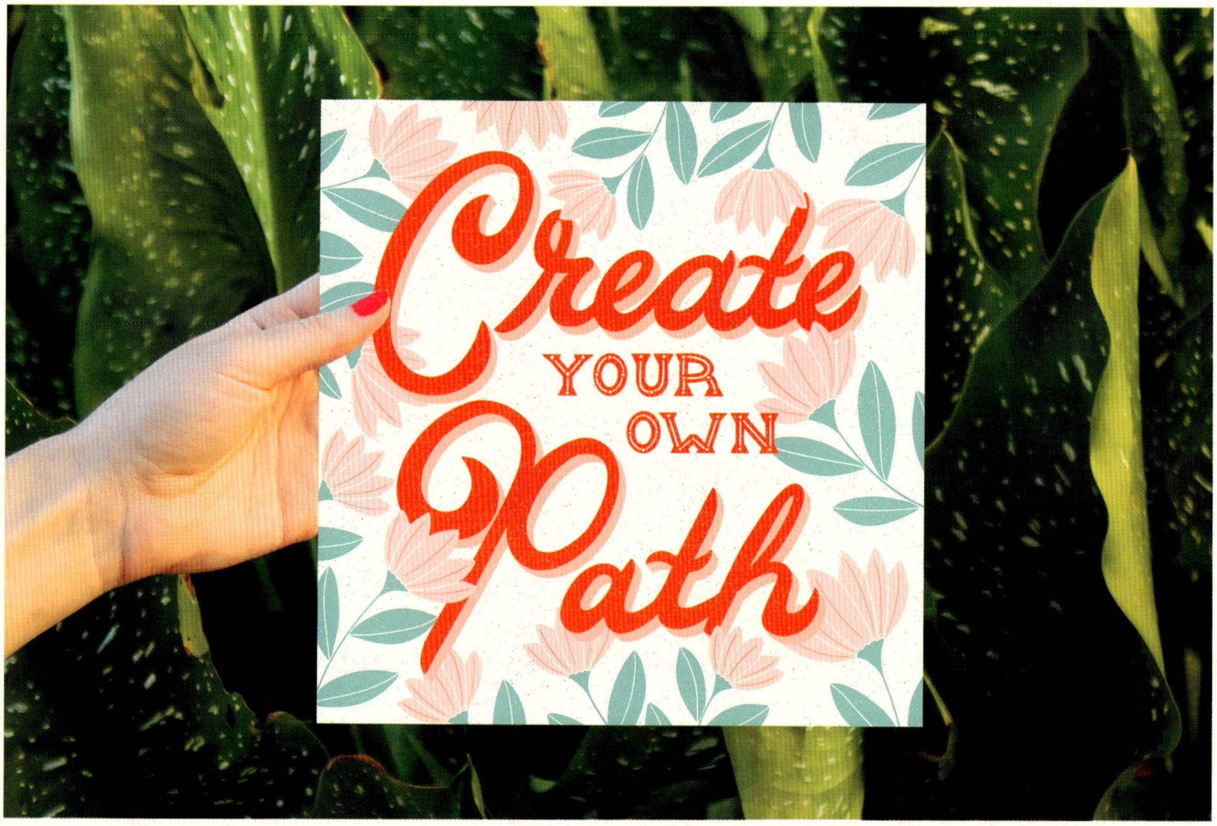

Sharing your work is a great way to get feedback, find potential clients, and engage with other letterers online and in the real world. There are endless ways to present and use your hand lettering pieces, many of which you'll discover as you begin the process of sharing your work online. In this chapter, we'll look at a few of the best sharing options and discuss some important things to consider when you're finally ready to present your work to the world.

Places to Share

Of course you can always share your work on social media platforms, your website, and the Facebook group mentioned in chapter 1, but there are also plenty of real-world applications for hand lettering. Next time you go to a grocery store or gift shop, look around at the product packaging, magazine covers, and greeting cards. Hand lettering is everywhere! There is a growing demand for beautiful lettering in all kinds of physical and digital applications, so as you expand your lettering portfolio, consider both the conventional and unconventional ways to share your work.

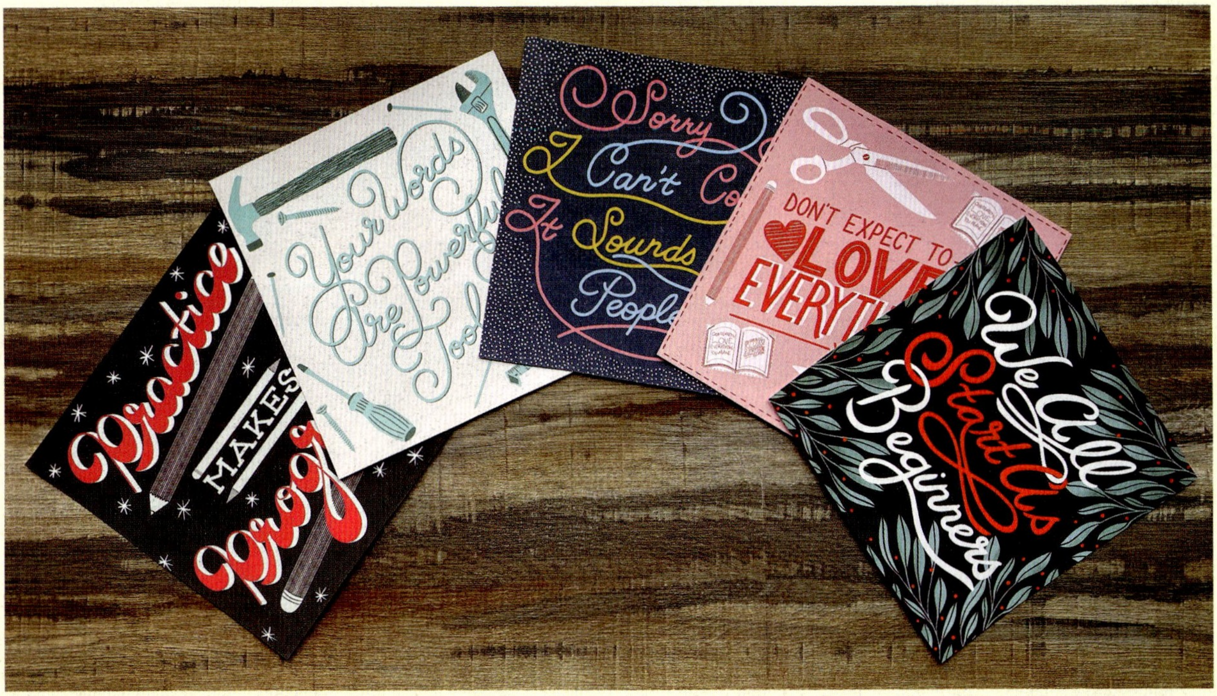

For example, you could do any of the following:

- Reach out to local companies, and ask if they would commission you to hand letter a logo or promotional materials.
- Send your lettering portfolio to art licensing agents, and ask if they would represent you and help you find clients.
- Create a series of greeting cards, and present them as samples to local shops and galleries where you would like to sell your work.
- Create a flyer or poster for your band, church, book club, or local event.
- On your website, offer your lettering as prints for sale or allow free downloads of your pieces to help grow your email list.
- Start a business for hand lettered invitations, cards, posters, and so on.

The options are only limited by your imagination! Let's look at a few different ways to share your work online and in print, and cover some of the important considerations for each approach.

Sharing Digital Images

As we covered in chapter 3, when exporting images from Procreate to social media apps, the JPEG file format is recommended for most online uses. Most social media sites downsize your images considerably, so you don't have to worry about changing the size of the image first.

However, what if you share images on your website or another online portfolio? In this scenario, it's important to protect your work from being stolen, so be sure to downsize it so no one can save the original image and then reuse it somewhere else without permission.

To downsize an image, follow these steps:

1. Export the lettering composition as a JPEG file in Procreate.
2. Create a new canvas at 4″ × 4″ at 300 DPI. You could use any size here, but be sure to use a size that is just big enough for your intended use but not so big that someone could easily steal the image and print it out at full size.
3. Tap the **Actions** menu, tap **Add**, and tap **Insert a Photo**.
4. Select the lettering composition you exported in step 1.
5. Save the new, smaller file as a JPEG.

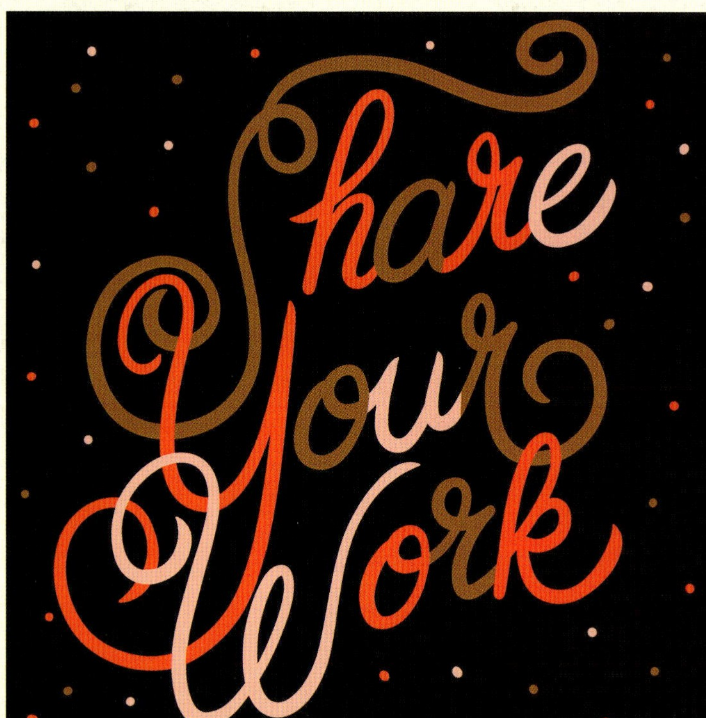

Now that you have a smaller version of the file, you can freely share it online without worrying that someone will use the original at full size. Some letterers also like to include their signature on each composition, so if it gets shared online without your authorization, at least everyone will know who the creator is.

When you first start sharing your work with the world, it's normal to feel some anxiety about the images being stolen or reused in ways you don't approve of, but it's important you don't allow that feeling to prevent you from sharing at all. Remember that while there is always a possibility that someone will reuse your work in a way you don't like, it's also possible that a client, a company, or an art buyer will see your work and will want to work with you. Don't let fear dampen or outshine your goals of finding great opportunities and sharing your beautiful compositions with the world!

Sharing Time-lapses

As we talked about in chapter 3, you can share Time-lapse videos that show your whole lettering process from start to finish. This can be a great way to show your followers how much work you put into your lettering projects, but keep in mind that showing your Time-lapse also gives away your process for others to copy. Therefore, it may not be the ideal way to share certain compositions, especially those you plan to eventually monetize in some way.

I share many of my Time-lapse videos in the Facebook group mentioned in chapter 1, so check out the group to see the full processes of my lettering compositions featured in this book.

Printing Your Work

Printing your pieces on greeting cards, posters, gift wrap, and many other products is a great way to show off your work to friends, family, and even businesses that might be interested in your work. There are many options for printing, so we'll look at just a few of the most popular ones

If you have a home printer, you can do a test print of a finished composition to see if the printer produces high-quality prints. If the print looks good, you could certainly use your home printer to print your work, although keep in mind that regular printer ink is not archival, meaning it will fade with time, especially if exposed to light. If the print is blurry or dull, it might be better to seek out a local professional printer or use an online printing service for your work.

Some things to consider before printing are the vibrancy, brightness, and saturation levels of the image. Many inks and papers will dull the colors slightly, so you may need to increase the saturation and brightness of the image (in the **Adjustments** menu) before printing, and you should perform several test prints until is looks it right. Be sure not to use the last sheet of your favorite paper on the first print!

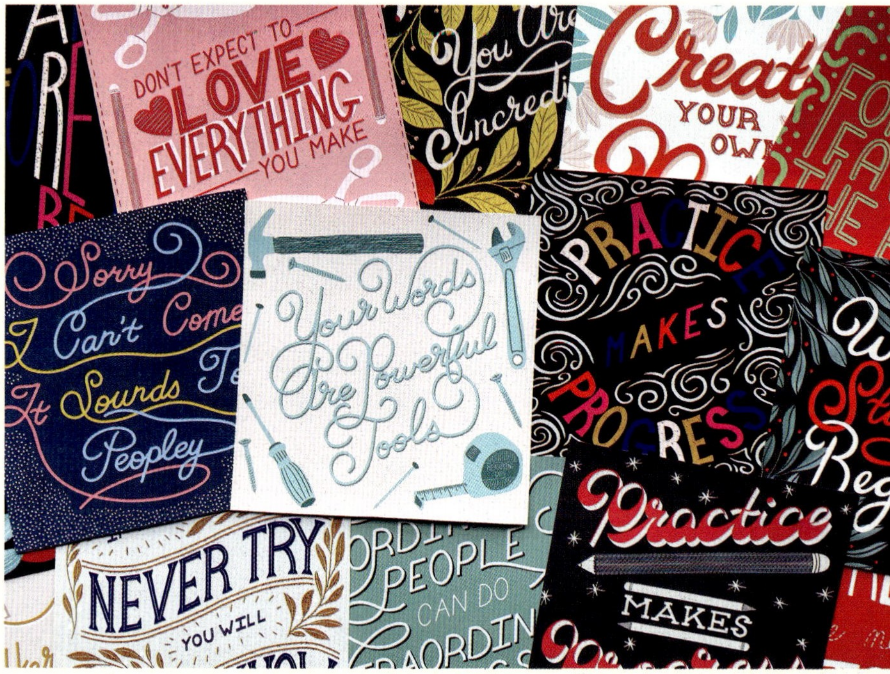

You can see in the bottom image that the colors on the screen are darker and more vibrant than the colors on the print. This is a common occurrence when printing on paper, and many print companies will compensate for this difference by calibrating their printers to print darker than the actual image file. However, not all printers do this, so it's best to make a test print if you have specific color needs. In this case, if I want my print to have the same coloring as seen on the screen, I would duplicate the document and create a darker, more vibrant version using the **Hue, Saturation, Brightness** tool, and then I would do test prints, making adjustments until I achieve a satisfactory result.

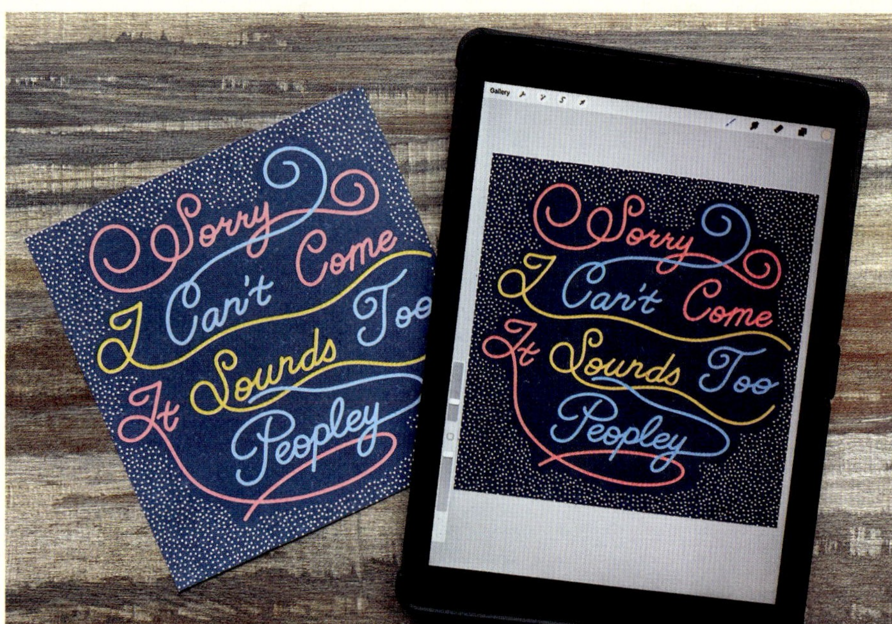

Colors might become duller when printed, so making the digital image more vibrant can help the printed colors better match the colors of the original image.

Most cities have professional print

shops or office supply stores that can work with you to be sure you get a high-quality print. Some things to consider when talking to a print shop are:

- What is the intended use for the print?
- Does it need to last for years, or is it just a sample to show to clients?
- What size paper do you need?
- What surface do you want to print on (glossy, matte, textured, etc.)?
- Are you concerned about color vibrancy being lost?
- Can the image be reprinted at no cost if it doesn't look right the first time?
- Are there discounts for large orders?

Of course, there are many great options online as well, so check out online sources for printing if you don't have local options available. Some of my favorites are FinerWorks.com and GicleeToday.com.

Sharing Printed or In-Progress Work

Once you print out your work, you'll have a beautiful print to share both in person and online. You can then take your prints to interesting settings and photograph them one at a time, or show multiple prints in one photograph.

The best lighting for taking photos is overcast or indirect daylight, so go outside or near a bright window to take a high quality photograph. Take lots of pictures, and don't be afraid to try some of the more adventurous ways of showcasing your work. To add variety and character to your photographs, experiment with various backgrounds like plants, bricks, wood, or stone.

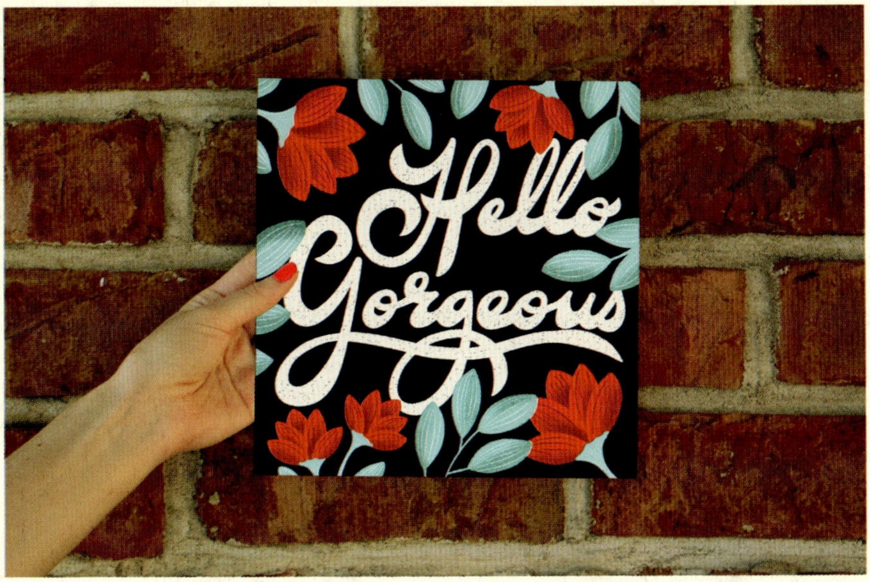

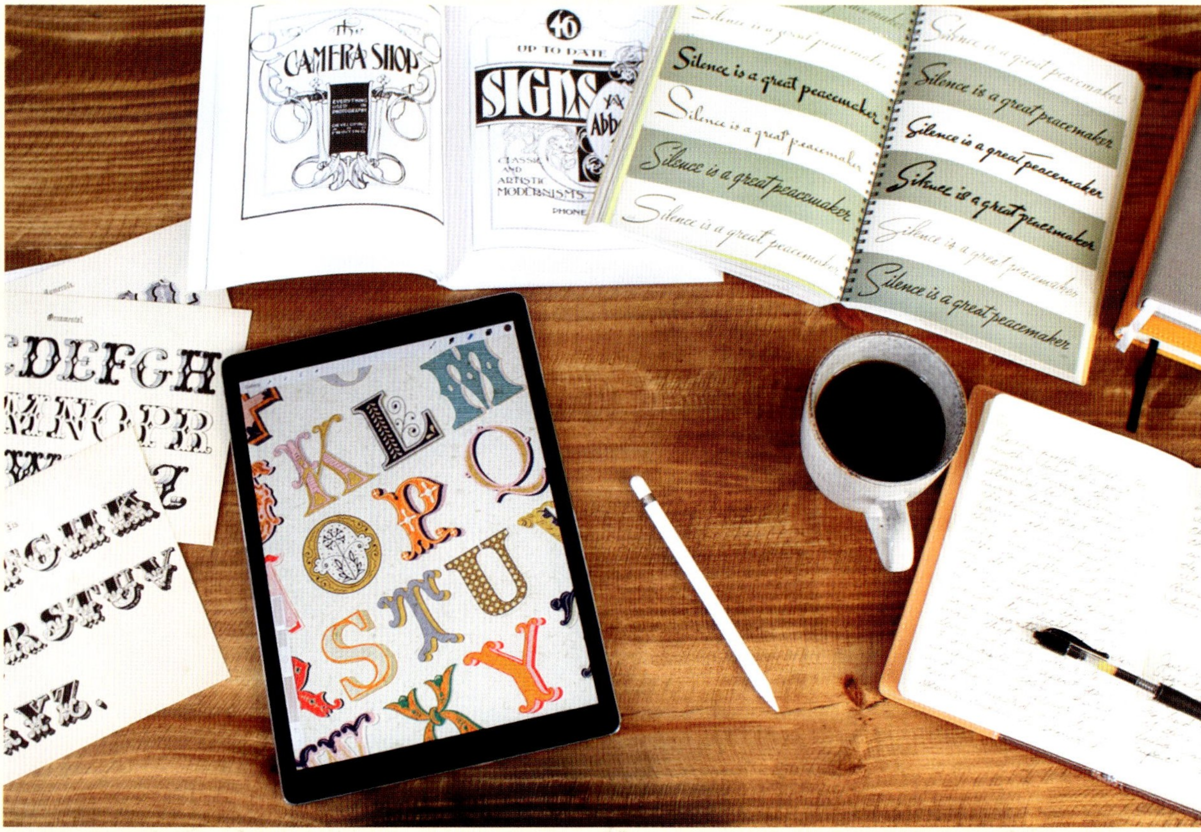

You can even display your process and inspiration by scattering some of your favorite inspiration elements around a table or desk and taking a photograph. People love to see an artist at work, so show your followers your desk, inspiration, favorite drink, and even a peek at your sketches and notes! Showing parts of your process can also help interested buyers see how much planning it takes to create a lettering composition, which increases the perceived value of your work.

Print on Demand

If you want to sell your prints online without having to invest in a printer or website, there are many great print-on-demand services that allow you to offer your work for sale on their websites. These companies print the work only when a customer has ordered it, so you don't have to pay anything up front for stocking your store. Some of my favorite print-on-demand websites include RedBubble.com, Society6.com, and Casetify.com. These companies allow you to sell your work on a wide range of products like art prints, clothing, furniture, wallpaper, buttons, and so much more.

Once you set up your print-on-demand store, you can use social media and your website to market your work and find interested buyers.

While all of the above options are great ways to sell your work, the only way to know which one will work for you is to try them. You can get advice about various platforms for selling your work in the Facebook group mentioned in chapter 1.

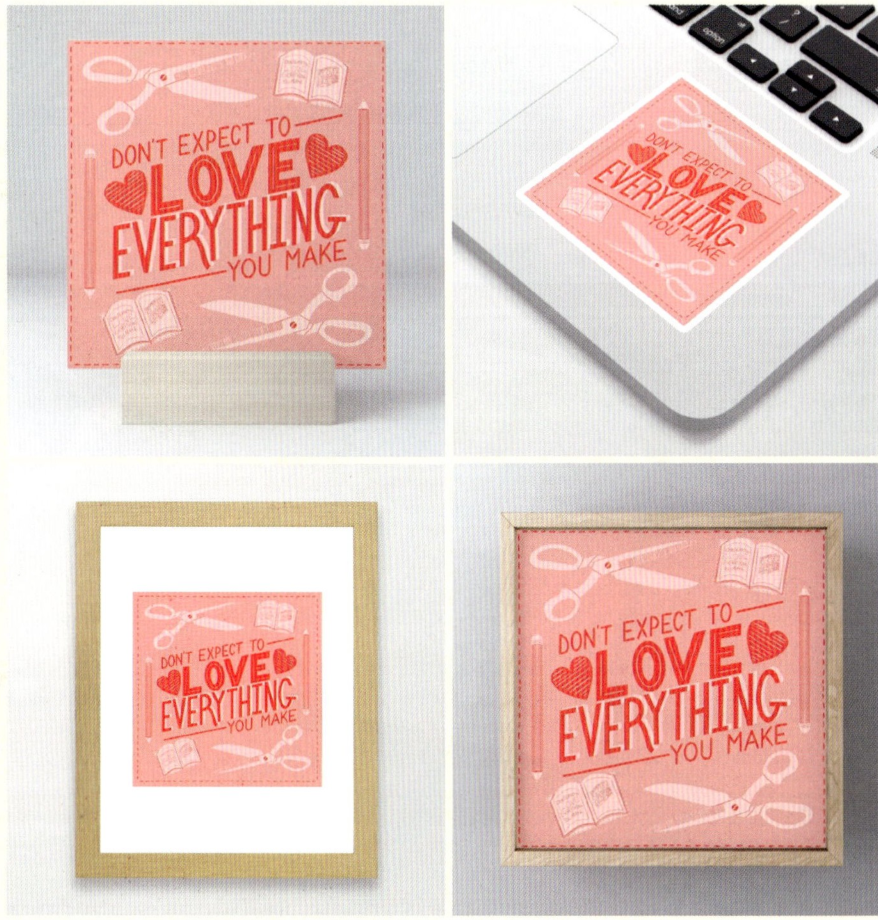

Mockups made using society6.com

Critiquing Your Work

After I have finished a new lettering composition, I put it away and I don't look at it for a few days. Right after you create something you may be so attached to the final result that you find it difficult to consider changing anything. Therefore, remember not to rush into critiquing, nor to do it at a time when you're tired or in a bad mood. When you are ready to critique your work, sit it down with a hot cup of your favorite drink, put the work on your desk or hang it on the wall so you can consider it carefully, and take some mental or actual notes about what could be changed to make it better.

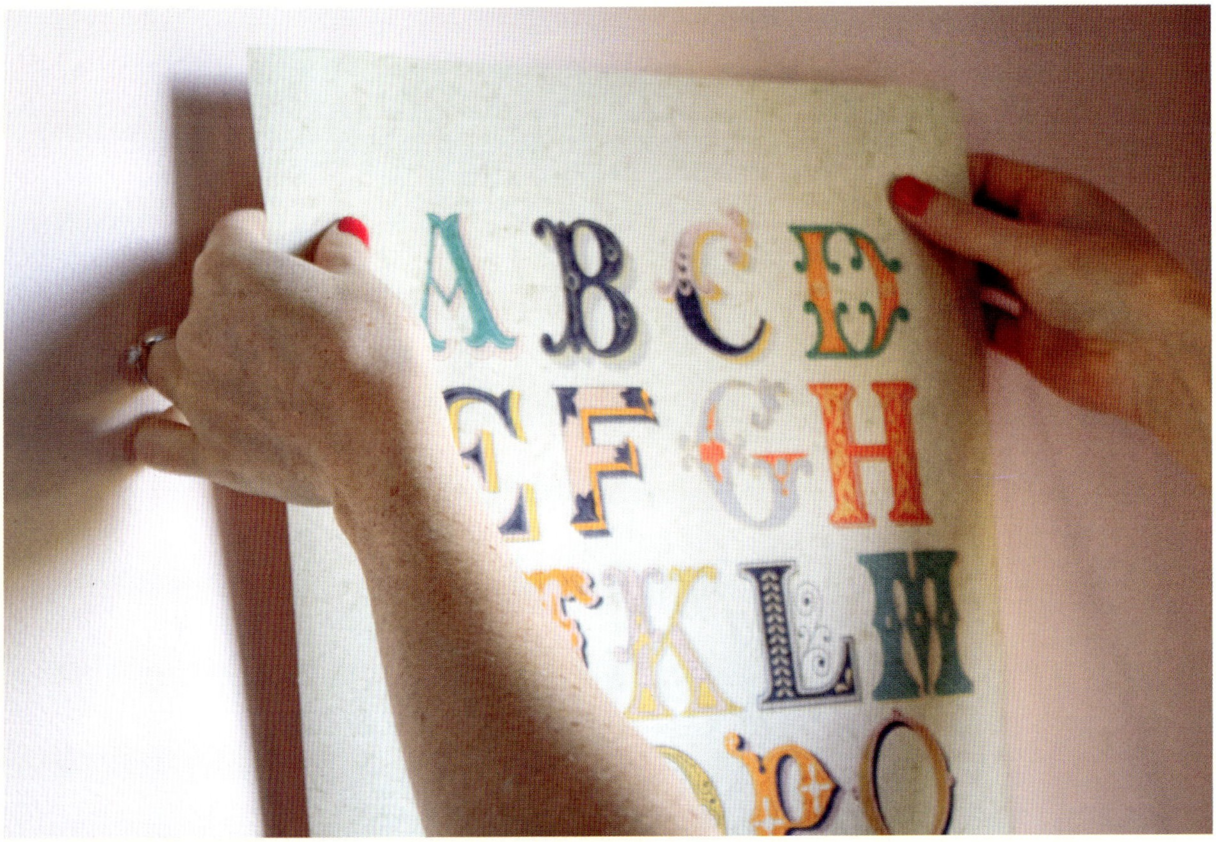

The first thing I like to do is to go through the design principles covered in chapter 5. Is the composition balanced? Does it have enough contrast? Is the color palette harmonious? Did I use scale and contrast to create emphasis on the most important words? Try not to spend too much time critiquing—just get started on making adjustments based on your observations. The longer you stare at a piece, the more problems you'll see, so just choose two or three of the most important things to adjust and go from there.

Remember that you are on a path to slowly improving your lettering, so not everything you make will be beautiful. You have to create some unsuccessful work in order to learn important lessons about lettering and composition. Sometimes your critique will become more of a lessons-learned session rather than a plan to alter the composition. It's okay to throw a lettering project in the trash and start over! It's also fine to critique only a few of your final compositions. Not everything you make has to be analyzed and questioned, so feel free to focus your time on creating rather than critiquing!

Most artists and designers share only a fraction of their work with the world. The rest is hidden away and chalked up to practice. The next time you make something you don't like, instead of viewing it as a waste of time, congratulate yourself for learning the lesson that piece taught you. Remember, if you have trouble critiquing your own work, you can always reach out to others in the Facebook group mentioned in chapter 1.

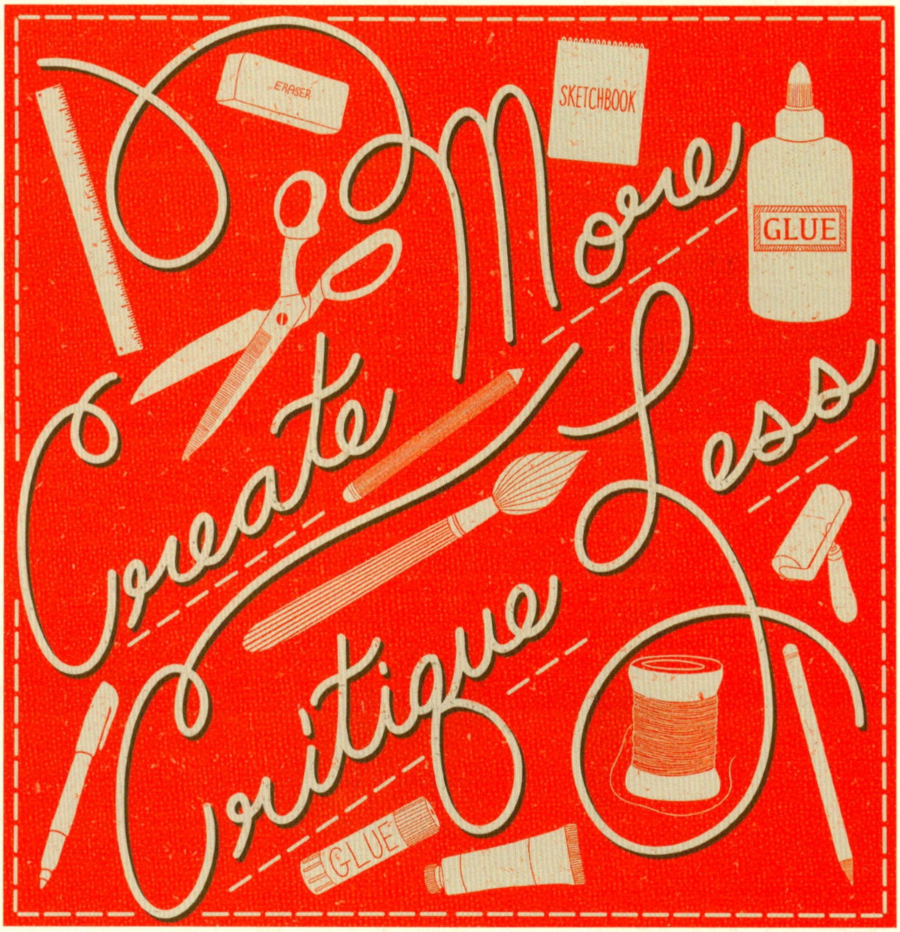

Critique vs. Criticism

The more you share your work with the world, the more comments and suggestions you'll get from others. Some will be helpful and constructive, while some will be blatantly rude or unintentionally hurtful. It's important to develop a thick skin and to recognize the difference between critique and criticism.

A **critique** contains a tangible and clear suggestion or observation that could possibly improve the work. For example, someone critiquing your work might say, "What if there were more berries on the left side of the canvas to balance out the ones on the right?" or "What if you made this letter a bit larger or changed the spacing so there is more breathing room in the middle?" While you might disagree with these types of suggestions, they are clear and justified by design principles, and they are an attempt to be helpful. While a critique may still contain a negative view of the work, it is based in knowledge of design principles and (hopefully) includes clear actionable solutions.

Criticism is not based on design principles and is often formed from an uninformed opinion. For example, someone might say, "I don't like these colors" or "It looks like a big toe." These types of vague and frivolous comments are not helpful and can plant a seed of negativity in the letterer's mind. Remember as you receive criticism, that art is ultimately subjective. Everyone has their own personal color and design preferences, so no matter how amazing your artwork might be, someone is going to hate it. Rather than taking criticism as a reflection on your work, consider that your artwork is just not for that person.

It's also important to consider who is doing the critiquing or criticizing. Critiquing takes training and knowledge of art and design principles, so try to develop the habit of placing more weight on the opinions of those you trust and respect, or who has some knowledge and experience in the field of art and design, rather than allowing every opinion to affect you equally. Remember that your Aunt Mable, as nice as she may be, is probably not qualified to critique your work. So don't take her comments too seriously.

Improving Your Work

The only way to improve your work is to keep lettering, critiquing, and making more compositions. Looking at beautiful lettering online will help you get an idea of how to improve, but it won't make your work better. Just like any skill, lettering has to be practiced to be mastered. If you ever feel frustrated that your lettering isn't improving fast enough, the best way to address that frustration is take out your iPad, open your Procreate app, and begin a new challenging composition.

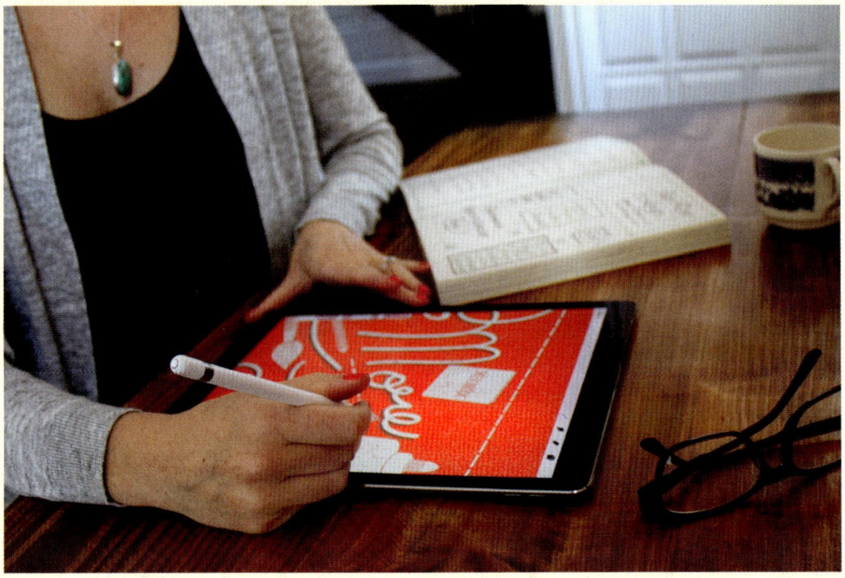

Also keep in mind that improvement often comes in waves. You might practice for weeks and feel like your lettering has not improved at all, then suddenly you look back at something you made a month earlier and realize you are light years ahead of your past skill level. Try to avoid focusing too much on short-term improvement, and instead look back every few months or so to judge your progress.

You might even consider creating a more structured long-term challenge for yourself, like committing to spend a certain amount of time on lettering every day for 30 days. You could spend 30 minutes a day practicing drawing letters, or try to complete one lettering composition per week. Whatever you decide, choose something that fits into your schedule so you'll be able to stick to it. Before you know it, you'll be surprising yourself with how beautiful your lettering has become!

Drawing Out Your Style

We often hear the phrase "find your style" in relation to art and design. I try never to use this phrase because it makes the process sound like you have to go out and search for your style, when it's exactly the opposite. Your style is not something "out there" that you have to find. It's something inside you that you can draw out by creating work and analyzing it. Of course you need some inspiration from the world to help you develop your style, but the answers to your questions about your style are all within you. The great news is, you already have a style even if you don't yet know what it is! Your job is to let your style out by giving yourself lots of opportunities to learn about your choices and decisions as a creator.

Just like improving your work, the only way to develop your style is to make lots of compositions and slowly figure out which colors and letterform styles you prefer. Your style will emerge as you create more compositions, and soon, people will recognize your work by the colors, illustrations, and letter styles you use.

Your style is also found in the unique and offbeat choices you make as a letterer. Don't be afraid to try something weird in your lettering, because often those weird ideas are the ones that differentiate your work from everyone else's.

Above all, stay true to your personal style. Following trends can help you get started, but the only way to differentiate your work from everyone else's is to combine your lettering, color, and drawing styles into a unique combination that only you could create. Think about the most notable artists and designers in history. What did they have that no one else had? Usually, it was a willingness to break the rules and try something no one had ever tried

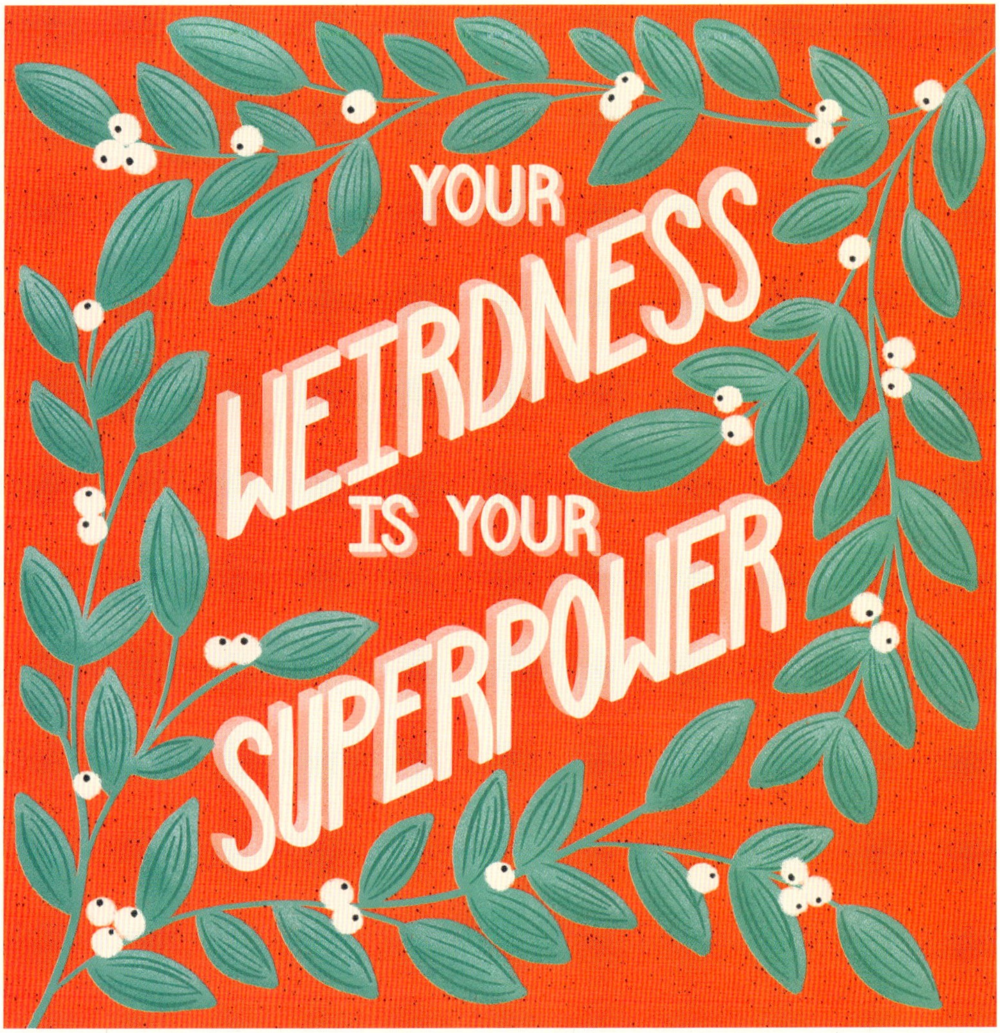

before. Therefore, if you get an interesting idea but are worried that it breaks the rules, don't hesitate to try it! Those risk-taking moments are the ones that will define your style and make your work stand out in the world.

References

All of the images referenced on this page were sourced from Archive.org, a 501(c)(3) non-profit building a digital library of cultural artifacts in digital form. They provide free access to researchers, historians, scholars, the print disabled, and the general public. Their mission is to provide universal access to all knowledge, so that those without access to libraries can share in the wealth of information in print. Check out their incredible database at Archive.org for endless lettering inspiration!

Page 8

Center Alphabet:

J.L.M., Lauweriks. "Quadratuuralfabet, Alphabet," *NAI Collection*, 1900.

Outer Alphabets:

Delamotte, Freeman. *The Signist's Book of Modern Alphabets, Plain and Ornamental, Ancient and Mediæval, from the Eighth to the Twentieth Century, with Numerals*. Chicago, F. J. Drake & co., 1906, pp. 28, 34, 62, 66, 74, 76, 82.

Page 30

American Type Founders Company. *Specimens of Type, Borders, Ornaments, Brass Rules and Cuts, Etc. : Catalogue of Printing Machinery and Materials, Wood Goods, Etc.* Chicago, American Type Founders, 1897, pp. 463, 476, 631, 633, 715, 749.

Page 31 (top left)

Newbery & Company. *Handbook of Plain and Ornamental Alphabets*. London, Newbery & Co., 1850, p. 10.

Page 31 (top right)

Newbery & Company. *Illuminated Initial Letters & Ancient and Modern Alphabets*. London, Newbery & Co., 1850, p. 10.

Page 31 (bottom left)

John Mauritz, Bergling. *Art Alphabets and Lettering*. Chicago, Blakely-Oswald Printing Co., 1914, p. 3.

Page 31 (bottom right)

Thomas, Newman. "Bee Culture." *American Bee Journal*, vol. 276, 1861.

Dingee & Conard Co. "Our New Guide to Rose Culture." *Henry G. Gilbert Nursery and Seed Trade Catalog Collection*, 1898.

Forbes, Archibald, and Hillard Atteridge. *Battles of the Nineteenth Century*. London, Cassel and Company, 1901, p. 232.

Directory Collection, Indianapolis City. *Logan's Indianapolis Directory*. Logan, 1867.

Joseph M., Wade. "Poultry Birds Natural History." *Fanciers' Jounral of Land & Water*, vol. 4, no. 7, 1877.

Page 32 (top to bottom)

"A Wholesaler's and Retailers' Journal." *Pacific Wine and Spirit Review*, Vol. 34, No. 1, 1895, p. 3.

The San Francisco, Oakland and Alameda Business Directory. San Francisco, Dalton & Co, 1880, p. 389.

Wm. H. Page & Co. *Specimens of Chromatic Wood Type, Borders, Etc.*. Wm. H. Page & Co., 1874, p. 72.

Wm. H. Page & Co. *Specimens of Chromatic Wood Type, Borders, Etc.*. Wm. H. Page & Co., 1874, p. 59.

"A Series of Picturesque Views of Seats of the Noblemen." *The County Seats of the Noblemen and Gentlemen of Great Britain and Ireland*, vol. 1, 1866, p. 7.

Page 70

John Mauritz, Bergling. *Art Alphabets and Lettering*. Chicago, Blakely-Oswald Printing Co., 1914, p. 49.

Page 74 (top)

The San Francisco, Oakland and Alameda Business Directory. San Francisco, Dalton & Co, 1880, p. 389.

Page 111 (top)

American Type Founders Company. *Specimens of Type, Borders, Ornaments, Brass Rules and Cuts, Etc.: Catalogue of Printing Machinery and Materials, Wood Goods, Etc.* Chicago, American Type Founders, 1897, pp. 715.

Page 127 (top)

"Advertisement." *The Gardeners' Chronicle: A Weekly Illustrated Journal of Horticulture and Allied Subjects*, 1895, p. 38.

Page 128 (left to right)

Florist's Publishing Co. *The Florists' Review*, 1912, p. 531.

Illinois Agricultural Association Record, 1920, p. 299.

Chicago, Florist's Publishing Co. *The Florists' Review*, 1912, p. 266.

American Florists Company. "Advertisement." *The American Florist: A Weekly Journal for the Trade*, 1885, p. 129.

Florist's Publishing Co. *The Florists' Review*, 1912, p. 266.

Florist's Publishing Co. *The Florists' Review*, 1912, p. 1400.

American Florists Company. "Advertisement." *The American Florist: A Weekly Journal for the Trade*, 1885, p. 321.

"Advertisement." *The Canadian Druggist*, 1889.

Florist's Publishing Co. *The Florists' Review*, 1912, p. 144.

American Florists Company. "Advertisement." *The American Florist: A Weekly Journal for the Trade*, 1885, p. 1298.

Florist's Publishing Co. *The Florists' Review*, 1912, p. 1168.

Page 128 (bottom)

"Advertisement." *Hardware Merchandising*, 1920, p. 68.

About the Author

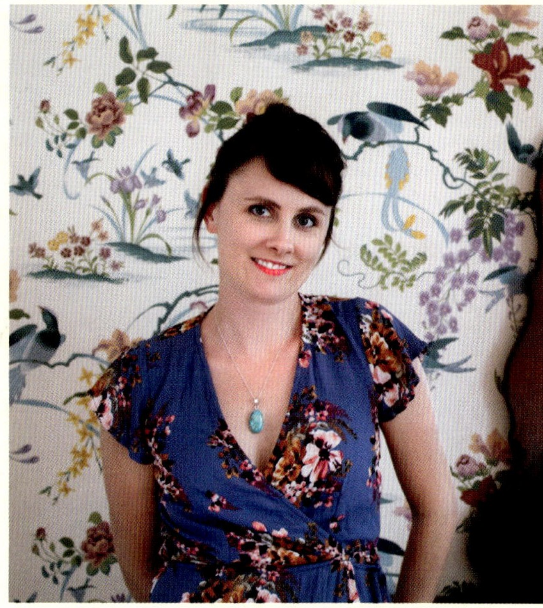

Liz Kohler Brown combines her skills as an artist and designer to create unique lettering projects, surface designs, and illustrations. She studied art and design at Appalachian State University, Penland School of Crafts, and Arrowmont School of Crafts. After earning an MFA from East Carolina University in 2013, she followed her passion of teaching workshops and classes around the world, online and in person.

Liz is a Top Teacher on Skillshare, a designation for the top 1% of teachers. She has created 50-plus Skillshare classes on iPad Art & Design and built an online community of artists and designers who share their work, offer support, and provide feedback to help each other improve and advance their creative goals. You can connect with Liz on Instagram @LizKohlerBrown and get loads of resources for iPad art and design at LizKohlerBrown.com.

Acknowledgments

I couldn't have written this book without my trusted editor, best friend, and husband Ryan. No one could have possibly been more invaluable (and brutally honest) at the times when I needed it most. He spent weeks reading, re-reading, editing, and offering helpful critique on every aspect of this book. I spent many hours lying on the couch in his office saying I couldn't write a book, and he spent many hours convincing me that I could. While I married him for love (and his good looks of course) I was incredibly lucky to have found the partner who made up for all my shortcomings as a writer, creative, and business owner.

The artists and designers who have watched my classes over the past few years have totally changed my life and work forever. Their inspiring messages, gorgeous projects, and often-needed encouragement has kept me making classes and bettering my work so that I could eventually write this book. Without the support of these kind and loyal viewers, I would not be where I am today.

Index